CONTEMPORARY THEATRE REVIEW
AN INTERNATIONAL JOURNAL

Aims and Scope

Contemporary Theatre Review is an international journal concerned with all aspects of theatre — from text-based drama and current developments worldwide, to work of an interdisciplinary or cross-cultural nature. The journal includes primary material, production notes, documents and interviews as well as research. **Contemporary Theatre Review** complements the companion **Contemporary Theatre Studies** book series.

Notes for contributors can be found at the back of the journal.

First published 1996 by Harwood Academic Publishers

This edition published 2016 by Routledge
2 Park Square, Milton Park, Abingdon, Oxon OX14 4RN
711 Third Avenue, New York, NY 10017

Routledge is an imprint of the Taylor & Francis Group, an informa business

ISBN : 978-3-7186-5845-9 (pbk)

Contemporary Theatre Review, 1996, Vol. 5,1 pp. 1–3
Reprints available directly from the publisher
Photocopying permitted by license only

Introduction

Nicole Boireau

The abundance of material offered here shows that editing a volume on taboo-breaking in recent drama is no foolhardy enterprise; outrageousness even seems to be second nature to drama, in the English-speaking countries the articles refer to. Indeed, the art of theatre has consistently transgressed established rules (the rules of the Gods or the rules of the City) ever since Dionysian celebrations gave birth to the art of tragedy, and one can infer, without being exaggeratedly bold, that it will continue to do so.

Drama explores the tensions between the real and the ideal, between the desires of men and the laws of the gods, between individual freedom and repressive systems. Breaking the rules is a vocation equally shared by the tragic hero and the comic spirit. Challenging established values, questioning ready-made assumptions and subverting representational codes is the purpose of art.

Censorship is the way societies try to protect themselves from the attacks of the theatre and/or of the written word. Taboos are generated by all societies; they are internalized and defended by those who benefit from the imposition of rules. A very broad definition of the word "taboo" would involve what is morally forbidden, be it in the social, political and religious fields.

Twentieth century drama opens up a privileged territory for a reflection on this subject as it has offered a number of exemplary taboo-breaking dramatists such as Jean Genet and Joe Orton, among others. Yet, the object of the present volume is not to draw up a list of famous censorship cases, nor does it aim at drawing the line between what can be considered a taboo or not. Indeed, we would be trapped in a very sterile debate, as what is understood as a taboo at one end of the social and political spectrum might be sheer conformity at the other end, depending on which side of the fence of History one chooses (or is forced) to stand.

Throughout the centuries, nudity, coarse language, sexual self-determination, crossing racial and social barriers, legitimizing or condemning all political systems have been, among others, so many fluctuating limits transgressed on stage. If we consider that the drama of the post 1968 era, marked by the abolition of theatre censorship in Britain, has broken all taboos in terms of obscenity, verbal and visual, what territory can possibly be left for the artist to explore? Yet, like History, the history of taboo-breaking is not linear; taboos have the ability to rise from their own ashes and to re-emerge, a decade or so later (let us just think of *The Romans in Britain* case, in 1980, a sort of "Dirty Play Controversy" revisited), simply because moral victories are not necessarily long-lived, new generations bring about new taboos, unpredictable new approaches, new definitions and, of course, raise new questions.

The crises and changes the world has gone through, in the last twenty-five years, have radically modified the intellectual climate, no longer structured by the polarized, clear-cut issues of the Cold War and the class struggle. The contributors have therefore adopted the broadest possible of operating viewpoints, in order not to define limits, but to show their fluctuations. This volume aims at examining the way recent drama has questioned aesthetic, cultural and political certainties. Isn't Edward Bond providing us with the right perspective, when he states that it is "the nature of the boundary", which "must be interrogated," in his "Notes on Post-modernism"? Is this not the way the function of taboo-breaking in drama at the end of the century should be assessed?

After all taboos have been broken, after all possible shock-tactics have been used, what is left to the inspired artist is the urgency to question the validity of inherited humanist culture, and to blur the frontiers a little more. After the spectacle has been disrupted, outrageousness still remains a means to an end and new questions need to be raised: are there any sexual, social or political taboos waiting to be broken? Have all the essential questions been asked? How can a new radical discourse be reinvented in the theatre? Indeed, new Europe is craving for new modes of thought, for new prophets, for dramatists who can "analyze" more than they can "polemicize", as playwright David Edgar recently put it, and who can make the question more vital than the answer.

The twelve articles contained in this book cover the related areas of aesthetics and politics, both on the stage of the world and in the world of the stage. Each contributor shows how drama subverts the foundations of accepted modes of perception and how it meditates on its own conventions. Taboo-breaking in theatre practice is the field John Arden and Margaretta D'Arcy have chosen to discuss, drawing from their own personal experience. When it goes beyond limits, and blurs the frontier between illusion and reality, performance art can involve physical violence done to the audience, as MaryBeth Inverso critically shows in her article. In this essay on Peter Barnes, John Elsom reflects on the use of sensational shock-tactics in the post-censorship age. A "Theatre of Catastrophe" emerged in the late Seventies, with Howard Barker as one of its major representatives; Georges Bas has chosen *Victory* as "a ground for moral revaluation", to show how the meaningful interplay of obscenity and horror serves a vision of history. Edward Bond's lurid dramatic world is unconventionally examined through his approach to female characters by Ruth Freifrau von Ledebur. Christine Dymkowski offers a challenging counterpart, with her exploration of Sarah Daniels's pungent plays about sexual politics. Even more outrageous in his orgasmic obsession is Steven Berkoff, who "unleashes the savage forces" in Nicole Boireau's article.

In (literally) breaking through barriers, recent political events have introduced new responses to the state of the world. In problematizing politics and culture, English-speaking drama at the end of the century has reshuffled the cards of History. Savage satire of the Thatcher decade, a prevailing streak in recent drama, is Monique Prunet's field of investigation. Wolfgang Lippke discusses Howard Brenton's play *Berlin Bertie*, which analyzes the political bankruptcy of Western democracies after the fall of the Berlin Wall. If truth and "fixed borderlines" are nowhere to be found, "confusion is not an ignoble condition", as Christa Velten claims in her article on Brian Friel's *Translations*. Cutting across cultural barriers is a taboo-breaking enterprise which Nicole Vigouroux-Frey tackles in her discussion of Wole Soyinka's violent art of dialogue. So does Albert-Reiner Glaap in his study of the thought-provoking black-and-white issue in Canadian playwright Wendy Lill's *The Occupation of Heather Rose*.

All the articles deal with the shifting of boundaries, more than with the boundaries themselves. In doing so, they try to do justice to the enlightening power of drama at the end of the twentieth century.

This issue was commissioned by Rick Takvorian.

Contemporary Theatre Review, 1996, Vol. 5,1 pp. 5–16
Reprints available directly from the publisher
Photocopying permitted by license only

Taboos of the Theatre-production Ambience

Margaretta D'Arcy and John Arden

The article is in three parts and a summing-up. As it is by two authors, each of them has a section, presenting their own personal experience of taboos in theatre work, how they first came up against them, how this was related to taboos in their everyday lives, and how they have tried to "go beyond" them.

The third section contains a list in chronological order of a number of their productions, briefly summarising the types of taboos challenged and showing how there has been a cumulative effect – each challenge, when built upon for subsequent work, has created new challenges. The summing-up restates how taboos may be breached in the contents of plays only to be consolidated anew and augmented by further and more deeply-rooted ones, aroused as a result of the general ambience of production.

KEY WORDS Censorship, Culture, Establishment, Feminism, Gender, Playwriting, Royal Court Theatre, Production

Dismantling Taboos

Margaretta D'Arcy

Dictionary definition=taboo=restraint, ban, ostracism.

I have experienced all three categories and have adapted and absorbed them into my cultural attitudes and way of life. Our culture conditions us from birth to accept taboos, not in accordance with common sense, but in order to preserve authority for the military/industrial complex which rules us all. The complex itself is bound up with taboos, to protect itself against any questioning of its logic or its proclaimed purpose "to benefit the human race". Class, race and gender divisions are all used to prop it up.

In my own case, my very existence stems from the breach of several taboos; my father was an Irish nationalist Catholic and my mother was born in the East End of London into a family of orthodox Russian Jews who had fled the military service of the Tsar and the Austrian emperor. No Catholic may marry a Jew; no Jew may marry a Catholic; a good Irish patriot would not marry someone brought up in England. And so, through no fault of my own, whatever I did broke some taboo in my kinship-structure: therefore from an early age I became very conscious of taboos, deliberately choosing whether to accept or break them.

Even my nationality came under question: my mother had had me in England; she rejected the Catholic teaching that the unborn child held equal status with the mother. I left the Church without any feeling of guilt because of its views on sex and women; in the same way as I left Ireland and emigrated to England – alongside other thousands of young people – my country had no room for me, so I departed with no room for my country in my heart. And yet when the English theatre tried to remove my Irishness, I wouldn't go along with it.

My first theatre job in England, Hornchurch Repertory Company, 1953: the Christmas pantomime, a popular artform supposedly defying all taboos and then patching them up at the curtain-fall when the cast all sing the National Anthem; I refused to sing. A terrible thing to do for one who was just starting out on a career in the theatre. I was an inexperienced, lowly member of the company: I had challenged the entire premise of the theatre, that in a show all individuals are all part of the show and do not display their personal attitudes. It was dealt with by stereotyping me as an Irish savage – I was given the name "Bogs" by one of the senior actors (a *double entendre*, Irish swamp and English lavatory). But the homosexuals in the company were extremely supportive of me: becoming an outcast in one culture, I was made room for in another. I was not sacked. The director, Stuart Burge, belonged to the George Devine/Michel St Denis school, itself making waves and breaking the taboos of traditional West End theatre.

(Stuart had brought young movie starlets into the live theatre, protegees of Stephen Ward the osteopath whose pimping in high places toppled Minister of Defence Profumo and created a national scandal. Stephen Ward in the end accepted his taboo; by committing suicide and saving the faces of leaders of the establishment.)

The theatre has one all-embracing taboo: "The show must go on!" The punters have paid their money and expect to see its value. They have a wage-relation with the actors (which Karl Marx called "robbery"), and the value they look for is the illusion that the actors are other than they are. By 1958 I was working at George Devine's Royal Court (1958). His life was shortened by endless battles and frustrations with his board of management. There was no subsidised theatre then; the board was composed partly of theatre people who knew it took time to build up audiences, partly of business men who wanted the glory of this new postwar generation of voices from the underclass wishing to tear down the old order, but only if it meant "bums on seats". The established critics felt uncomfortable in this era of new values, because they were going to have to *think*, and declare their own values in print.

Which side would they be on over the issue of the H-bomb? This was the time of Nuclear Disarmament rallies and the massive civil disobedience of the first Committee of 100 headed by Bertrand Russell, in which many of the Court's actors, directors and playwrights (including myself and John Arden) were members. A number of them were in fact picked up one night, whisked before the magistrates, and "interned" in prison for three months – Arnold Wesker, for example, Robert Bolt, Christopher Logue ...

Ivor Browne, one of the last of the old-school critics, foamed at the pen against the Royal Court because some of us actors did not use stage makeup, wore our own clothes for performances, and – taboo of all taboos – used the front-of-house instead of the stage-door to reach the dressing-rooms. Also we went to the management, questioned them publicly over cutbacks on office staff, and told them we did not want expensive first-night bouquets. It all came to a head in a Sunday night show put on under the direction of Anthony Page, Keith Johnstone, and Anne Jellicoe, by a small company of young actors within the main company. I was part of this: the main item on the bill was a satire on the critics' reviews of Royal Court plays. Attacking critics from the stage was a serious breach of taboo. The electrician refused to work, and the critics (of course) condemned it with one voice.

That was the last time I played in orthodox theatre. I found that the new order had begun to lose its nerve and was allowing itself to be absorbed by the old dispensation: it was too confusing, too stressful for me; my last breach of taboo was to tell the profession that I was going to create my own type of theatre in my home, with my children as part of it, choosing my own time and times. To leave without being cast out means they cannot woo you back. I was not consciously rebelling; I was just doing what was comfortable; the real rebels are those who *don't* break taboos; they are rebels against their own common sense, selling their common sense for "a cheque in the post".

Creating my own theatre brought me up against the gender taboo. I had a personal and professional partnership with John Arden. As he was recognised as a playwright, his helping me with my projects meant that I disappeared as a person in my own right and became merely a component of "the Ardens". This was partly my own doing: I did not understand (as now I understand) how thoroughly insidious was the dominant culture as recorded in the press. People in Britain take press-reports as fact; when they meet the subject of the reports they see her only in the light of what they have read. It is the differences between an oral and a written culture. On the other hand, for the Irish, the colonisation of our country and subsequent censorship, combined with the equivocations made necessary by Catholic theocracy, have meant that we never took very seriously the things the press wrote about us.

At last I came to realise that before national colonisation there was gender colonisation, and that we women had been colluding with our own invisibility by not openly counting our work and claiming it. I claimed my work and so brought down the wrath of the British theatre establishment upon myself – wives were supposed to be hidden helpmates – if they weren't, they were called stumbling-blocks and hindrances to their wimpish men.

In 1981, in London, women-in-entertainment gathered together to recognise that women were discriminated against in the business, not only as directors and managers, etc.; but also that our fundamental area of creative imagination and experience was hidden and suppressed. Our task was to change this. Back in Ireland I organised a weekend seminar where we discovered that female theatre-workers (taken as part of the whole industrial work-force of the west) were at the top of the list for ill-health, mental and physical, and had the highest rates of suicide. 98% were out-of-work. In other words, Showbiz was a Woman-Killer. We found, too, that those women who regularly went to the theatre as audience belonged to the higher socio/economic groupings, with higher rates of education and social status, for whom the Drama is an escape from the stresses caused in their own lives by the military/industrial complex; whereas women from the lower strata, and unwaged women-in-the-home, needed above all convivial interaction and participation, letting the hair down, playing around, to energise their suppressed feelings of rebellion.

By the '80s, the words "play" and "player" had disappeared from the vocabulary of theatre – it now was "drama", "performance", "performers", "texts", "drama workshops", etc. We had been culturally conditioned to eliminate "play", except for the training of mothers and carers, nice little girls as in the nursery-rhymes –

> There was a little girl, she had a little curl right in the middle of her forehead;
> When she was good she was very very good, when she was bad she was horrid.

What are little girls made of?
Sugar and spice and all things nice.

"We're all bad girls: take the toys from the boys!" became the new international slogan for some of us. The focus, of course, for being a bad girl was at Greenham Common, where women, through direct action against the cruise missiles, brought collective theatre into politics; and the military/industrial complex squealed, "This is unfair, they're not playing our games and keeping our rules!"

I have been going to Greenham since 1983, involving myself with theatre-in-politics there, and then the extension of it in the courts and jails. Death-theatre versus women's life-theatre. Yes, in our theatre women have died. We say murdered; like Helen Thomas, crossing the road to post a letter in 1990 on a Saturday afternoon, clear vision, and yet the West Midland Police, driving their van to a charity horse-show, ran her down – her mother is still fighting to have the full truth of that strange accident brought out in the courts. Cruise missiles have gone; but Trident, costing billions of pounds, is still to come. Women are still there, with their demand: *Return the land to the people: pay women, not the military!* D-notices (Ministry of Defence unofficial censorship) have hidden this continuing theatre from exposure in the press.

In Galway, Ireland, helped by a pension for artists from the government, I began to develop the spirit of play for women. I was guided by a remarkable local traditional musician, Breda Lewis, who refused to conform to the more businesslike music-sessions in the pubs – all musicians, experienced or not, are welcomed to her group. The practised fiddler has to be patient for the novice. Everyone has music inside them, and it must have the opportunity to come out. With that as our model, we took to the airwaves as Radio Pirate-Woman; to hell with the law and licenses and censorship-regulations. Using radio as theatre, going on the air in blocks – not being ground down to keep broadcasting all the time – linking up with women all over the world, and being accepted as a member-station of the World Association of Community Broadcasters (AMARC), we can commune, help, learn, organise, have fun, be good or bad as we want. This is theatre beyond the taboo.

Anyone who uses imagination-versus-force to change the world has gone beyond the taboo. And the biggest taboo to go beyond is the assumption that we all want to *work according to someone else's concept of work*. The breaking of the taboo is to assert: "I do work. Pay me for what I do; not for what you tell me to do." I have become linked, through Greenham and the radio, with Selma James's and Wilmette Brown's organisation, International Wages for Housework (set up in 1972), which has worked out the political theory behind this demand, and has shown by analysis that women do 2/3 of the world's work, get 5% of the world's income and own only 1% of the world's assets – in other words, the military/industrial complex is built on the robbery of women's unpaid labour. How to change that? At the time of writing, bills are going through the EC Parliament and the US Congress "On the Assessment of Women's Unwaged Work in Gross National Products". Who *is* to assess it? and what will be the consequences to the world when women en masse can evaluate their contribution? The framing of, and the answers to, these questions is for me Real Theatre.

Intentions and Discoveries

J. Arden

My mother once gave me a loving but severe reproach. I was perhaps seventeen years old. I had begun to affect a sort of highly-coloured Rimbaudesque (or even Villonesque) eccentricity and slovenliness of costume, intended to suggest a determined interest in the ARTS. A genuine ideological statement; but also a calculatedly practical one. I hoped it would allow me to evade the heavy games-playing ethos of the school she and my father had put me to. Nobody looking at me in such a guise could possibly expect me to be athletically disposed, and I was growing a bit too old to be *coerced* any more onto the sports-field. I thought, to begin with, I was breaking a taboo; in fact I was not; I had merely slipped myself tactfully into a slot of acceptable dissidence, and my "statement", in short, proved non-confrontational.

But not with my mother. She was very seriously distressed. "But you look so *conspicuous*!" she pleaded. "It is so important for a young man not to *stand out*." No-one would employ me if that was how I proposed to present myself. People would think I was throwing all her values, all her sacrifices, in her face. I seemed to be a child for whom nobody had ever *cared*. I was an only child, of course, and she and my father had greatly cared. I couldn't bear it. I was most certainly not intending confrontation outside the school environment; nonetheless, most unwittingly, I got it. I backed off. I allowed myself, while in my parents' house, to dress according to their standards. I became, once again, inconspicuous; and then after the holidays I broke out in full flower among my schoolfellows. In the long run I risked nothing, but I ought to have felt rather foolish and deceitful. (I don't remember whether I did or not; most probably I believed I had triumphed.)

All of which should have taught me something. That a truly valuable breach of taboo is not best achieved by striving for it – all you are likely to gain is a growth of your own self-conceit and a laying of yourself open to ignominious compromise. Whereas the real taboos creep up on you, as it were out of ambush; it is only after you have assailed them in ignorant simplicity that you are made to realise what you've done. And then it is a question: are you acting from authentic principle? For if not, nine times out of ten, your confrontation will fail. I ought to have understood, as I understand now, that my mother's values were ones that no family piety should have allowed me to accept, because they were grounded in social arrogance masquerading as timidity, combined with over-possessive affection (a far more potent and enduring mix than any macho peer-pressure from rugby-football-crazed school traditionalists) and were in any case not at all representative of the true strengths of her character. Had I then considered a proper strategy for releasing myself from them *on principle*, I might have avoided all the storm-and-stress between us that erupted some ten years later when I announced to her, one after the other, (a) that I had contracted a civil marriage with a professional stage-player who was not only Irish but also Jewish and at that time a practising Catholic, and (b) that I was abandoning a respectable career in an architect's office for the freelance hazards of a playwright's life.

Now I have never believed that a playwright's life necessarily involves a permanent *and conscious* struggle to get "beyond the taboo". In fact I have found something like that happening time after time, but not because I have deliberately sought it out. In almost every case this has been due simply to my having originated, or been introduced to, what seemed a good idea that ought to work, so why not try it? And then suddenly someone has come along and said, in effect, "Hey, take it easy, we can't do that, you know." It began with the very first play of mine to be professionally produced, a radio-piece called *The Life of Man*, a winner in a BBC competition for new work in 1956.

It was a legend of a disastrous mid-nineteenth century sea-voyage, and I thought to narrate it through the ramblings of the sole survivor, a decayed and drunken ship's-officer who picked up a young woman in the slums of Liverpool and insisted (like Coleridge's Ancient Mariner) on telling her his tale instead of making love to her in a normal fashion. A dramatic technique which I hoped would enable me to give the story the right ambiguous quality – was one to believe it or not? or was the officer inventing its queer details to hide his own collusion with the crimes of a murderous captain?

Well, having won a prize with this script, I was invited by the BBC to come to their Manchester studios to receive it; there were to be press-photographers and congratulatory speeches, and a fancy lunch for all the successful competitors. I arrived from London the evening before, a hotel-room had been reserved for me, I went to bed in it feeling very jolly; and at about midnight I was awoken by a phone-call from a senior BBC producer. "You're not asleep yet, are you? oh good, because it's really rather awkward but I thought I should tell you before the press-conference tomorrow – the judges gave your script the prize, but of course they're just a bunch of writers like yourself, *they* don't have to present the play and I do, and I'm afraid I have to tell you that it can't possibly be put over the airwaves in – in quite the form you've written it. It's all that business about the prostitute – so *direct*, you see, explicit – out of the question to mouth so clearly what she expects the sailor to do to her – I'm afraid a great deal of her highly entertaining conversation with him will have to be conducted on – on similar but different lines, you do understand, I *hope*?"

I was threatening a long-accepted taboo.

And moreover I was not to be permitted to get away with it.

Although the competition-winners had all been assured that their plays would be presented, the small print in our contracts gave the BBC the right to amend the text to suit its rules of sexual propriety: and that was that. My choice was unequivocal: I must purge my play of "dirty talk", or I must allow someone else to do so, or I must accept there would be no broadcast. I was outraged and nonplussed. I thought highly of the story; I was desperate at the thought it might disappear, which was surely very silly of me, but how many young writers with their first play can afford philosophical detachment? Looking back on the affair, I realise it was a small matter, technically speaking. The dialogue objected to was only in parentheses during the main narrative, which would hardly be affected by the required alterations; if the alterations were cunning enough, the licentious spirit of the encounter between woman and sailorman need not be essentially diminished.

I agreed to amend the script myself.

But then I allowed myself to agree to something further. I promised not to mention this little difficulty to the press at the prize-giving. I felt at the time that the first concession was justified – *force majeure*, the words of the contract, and all that – but the second one? There was nothing in the contract about the second one. Perhaps it was my duty as a writer to speak out for freedom of expression for the poetic drama? denounce the public prudery and censorship-tendency of the age? make a nice little scandal for the media, and bust-up the BBC's complacent patronage-festivities? (Indeed an assault upon one of the strongest of all British taboos!) I scarcely thought I had the *leverage*; I was sure I didn't have the courage; I did very much despise myself; but I didn't say a word.

To this day I don't know whether I was right or wrong. I hadn't set out to challenge the BBC, only to stimulate and entertain its audience with what I thought an entertaining tale which I had told as vividly as I could. So I had run up against a taboo imposed by the established structure of the broadcasting organisation upon the content of my individual writing; and I failed to make a breach in it, because (I suppose) the time was not yet ripe.

Three years later, and no less innocently, the content (with which I include the style) of my *Serjeant Musgrave's Dance* broke taboos left and right, and was nonetheless accepted in toto by the enlightened management of the Royal Court Theatre, where George Devine sturdily upheld the playwright's right (no, *duty*) to present such challenges. As a solitary child immersed from an early age in ballad-poetry, the Elizabethans and Celtic saga, I had long hoped for a theatre which would mix verse, prose, anti-militarist anti-imperialist political comment, violent action, strongly-marked costume and decor, into a new sort of mid-20th-century unity; the play piled itself out of my imagination all in a run like a lava-flow from Mount Etna. It never occurred to me there was anything odd about it until actors at audition began clearing their throats dubiously. When the critics arrived they were baffled; bafflement expressed itself as loathing; it appeared I was throwing all their values, all their cultural civilisation, in their faces; the production lost more money for the Royal Court than anything else the theatre had done.

And then, didn't it grow to be famous? and everything I have done since has been seen, more or less, as a "falling-off".

It took quite a time for me to realise that *Musgrave's* content and the Royal Court's comparatively conservative traditions of production were at odds. New types of play need a new type of theatre; little by little, through my work with Margaretta D'Arcy, I came to discover one.

And thereby discovered all sorts of other taboos which extend far beyond a writing's content: not only the way it is presented; but to whom it is presented; by whom, and under what socio/economic circumstances, the presentation takes place. Sometimes, when they are firmly challenged – and the challenge has strong principle behind it – you find the taboo collapses surprisingly swiftly. Sometimes it doesn't: it is founded upon so deep a characteristic of the society we live in that only an outright and widespread revolution would serve to shift it. And we can never altogether foresee which it's going to be. All imaginative theatre-work involves some sort of probing. Impossible to know that you've pierced a tender place until you hear the subject yelp. But a yelp is not necessarily serious resistance. When you meet *that*, you recognise it soon enough.

A Chronology

(by M. D'Arcy & J. Arden)

Here are some of the stages in our progressive discovery of taboo within theatre, falling into three categories; content, presentation, economic/working relations.

I. To break down barriers between performance/performers and audience; between professional and non-professional; between fixed and fluid concepts of space/time.

1. *The Kirkbymoorside Entertainment, 1963*

A two-month get-together of artists interacting within a north Yorkshire small-town community.

The taboo was broken in the presentation: the events were all held in our small cottage, with everyone who needed it fed and bedded on the premises. No taboos were imposed on content, no standards "of excellency" demanded. So most of the press and TV treated the whole affair as *violent anarchy* because we made no rules about drugs, drink, or sex. All told, about 50–100 participants, poets, musicians, actors, a fire-eater, a magician, children, film-makers.

2. *The Vietnam War Game, New York University, 1967*

An unbroken anti-war eleven-hour goulash – the basic ingredient was an improvised hillbilly "soap-opera" interspersed with serious political analyses, films, music, the Bread-and-Puppet Theatre, Joe Chaikin's theatre-group, the Harlem Baptist Choir – the lead-percussionist from the Philharmonic Orchestra played throughout. Literally hundreds of participants.

Breach of taboo: content. Committed agitprop politics in a university drama-department. Also, the surrealist style and the "hillbilly" element offended the orthodox urban left.

3. *Muggins is a Martyr,* Unity Theatre, London (founded and owned by a Communist Party trust), 1968

A satire on contemporary British politics, attacking Harold Wilson's Labour government, written and performed in collaboration with the Cartoon Archetypical Slogan Theatre, a Trotsky-orientated group. Breaches of taboo:

(a) content. Both Communists and Trotskyites objected to a strip-tease scene, the first full-frontal nude moving on the British stage (legal, because Unity was a *club*).

(b) presentation. Use of street-theatre, and performances outside the theatre by local children before the show. In the final performance we threw the script out and improvised the whole thing.

4. *The Hero Rises Up*, the Roundhouse, London, 1968

Ballad-opera, an anti-imperialist view of Admiral Nelson and his victories. Sponsored by the Institute of Contemporary Arts (ICA). Breach of taboo: economic/working relations. As the show only ran for five nights, it was clearly uneconomical, there was no way the expenses could be recouped. Despite strong objections (amounting to sabotage) from the ICA, we had two entrances, one for those who didn't want to pay, the other for those who thought they ought to. Thus the audience itself was involved with the economics of the theatre.

II: To wrest control from the dominant state and culture.

1. *The Ballygombeen Bequest*, 7:84 Company, England, touring production, 1972.

Breaches of taboo:

(a) content. The play attacked British policy in the north of Ireland and the Irish government's collusion with that policy. An attempt was made (in vain) by the British Army to get the play stopped at the Edinburgh Festival because of a scene of soldiers' torture of an IRA suspect.

(b) presentation. The production was topically linked, by narration from the stage and by programme notes, to an actual eviction of an Irish family by a British landlord. When the Army's case against the play failed, the landlord was alerted by the right-wing press and brought a civil libel action against us as authors (but not against 7:84, who had taken the play off as soon as the writ was issued, to preserve the actors' jobs – but the Arts Council did temporarily withdraw its grant from the company). The lawsuit lasted for five years, ending in an out-of-court settlement; during which time the play was necessarily suppressed.

2. *The Island of the Mighty*, Royal Shakespeare Company at the Aldwych Theatre, London, 1972

Breach of taboo: economic/working relations. We, as authors paid to attend (and work on the script) during rehearsals, went on strike because of our working conditions – a collision with management over the interpretation of the script's presentation. We had the support of our trade union, the Society of Irish Playwrights, affiliated to British Equity. British Equity eventually withdrew recognition from the strike; we have been an *unofficial* strike ever since. This was the first time ever that industrial-type strike took place in the British theatre. We also had support from artists in "fringe-theatre" (*not* from 7:84) who interrupted a dress-rehearsal demanding that the audience should take a position on the dispute. The last time anything like this had happened was when Jean Genet (in 1957) was barred from the London production of his *The Balcony*, which he thought a travesty of his play, and where he was thought likely to provoke an uproar. Attitudes were hardened against us because of the *Ballygombeen* controversy, the entire political climate in the UK on Irish matters, the growing popular resistance to British policy throughout Ireland, and the authors' then membership of the Official Sinn Fein Party in Ireland.[1]

3a The Non-Stop Connolly Show, sequence of six complete plays; Liberty Hall, Dublin, followed by tour in Ireland, 1975.

Taboos breached:

(a) content. The plays placed Irish rebellion as part of international struggle, contrary to the conventional Irish nationalist view; as well as challenging the Irish revisionist view (that Connolly's Easter Rising of 1916 had been a political setback). Also, one of the authors (J.A.) was English: and M. D'A as Irish co-author was totally ignored in consequence. She was, as well, politically suspect to elements of the Irish republican left because of her involvement with a Trotskyite party in England; and because she had been expelled from the Official Sinn Fein Party, which (ironically) was sponsoring the Connolly plays.

(b) presentation. The plays, run in sequence for the one occasion in Liberty Hall, lasted twenty-six hours and a half. Subsequently, because of problems in economic/working relations (see below), new forms of presentation had to be created for the tour. A diminished cast meant that members of the audience had to become an integral part of the plays; volunteers were required, to read parts at sight.

(c) economic/working relations. At this time the Irish political scene was extremely dangerous, internecine feuds and assassinations – a struggle for dominance within the Republican Movement – were going on in the very venues where we performed. Many actors left the tour.

3b The Non-Stop Connolly Show. Almost-Free lunchtime theatre, London, 1976.

The plays were broken down into fourteen parts and put on twice, throughout successive fortnights, as rehearsed readings. Breach of taboo: economic/working relations. To get over the difficulty of large-cast readings of a different section of the plays each day, any actor who wanted to take part could turn up during the morning and receive a role. The audience played a role as well; in political discussions held every day after the reading.

4 A Pinprick of History (devised by M.D'A.), Almost-Free lunchtime theatre, London, 1977

Breach of taboo:

(a) content. The play dealt with recent Irish politics, not only giving overt support to national-liberation struggle but also attacking the British cultural left over its silence on human rights in Ireland.

[1] M. D'Arcy had been to see *The Balcony* on the evening before her marriage.

(b) presentation. It was framed within the supposed proceedings of "The Dialectical Association of Pinpricks of History", of which all the audience were assumed to be members. An opportunity was offered to "the association" to suggest other issues for dramatisation, instead of Ireland. When someone from Egypt asked for the Camp David Agreement to be handled, the actors accordingly improvised a brand-new piece on that subject. The Arts Council declined to give financial support – refusing to accept *Pinprick* as a "play".

5 *Vandaleur's Folly*, 7:84 Company, touring in England and Ireland, 1978.

Taboos breached:

(a) presentation. The play was a historical story of a socialist co-operative that had existed in 19th-century Ireland at a time when British policy was changing from overt repression to token reformism. The same thing was happening in the north of Ireland in 1978, organised by a Labour government. In order to show how repression continued under the guise of democratic reform, up-to-date blow-ups of news-cuttings about recent denials of civil rights etc. were displayed in the venues as part of the decor.

(b) economic/working relations. Our tour-date in Belfast was part of the Belfast Festival, a phenomenon of the government's new policy of cultural normalisation combined with criminalisation of political prisoners. The actors now began to get frightened because of the Prevention of Terrorism Act and pressures from their agents who did not want them labelled as IRA fellow-travellers. So they took down the news-cuttings – they were entitled to do this as they were a "collective" in which we, as author-directors, had no part during the tour. But we had been personally invited to participate in the Festival. As an author, therefore, and festival-participant, M.D'A. made her own interventions against censorship. After the decor was mutilated by the actors, she handed out to the audience leaflets against the criminalisation of prisoners. At the same time, two political paintings had been removed from an exhibition in the Ulster Museum 'by the Festival Committee'.

During a poetry-reading in the same gallery M. D'A. wrote "H-block" in one of the wall-spaces replacing the banned pictures this was also a statement against the banning of a march about the prisoners – and she got put into jail as a result. She thereby broke an additional taboo, in the eyes of the Belfast *literati*: writers are not supposed to fetch themselves outside the boundaries of their work to reinforce the content of the work by individual political action.

To Sum Up

(by M. D'Arcy & J. Arden)

A theatrical experience is an attempt to demonstrate by creative imitation of life an alternative "Possible World". But the structure of the "theatre-society" in which this is done will normally reflect the values of the larger society which has established it, and therefore is bound to act as a control upon any dissident ideas of the individual theatre-artists whom it includes. It follows that the ambience of production and presentation has a more important potential for dissidence than the content of the work performed.

When the ideas can no longer be contained within the structure, and activity takes place towards breaking the structure down and replacing it with a new structure, the ultimate TABOOS encountered throw into question the whole nature of "art" itself.

Contemporary Theatre Review, 1996, Vol. 5,1 pp. 17–25
Reprints available directly from the publisher
Photocopying permitted by license only

Beyond Offending the Audience: Violating the Audience Body

MaryBeth Inverso

The most recent survey of performance art theory to appear in the United States, the Spring 92 issue of *Discourse: Journal for Theoretical Studies in Media and Culture*, while it treats a number of performance-related issues – auto-destructive art, Viennese Actionism, even "what is left of performance art" – pays astonishingly little attention to the body of the audience and virtually no analysis is applied to the question of the function of the audience body in/during high-risk performance.

This essay offers an overview of the phenomenon of so-called pain or risk art as produced in the United States and Europe with special attention to the stresses and dangers brought to bear against an audience often perceived by the artistic community as a mere consumer of art, if not downright recalcitrant. The articulation of this rarely acknowledged hostility is itself the breaking of a taboo.

KEY WORDS performance art, body art, risk/pain art, autodestructive art, Viennese Aktionism, Calif. performance art of the 70s

Nonetheless, a few boundaries ...

This essay is devoted to an aesthetic phenomenon which arose in the late 60s, flourished in the 70s and practically disappeared with the onset of the 80s. The nomenclature devised at the time to define this curious, mongrel form was, not surprisingly, various – here is a sampling: "Body Art," "Performance Art", "Living Art", "Conceptual Art", "ProtoPerformance", "Performance Events", "Body Works". One feature which did seem universal, however, was a persistent disattendance to traditional classifications and generic distinctions. Laurie Anderson, one of the most successful American performance artists, values its ill-definedness "It crosses over lines, and that's what really makes it live". As for the practitioners, many had had little or no prior association with the Performing Arts as such – they were more often likely to be sculptors, painters, even writers. An even odder characteristic of this new genre was the fact that the performance event could transpire without the presence of an audience. Often as not, the artist would photograph or videotape an event which would otherwise have remained invisible and inaccessible to would-be spectators. In other cases an audience would not only be present, but would be conscripted as participants. In a few instances, the event was neither witnessed nor recorded – the performance was declared as having taken place by the mere fact of the artist's claim that it had. Some observers argued that in order for the phenomenon to qualify as performance art, the event had to be sustained over a period of time or else be repeated (or be at least repeatable); others just as vehemently insisted that the performance was not theatre and therefore could not and should not be reperformed.

Actually, some types of performance art are centuries old – for example, the performance of the juggler, the trapeze artist, or more recently, the stand-up comedian. Sally Harrison-Pepper in her *Drawing a Circle in the Square* argues that urban street performers are performance artists in their own right. These street artists are primarily, however, daring entertainers who create, as she puts it, "an oas[i]s of fun and energy in the midst of vagrants, burglars, and traffic" (1990).

But the specific type of performance art that I here propose to examine can hardly be described as an oasis of fun – either for performer or for audience. These more extreme varieties of performance art can be grouped together as a kind of subgroup of performance art. Their signal trait is that they centralize the human body – most often that of the performer, though sometimes that of the audience. Furthermore, this centralization comes about as the result of actions that are taken by the performer against his or her own body or that of the audience. The body is abused, traumatized, sometimes even mutilated while the abusive action itself constitutes the performance itself. Often described as "pain" or "risk" artists, these performers call to our attention some of the interesting and often disturbing questions which arise when matters of aesthetics and matters of ethics interface.

Of Itching Powder and other Audience Tortures ...

Futurist Fillipo Marinetti once proposed (not unseriously) that "the audience constantly be taken off guard by such devices as "the use of itching and sneezing powders, coating some of the audience's seats with glue, provoking fights and disturbances by selling the seat to two or more people".[1] While Marinetti's tactics have the effect of desacralizing the audience's identity as a god to be pleased, they open the door to the practice of audience manipulation, practices which could easily assume a threatening hue.

In a 1978 article, "The Actual as Bizarre: Assaulting the Sensibilities of the Audience," Theodore Shank documents a performance piece, *Great Suicides of our Time*, performed in 1977 by Jail Warehouse, a London-based performance group. As will shortly become evident, this piece is a more than usually clearcut example of audience manipulation by means of the body. His description is worth quoting at length:

> The audience of about twenty is led outdoors in the dark, where, after being coerced into giving up their valuables – or at least a few coins – they are taken into a tiny abandoned shack where they sit around a table ... [T]he spectators are offered a filthy meal of a hastily cooked hamburger and a watermelon that has been chopped to bits. When the banquet has been served, the performers leave the building, closing the door behind them. A pipe is inserted into a hole in the wall, and smoke begins to pour into the building. At first, the audience does nothing, expecting the performers to return. Finally a spectator goes to the door and tries to open it, but it is being held closed by someone on the outside. The audience begins to be somewhat concerned. They know they can open the door by force, but "they are reluctant to disrupt the performance." Eventually, as the smoke becomes suffocating, several people force the door open, and the audience goes outside. It is no longer a performance. (Shank 1978)

I would argue that, at least in this case, more than the audience's "sensibilities" is under attack, yet Shank offers no comment other than to note that the involvement

[1] Quoted in Kirby (1971) 22.

of its non-visual senses tends to make the audience's experience of the performance event seem more real than illusory. This odd omission of concern for the audience body (both on the part of the performer and of the critical observer) is likewise readily observable in other documented performance pieces.

Another particularly useful example of this sort of event performed "against" the audience is John Duncan's *Scare* (1976). Linda Frye Burnham describes the piece: "On two successive nights wearing a rubber mask, he [Duncan] knocked on the doors of two people he knew well. When each man arrived, he shot him with a gun loaded with blanks" (1980). Duncan's objective was even more problematic than the performance act itself. His explanation was that after having suffered and survived a mugging, he experienced a euphoria "that he wished to create for others" (Burnham, 1980). The motivation expressed here is clearly not hostile; nonetheless, it is, all the same, chilling in its childlike egocentrism and its manifest inability to recognize an act of terrorism as such.[2]

Vito Acconci's 1969 *Following Piece* works somewhat along the same lines though the methodology tends to be tamer. David Bourdon describes the piece: "Each day he would choose at random a person on the street and follow him wherever he went, no matter how long or how far, until that person entered a private place" (1973). In another piece entitled *Performance Test,* which Acconci performed in an actual theatre, "he sat onstage and stared at each member of the audience – from left to right, front to back for fifteen seconds" (Bourdon 1973). In *Proximity Piece,* which he performed at a museum exhibition, Acconci "sidled up to spectators and stood uncomfortably close to them until they moved away" (Bourdon 1973).

A California performance duo which billed itself as "Bob & Bob" manipulated its audience in ways that managed to be simultaneously sinister and funny. During one gallery performance, the audience was literally tied to their seats while forced to view a "documentary" about the duo. Linda Frye Burnham recounts a very unusual audience ordeal undergone by the spectators of their 1979 event *Sex Is Stupid:* since the event was coincident with an exhibition of their paintings, "they required that the audience be drunk, reasoning that they would buy more of the work if under the influence. If not intoxicated, audience members were escorted to a waiting room where they had the opportunity to drink until the desired state was reached" (1980).

The salient feature which unites these seemingly discrete, unrelated performance events is that in each case there is a deployment of the threat of death (in *Great Suicides* and *Scare*) or at least of pain or discomfort against the audience. Judith Barry's discussion of this issue makes it clear that during the heyday of risk/pain performance art, the matter of the safety of the body was treated with cavalier indifference:

> As some early performance pieces sought to involve the spectator as thoroughly as possible, questions about the responsibility of the artist as a producer became important. How responsible was the artist or the gallery for the safety of the audience or the artists? This form of question was discarded as being antagonistic and antiformalistic. Consequently, what was implied in the questions (the relationship of artist to the production process) was never voiced (Barry, 1980).

[2] We can see the same sort of "let's see what happens" mentality in Chris Burden's piece *747* during which he fired at a jet plane.

Anthony Kubiak, writing on terrorism and on coercion as theatre history, clarifies the difference between the interrogation cell and its representation on a stage:

In the final analysis, we are still faced with a theatre whose violence, no matter how "real", still exists primarily as a sign of itself ... (It is also worth noting that the theatrical ordeal, no matter how intense, is undergone voluntarily, while the very terror of torture rests in part on the victim's absolute lack of control). (1991)

Elaine Scarry similarly insists that lack of "consent" is an absolute component of the structure of torture: "The prisoner of torture has at no time consented to contribute his body to the fiction of the regime's power produced through his pain" (1985). We can accept, at least provisionally, Kubiak's argument that violence in the theatre is but "a sign of itself". However, from the standpoint of the audience, how much of the "theatrical ordeal" for *them* is voluntary? Ronald J. Pelias raises the same question albeit in legalistic terms: "What implicit contract exists between performers and audience members in terms of what the audience will be asked to do when they attend the performance"? (1992) Translated into blunt economic terms, how much, if any, protection is purchased with a theatre ticket?

The rhetoric which performance artists and theorists have produced is relatively scant (for reasons which will become apparent), but the commentary one finds does suggest that that ticket is construed, or can be construed, as the visible representation of a total surrender to the whole of the performance event. The following remarks by two members of COUM Transmissions, a performance arts group, barely conceals its contempt for and hostility toward the spectator:

People always pretend to want to be lifted out of themselves, but in reality they are terribly afraid of anything REALLY happening to them ... People like the sham artists who soothe them with aesthetic platitudes. They dread having to face reality in any form ... (Orridge & Christopherson, 1979).

The violation of the audience's body, its space, or its sensibilities, given such an orientation, becomes an unacknowledged agenda. "The purpose," (of "theatricalized spectator-manipulation") claims Kenneth Coutts-Smith, is to forc[e] novel perspectives through the effects of shock and cultural trauma" (1979). Josette Feral in "Performance and Theatricality: The Subject Demystified," couches her agreement in terms more physical: "It attempts to wake the body – the performer's and the spectator's – from the threatening anaesthesia haunting it" (1982). Charlemagne Palestine, an American performance artist, in a 1978 interview, makes quite clear her expectations of an audience: "I like to feel that they're sucked in and that they're in danger. Their perception is in danger of being pierced and that they're in danger of thinking things they don't want to think and feeling things they don't want to feel" (1978).

There were a few dissident voices from within the community of performance artists. John Duncan, for example, was taken to task by feminist colleagues for the scare tactics of *Scare*. According to Linda Frye Burnham, they questioned his right "to assault an unprepared audience with unexplained violence" (1980).

Such objections, however, seem to have been the exception. Most of the critical attention was deflected to what these artists were doing to their own bodies. On this score the troubling issue of consent seemed to become a non-issue. As performance artist Chris Burden put it, art "is a free spot in society, where you can do anything"[3] So, with that never very seriously considered obstacle conveniently removed, commentators felt free to respond to and discuss the aesthetic infliction of self-injuries as mise-en-scene. Here, for example, is an almost rhapsodic response to photographs of Viennese Aktion performance artist Rudolf Schwarzkogler's "ritual of self mutilation":

> The ... folio of photographs ... embodies, to one's enormous surprise, a remarkable density of sheer lyricism ... It is more reasonable to assess the haunting power of Schwarzkogler's imagery (that of a mute and blind, gauze-wrapped, bandaged-and bondaged-figure, teetering at the very edge of self-recognition, the composite victim-torturer, acting out his elegant and poignant sado-masochistic role with absolute conscious authority and total consistency) as imagery defined completely in its own terms ... The freedom that he seized was not the fragile and transitory anarchistic "freedom" of a Dada-type egoic self-asseveration, but that absolute and rare liberty which is the ... fruit of an assertion of complete control both over a ... private bodily existence ... and a public social existence ... Schwarzkogler's manipulation was ... even to some degree a spiritual act ... (Coutts-Smith 1979).

One can't help but get a sense here that self-torture may become aesthetically beautiful and politically empowering. Joel Black in his study *The Aesthetics of Murder*, (which also treats suicide as an aesthetic phenomenon) contends that the postmodern artist "often employs bold, aggressive means to penetrate the surrounding world of hyperreality in order to reveal the "real" " (1991).

If one entertains his argument long enough – that "the social norm in post-industrialist society and in postmodern culture is no longer the ethical world of the real, but the aesthetic realm of the hyperreal" (1991) – one begins to see how Kenneth Coutts-Smith and others can reperceive the self-mutilation of a Schwarzkogler as an aesthetic act of transcendence. Kubiak explains the triggering of the aesthetic response even in such extreme instances by pointing to the fact that "the image seems so exquisitely reproducible or detached that it loses the impact of *real* violence" (1991).

Subtler Torments ... or, "Warps in the Participation Mystique"[4]

For other commentators, however, the suffering spectacle presented by the pain or risk artist – its "visceral immediacy", as Herbert Blau puts it – "confound[s] the idea of the artistic image" (1990). In this wise, the mere act of spectatorship may be fraught with a distress that exceeds mere empathy and may in fact be dangerous. For Blau, "[T]here is nothing more threatening to an audience" because at such moments "we seem to be decidedly in the unmooring presence of real pain" (1990).

One could, of course, advance the argument that the artist who violates only his or her own body is not assaulting the audience at all. In a literal sense, this is true. Nevertheless, there remains the real issue as to the degree to which an audience may be seduced into colluding with the artist. One begins to wonder whether the situation is substantially altered when an audience does appear to lend its consent to performance event.

---

[3] Max Kozloff ascribes the neutral tone of bodyworks literature, its "characteristic cool," to its "publicity function." See Kozloff pp. 30–32.

[4] See Blau p. 166.

The following brief illustrations of such willing co-conspiracy between artist and audience once again foreground the issue of audience consent, and ultimately suggests, as we shall see, that, freely given, non-extorted consent does not necessarily relieve the artist of his or her responsibility for the wholeness and safety of the audience. A good instance of this ethical/aesthetic conundrum is furnished by Chris Burden's 1971 piece *220*, in which the audience assumed the role of co-participants in the event. The following is Burden's account of the performance:

> The gallery was flooded with twelve inches of water. Three other people and I waded through the water and climbed onto sixteen-foot ladders, one ladder per person. After everyone was positioned, I dropped a 220 electric line into the water. This piece lasted from midnight until dawn, about six hours ... The thing I was attempting to set up was a hyped-up situation with high danger, which would keep them awake, confessing and talking ... I think everyone enjoyed it in a weird sort of way (Burden & Butterfield, 1975).

Jan Butterfield's commentary on the piece suggests that for her, "consent" signifies complete and thoroughly knowledgeable acquiesence. She points out that while Burden himself may have had the degree of physical control necessary to perform the piece, it was presumptuous on his part to assume that his participants were equally capable. Generally sympathetic to Burden's aesthetic goals and methodology, she expresses her own sense that in the case of *220*, a boundary had been transgressed: "In spite of the fact that the participants were involved of their own volition, I think the question of morality must be strongly raised in connection with this piece" (1975).

The "sucking in" of the audience, the elicitation of their consent to and perhaps participation in a performance event which involves assault upon only the artist's body raises still more questions about what constitutes violation of the audience. The performance piece *Rhythm O*, performed by Belgrade artist Maria Abramovic in 1974, is a case in point:

> Abramovic ... permitted a room-full of spectators in a Naples gallery to abuse her at their will for six hours, using instruments of pain and pleasure that had been placed on a table for their convenience. By the third hour, her clothes had been cut from her body with razor blades, her skin slashed; a loaded gun held to her head finally caused a fight between her tormenters, bringing the proceedings to an unnerving halt.[5]

What we encounter in a work such as this is the phenomenon of "reification". Once Abramovic surrendered performance activity to her audience while she herself assumed the condition of objecthood (in effect, corpsing herself), the audience seemed free to treat the vulnerable body as pure corporeality. For some observers of the 70s art scene, this development was perhaps the scariest of all. "Such reification," charged Richard Schechner, "is monstrous" (1980). For Max Kozloff, it was "derangement":

> [T]he urge to dissociate and depersonalize the body ... leads to considering others as less than human. Crimes that violate bodies depend, in one degree or another, on our propensity to turn people into things. It is by no means certain that some bodyworks even pretend to such derangement because they are directed inward. But at times the aura of it seems incipiently there, in reserve (1975).

---

[5] Several accounts exist, for one, see Blau 166.

I think we could safely assume that Abramovic's work would be excoriated by Kozloff in that its orientation was plainly directed outward.

Stanton Garner in his essay "Post-Brechtian Anatomies: Weiss, Bond, and the Politics of Embodiment" follows Elaine Scarry's lead urging that the suffering body "is no longer the seat of an externalizing productivity ... [but] ... becomes something inert, thinglike" (1991). Furthermore, "[to] inflict deprivation, confinement and violation against the body is to bring about a phenomenal collapse ... for as the body loses its status as the seat of a self-transcending subjectivity, it becomes objectified in its transfixing sentience, "subject" only to its liable corporeality" (1991). For Garner, as for Kozloff and Schechner, body art offers no resistance to commodification.

Our problem here is that while Kozloff, Schechner and Garner agree essentially, their attention is not directed toward the witnessing observer, but toward the pain-artist's suffering body. If we look for commentary on the issue of audience violation, we find far less unanimity. Bruce Barber articules these questions of audience contamination:

> The questions from the audience's standpoint in this instance may take the form of these: "To what extent am I put into the position of being an object by what I see before me – am I being harmed in some way by witnessing this act?" (1979)

Arthur Sabatini, as if in answer to these questions, takes the position that performance art bears a troubling likeness to actual terrorism and contends that manipulation, regardless of the affixing of the label "aesthetic", is, nonetheless, manipulation: "Although it is a cruelty to say this, the 'aesthetic' manipulation of people in a public environment (through installations or art-in-life performances) bears a resemblance to the disruptions caused by a bomb scare, hijacking, or explosion" (1986). Performance artists Genesis P. Orridge and Peter Christopherson raise but do not answer their own question as to whether "photos of Schwarzkogler ... [are] made acceptable by being framed on a white wall" (1979). Barber, on the other hand, confronts the issue head on and in taking Kozloff to task, insists that art is "insulated to a large degree", and that a critic's "feelings about what is right and lawful in art practice" do not sanction him or her as an "arbitrator" or "judge" (1979).

Herbert Blau's position at this juncture is particularly intriguing in that he is willing to take up the question of enforced participation in psychological terms as well as physical. Citing the example of Judith Malina's production of *The Brig*, he demonstrates how the imposition of a barbed wire proscenium barrier can project "onto the passive body of the spectator ... the form of social control being endured by the actors" (1990). To be sure, *The Brig* is a play, not a performance art piece, but it does illustrate how violence can be deflected onto the bodies and psyches of the observers. So palpable was this violation that, as Blau notes, reviewers such as Robert Brustein and Walter Kerr "transferred" compassion "from the actors to the audience" (1990). Brustein deemed *The Brig* a "punishment" not a play.[6] Blau finds

---

6 Quoted in Blau p. 166.

this reversal "curious," yet it does, in fact, make sense, given the disparity between the level of consent of the actors as opposed to that of the audience.[7]

Whether one speaks of physical pain or of psychic, the logical counterargument usually proffered is that the audience can refuse to participate, may, in fact, leave altogether. In practice that is not always true.[8] In many cases the structuring of a confining environment is deliberate – there have been productions, for example, whose playing space would have to be re-crossed by an exiting spectator, even if the performance were still in progress. There are performance spaces and places that essentially incarcerate and/or jeopardize the audience. I have attended performances in theatres in which the only escape route consisted of a narrow door which opened out to a narrow flight of steps which led to the pub below, five stories down. The audience is *not* always free to leave.

Judith Barry, in recounting performance events by feminist performance artists, provides the one lone example of a kind of performance art that refused to impound or abuse its audiences:

> Trust, intimacy and shared convictions between performers and audiences were of paramount importance to the success of these early feminist performances .... The audience had to trust in the emotional good will and psychological astuteness of the performer in order to be willing to undergo the painful intensity of many of the events. ... Finally, and very key, the combination of trust, intimacy and shared convictions ensured that anyone disturbed by a performance – whether a performer or member of the audience – would be given attention and support. It was an emotional and political atmosphere in which great risks could be taken and cathartic pain experienced in a safe situation (1980).

A safe situation ... such a demand or plea is not a call for sedative theatre or soporific performance art. In its drive to present violent images of the pain-wracked, commodified body, risk performance art succeeded only in gesturing toward itself. As Johannes Birringer remarks, "Instead of being able to break the mask of representation, some of the more radical and dangerous body art events... only reinforced the limits of transgression that were soon reached" (1991). To this I would add that risk artistry all too frequently gave little thought to the care of the spectator's body and psyche.

Laurie Anderson might well be speaking for the pain artist's audience in her *Like a Stream*:

> I don't know ... I've got a feeling this isn't what I paid my money for ... I mean ... I've got a funny feeling this isn't ... it just isn't ... you know ... what I paid my money for ...[9]

---

[7] Even the level of consent of the actor is to be questioned in some instances. Blau recounts moments when he observed actors abusing themselves and/or other actors: "There were times in performance when it seemed so painful that I wanted to leap on the stage and stop it." See p. 167.

[8] I have heard of productions whose seating policy consisted of purposely dividing and separating arriving parties of spectators. Audiences have been jammed three apiece into a cramped cubicle whose tiny windows provided the sole means of viewing the production; futhermore, this structure of cubicles was precariously perched atop a jerry-built platform. For these instances and much useful information, I am indebted to my colleagues who attended with me an NEH seminar under the direction of Herbert Blau in June and July 1991.

[9] The ellipses are not mine. (Anderson 44).

Bibliography

Anderson, Laurie. "Notes from 'Like a Stream.'" A.A. Bronson & Peggy Gale. 42–48.

Barber, Bruce. "Indexing: Conditionalism and Its Heretical Equivalents" A.A. Bronson and Peggy Gale. 183–204.

Barry, Judith. "Women, Representation, & Performance Art: Northern California." Carl E. Loeffler & Darlene Tong. (1980): 439–462

Battcock, Gregory & Robert Nickas, eds. (1984) *The Art of Performance: A Critical Anthology.* New York: E.P. Dutton

Birringer, Johannes. (1991) *Theatre, Theory, Postmodernism.* Bloomington: Indiana UP

Black, Joel. (1991) *The Aesthetics of Murder: A Study in Romantic Literature and Contemporary Culture.* Baltimore: The Johns Hopkins UP

Blau, Herbert. (1990) *The Audience.* Baltimore: The Johns Hopkins UP

Bourden, David. "An Eccentric Body of Art." *Saturday Review of the Arts* 1.2 (Feb 3, 1973): 30–32. Rpt. in Gregory Battcock & Robert Nickas. 183–193

Bronson, A.A. & Peggy Gale. (1979) *Performance by Artists.* Toronto: Art Metropole

Burden, Chris & Jan Butterfield. "Through the Night Softly." *Arts* 49.7 (March 1975): 68–72. Rpt. in Battcock & Nickas. 222–239.

Burnham, Linda Frye. "Performance in Southern California." Loeffler & Tong. 390–438

"Charlemagne Palestine." Interview with France Morin. Mar. 24–26, 1978. Bronson & Gale 100–112

Coutts-Smith, Kenneth. "Role Art and Social Context." Bronson & Gale. 217–236. Feral, Josette. (1982) "Performance and Theatricality: The Subject Demystified." Trans. Terese Lyons. *Modern Drama* 25.1, 170–181

Garner, Stanton B. "Post-Brechtian Anatomies: Weiss, Bond, and Politics of Embodiment." *Theatre Journal* (Mar. 1991): 145–164

Harrison-Pepper, Sally. (1990) *Drawing a Circle in the Square: Street Performing in New York's Washington Square Park.* University: UP of Mississippi

Kirby, Michael (1971) *Futurist Performances.* New York: E.P. Dutton

Kozloff, Max. "Pygmalion Reversed." Artforum 14.3 (Nov. 1975): 30–37

Kubiak, Anthony. (1991) *Stages of Terror: Terrorism, Ideology, and Coercion as Theatre History.* Bloomington: Indiana UP

Loeffler, Carl E. & Darlene Tong, eds. (1980) *Performance Anthology: Source Book for a Decade of California Performance Art.* San Francisco: Contemporary Arts Press

Orridge, Genesis P. & Peter Christopherson. "COUM Transmissions: Annihilating Reality." Bronson & Gale 65–71

Pelias, Ronald J. (1992) *Performance Studies: The Intepretation of Aesthetic Texts.* New York: St. Martin's Press

Sabatini, Arthur J. "Terrorism and Performance." *High Performance.* 34 (1986): 29–32

Scarry, Elaine, (1985) *The Body in Pain: The Making and Unmaking of the World.* New York: Oxford

Schechner, Richard. (1988) "Toward a Poetics of Performance." *Performance Theory.* Rev. Ed. New York: Routledge, 153–86

Shank, Theodore. "The Actual as Bizarre: Assaulting the Sensibilities of the Audience." *Drama Review* 22.2 (June 1978): 107–118

Contemporary Theatre Review, 1996, Vol. 5,1 pp. 27–32
Reprints available directly from the publisher
Photocopying permitted by license only

The Man who went Too Far

John Elsom

Peter Barnes's controversial play *Laughter!*, which uses slapstick comedy devices against the background of Auschwitz, failed in spite of its author's reputation. When it trivializes, instead of enlightening, humour cannot go very far. The article analyzes Peter Barnes's plays within the wider context of the battle between Modernism and Classicism. The Jacobean shock-effects used by Barnes in his plays lack real force, and only manage to preach to the half-converted. Veiled threats of new censorship laws under the Thatcher Era, the age of Political Correctness, made permissiveness an easy target for moralists. The article evaluates the shock-tactics *Laughter!* is a comment on, from the Swinging Sixties to the Anti-Clockwise Eighties.

KEY WORDS Paradox, Slapstick, Censorship, Dirty Plays, Modernism, Classicism, Jacobean, Shock Tactics, Political Correctness

Few British dramatists have been greeted by more fanfares than Peter Barnes in the late 1960s. The late Sir Harold Hobson, who occupied the critic's chair at *The Sunday Times* for forty years, described the opening night of *The Ruling Class* in 1968 at the Nottingham Playhouse as "a revelation". He was "suddenly and unexpectedly faced with the explosive blaze of an entirely new talent of a very high order". He likened the occasion to the premières of *Waiting for Godot* and Pinter's *The Birthday Party*.

After reading the typescript of *The Bewitched*, Ronald Bryden, the RSC's literary manager, wrote to his director, Trevor Nunn: "God must love us after all. I think this is a work of genius". Martin Esslin also described *The Bewitched* as "a work of true genius" and translated it into German to prove his point. Barnes was considered to possess all the talents. "Wit, pathos, exciting melodrama, brilliant satire, double-edged philosophy, horror, cynicism and sentiment, all combined in a perfect unity", wrote Hobson of *The Ruling Class*.

This critical honeymoon lasted for about ten years until 1978, when Barnes's *Laughter!* was produced at the Royal Court, two very black farces, side by side, the first set in the reign of Ivan the Terrible and the second in Auschwitz. Before either began, an Author, immaculately dressed, stepped out before the curtain to protest. Comedy trivialised suffering. "Laughter's the ally of tyrants. It softens our hatred", at which point a custard pie slapped on his face and his trousers fell down.

Some members of the audience laughed, others did not, while the rest were caught betwixt and between. Were we expected to laugh at the Author for being pompous or share his dislike of clowning? Should we enjoy or deplore the cruelty-slapstick? Are pogroms anything more than Tom-and-Jerry writ large? Peter Barnes had tossed us one of his grim paradoxes. Was the protective layer of humour which was supposed to help us to endure the intolerable anything more than the first grimace of a madman's cackle?

Laughter! ended in the concentration camp where two Jewish cross-talk comics, Bimko and Bieberstein, were dying the death, as they say, in a gas chamber. "The way to beat hydro-cyanide gas", wisecracks Bimko, "is by holding your breath for five minutes. It's just a question of mind over matter. They don't mind and we don't matter". Bieberstein curses "those foul, polluted German bastardized ..." and Bimko calms him down. "Hymie, Hymie, please. What you want to do – cause trouble?"

Laughter! was received by the audience in a stunned silence. It took a considerable effort in those days to stun audiences at the Royal Court, famous for being unshockable. Irving Wardle, the critic of *The Times*, remarked that it was an occasion when you felt "this sense of the earth moving under [your] feet", but my impression was that the feet were moving more than the earth.

The play was deemed to be in bad taste, not by the conservatives, who could be easily outraged, but by the liberals and the left, who were not accustomed even to using such phrases as "bad taste" except ironically. "Offending the audience" was a Sixties game, usually played with good humour on both sides, but there were occasions (and this was one) when audiences could be genuinely offended, which was either a measure of the play's success or its failure, according to one's point of view.

One Barnes supporter blamed the failure of *Laughter!* on the Jewish lobby, a paradox which Barnes could scarcely have written, a liberal congratulating himself on being able to laugh at gas chamber jokes which Jews found upsetting. Barnes's reputation suffered. He had trouble in finding the managements to produce his plays. Critics started to praise him more warily. He was reduced to writing radio monologues for the BBC, excellent in themselves but the equivalent, in terms of poorly paid literary effort, of several months down the salt-mines.

Laughter! was a kind of negative landmark, a play notable for the traces which it did not leave behind. It was like the line in the sand which showed how far the tide of permissiveness came up the beach before receding. After *Laughter!*, audiences were ready to take offense at plays thought to be offensive and the age of Political Correctness began. Blacks and Lesbians were Not Funny, nor were Mothers-in-Law and Vicars. In 1980, the National Theatre faced a private prosecution for obscenity over Howard Brenton's *The Romans in Britain* and was acquitted, but the fact that this case came to court at all set an ominous precedent. A law was passed to stop local authorities from promoting homosexuality by providing helpful books on the subject. Censorship returned.

The year in which *Laughter!* was produced, 1978, also has its political significance. A minority Labour government was clinging on to power, despite strikes, inflation and growing unemployment. Britain, it was said, was becoming ungovernable. In March 1979, a General Election returned Mrs. Thatcher to 10, Downing Street for her first term of office. Permissiveness had little to do with the economic or social problems which Britain faced, but it was an easy target for moralists to attack. Britain was decadent with all this promiscuity, blasphemy and drug-taking! Why at the Royal Court they were even making fun of Jews and gas chambers!

The anti-Thatcher alliance of intellectuals protested against these slurs on artistic integrity and the half-veiled threats of new censorship laws which lay behind them; but they were only half able to do so with conviction, for shock tactics had been part of Modernist dramatic theory for almost twenty-five years and the people whom they were trying to shock were those who supported Mrs. Thatcher. During the 1950s, there had been many battles with the Lord Chamberlain's Examiner of Plays over "bad language" and what constituted an obscene gesture. Samuel Beckett was asked to re-write *Waiting For Godot*. Joan Littlewood was reprimanded for an injudicious use of a broom in the musical, *Fings Aint Wot They Used T'be* (1959).

In these rude but courteous exchanges, the sympathies of the radicals were always with the shockers rather than the shocked. The Lord Chamberlain symbolised what was deemed to be what was wrong with Britain, its class system and its authoritarianism. The radicals were opposed to censorship in principle but also to those values which the Lord Chamberlain was supposed to defend, loosely characterised as the "British way of life". This implied respect for the Monarchy and the Anglican church, a defence of marriage and the Christian family, a deference towards authority and an observation of certain codes of behaviour; but the Lord Chamberlain's attempts to define what could and could not be permitted became petty and legalistic. He became a figure of fun. The word "bastard" was not allowed, but "illegitimate" or "born out of wedlock" were. Girls could stand naked on the stage but were not allowed to move. His authority did not extend to the private clubs around London, which flourished in his presence. It was from almost every point of view an intolerable situation.

Behind this bureaucratic struggle, another battle was raging between the Classicists and the Modernists. The Classicists might not have defended the Lord Chamberlain, but they would assert the right of the Guardians to guard. They would have insisted that a certain decorum should be upheld within the theatre, which partly meant avoiding stage violence and immodest behaviour. Modernists attacked such reticence on many grounds, but primarily because it was considered to be untruthful and a form of class protection. The standards of politeness prevailing in the West End conveyed the idea that society was calm and under control, whereas it was unjust, violent and sexy. Stage modesty was a kind of propaganda.

This local war (although it was less local than we thought) came to a head in 1965/66, with what became known as the "Dirty Plays" row at the Royal Shakespeare Company. The RSC was the second but unofficial British national company, whose director was Peter Hall, relatively young at 35. The official National Theatre was launched in 1963 at the Old Vic, under Sir Laurence Olivier, 58 years old and world-eminent. In the ensuing rivalry, the RSC was eager to experiment with ideas drawn from Artaud, Brecht, Genet and, in its Shakespearian productions, Jan Kott; while the NT upheld more traditional values. It was, or ought to have been, a battle between Modernism and Classicism; and this was how it felt at the time, although in retrospect many doubts creep in about Hall's radicalism or Olivier's conservatism.

The RSC's Modernism was more a matter of form than substance. It looked as if it was attacking the faults of the British way of life, but it advanced on such a broad front and with such lack of depth that it inflicted no damage. In the RSC's experimental Theatre of Cruelty evenings in 1964, Glenda Jackson stepped into a bath naked as Jackie Kennedy and emerged as Christine Keeler, a call girl in a recent British government scandal. This caused a furore, but the scale of the fuss disguised the silliness of the content. Peter Brook's *US* (1966) told us that the Vietnam War was a bad thing, but politely forbore to blame anyone for it.

Shock was prized as an end in itself, not as a means to an end. It was the Modernist's denial of Classical restraint. Of Peter Weiss's *The Marat-Sade* (which he directed in 1965), Brook wrote that "everything about this play is designed to crack the spectator on the jaw, then douse him with ice-cold water, then force him intelligently to assess what has happened to him, then give him a kick in the balls ...". The RSC's reputation was partly built upon mugging the middle classes without stealing anything, except more subsidies. The sequence of plays about violence, sex and the lives of politicians (themes not unknown to Shakespeare) provoked a section of the RSC's Board of Governors to call for Hall's resignation, which failed. The "Dirty Plays" row was won by the Modernists and "shock" became so familiar a feature of theatre-going that its absence alarmed more than its presence.

In this context, Peter Barnes became the critics' darling. His plays fitted most of the RSC's canons of Modernist taste. They were formidably literate. In *Leonardo's Last Supper* and *Noonday Demons* (1969), he scraped the barrel of dictionaries to find the Jacobean synonyms for whores and veneral diseases. In *The Bewitched*, he displayed a remarkable knowledge of the last of the Spanish Hapsburgs, Carlos, a mental defective whose failure to provide an heir led to the War of the Spanish Succession.

On one level, *The Bewitched* was a tour de force of historical re-construction, while on another Barnes's delight at providing startling images was both Jacobean and Modernist. Carlos's feeble appetites were stimulated at the end of Act One by an auto da fe, in which serious tortures were staged and rewarded by the father and mother of erections. "As the red wax bubbles and flows like blood, Carlos shifts position, legs apart. A monstrous phallus sprouts between them. The choir bursts forth triumphantly singing "Hallelujah! Hallelujah! The strife is o'er, the battle done ...' as the enormous phallus grows to become a massive eight feet long and two feet thick".

The second act provided what might be deemed the play's message. The real problem was not monarchies or aristocracies or impotent kings, but all forms of government. In his introduction, Bryden quoted Carlos's speech in which he denounces Authority:

> "No blessings come from't.
> No man born shouldst ha't' wield't.
> Authority's the basilisk, the crowned dragon,
> Scaly, beaked and loathsome.
> Born from a cock's egg, hatched under a toad,
> Its voice is terror, glance, certain death.
> Streams where 't drank once are poisoned
> And the grass around turns black.
> 'Twill make a desert o' this world
> Whilst there's still one man left t'give commands
> And another who'll obey them."
>
> (Act 2, scene xxii)

Bryden said that the play produced the effect on him "which A.E. Housman called the one infallible test of poetry: it made my scalp prickle with cold excitement."

Housman's test of poetry is widely taught in British schools and comes in useful at examinations because you do not have to say why you like something, only that it makes the scalp prickle. The sight of an eight foot by two foot phallus hanging over the edge of the Aldwych stage may have prickled some scalps, but Barnes's language had the appeal of a dubious antique shop. You wanted to know why so much effort had been spent on faking the wormholes and spraying on an odour of cats' piss. The deception was more elaborate than the plot required. When this erudition had been scraped away, what was left but a Sixties attack on "authority", a call for anarchy Beatles-style?

In his earlier play, *The Ruling Class,* Barnes attacked the hereditary peerage in Britain. In his lovable but dotty defence of *The Ruling Class,* Hobson pointed out that some members of the upper classes were actually members of Barnes's cast, notably Peter Eyre ("whose grandfather was Lord Acton") and Jonathan Cecil ("the grandson of the Marquis of Salisbury"), and so Barnes cannot have been so prejudiced against the peerage as the play implied. In a sense, that was what was wrong with *The Ruling Class* and *The Bewitched.* A fanciful, Eng. Lit. world was created upon the stage, which was supposed to be commenting on what was wrong with Britain but failed to do so. The trouble with the British House of Lords is not that it is filled with sadistic maniacs, but with "the Great and the Good" who believe that they represent Britain and can decide what is best for the rest of us.

The shocks were little more than frissons to the senses. They did not disturb at a deep enough level. Shock in the theatre, as elsewhere, requires a "mass" and a "force", the mass being public expectations and the force being the power for conversion. Barnes like the RSC spent too much time preaching to the half-converted, which was why he sometimes compensated for the lack of force in his arguments with an excess of baroque shock-horror on stage, rather like the Jacobean dramatists whom he liked and imitated.

The RSC was not alone among the British subsidised companies in the 1960s to seek such shock effects. Its chief rival in London was the English Stage Company (ESC) at the Royal Court. When the RSC farted in Roger Vitrac's *Victor,* the ESC belched in Jarry's *Ubu Roi.* The difference between them was that the ESC, with no pretensions to being a national company, could afford to be more radical.

In 1965, ESC staged the first performance of Edward Bond's *Saved,* in which a baby is stoned to death in a pram. It shocked on several levels. It was painful enough to watch at the time, but even more disturbing to remember and think about afterwards. Bond blamed capitalism for the cruelty whose effects stained the blankets with blood. The hooligans may have been working-class but they were victims of a society indifferent to their needs.

Saved contained such scenes of violence that it could never, under any circumstances, have received the approval of the Lord Chamberlain's Examiner of Plays. The Royal Court turned itself into a club theatre to stage it, but it was still not free from the attentions of the Metropolitan Police, who dressed in plain clothes to see if they could find anyone who was not a club member buying a drink at the Royal Court's bar. The ESC was eventually charged with the abuse of its club's licence, but won the ensuing court case. This in turn led to the downfall of the Lord Chamberlain's Examiner of Plays, a post abolished in 1968.

There is a telling difference between the shocking scenes in *Saved* and those in *The Bewitched* and *Laughter!*. Bond's scenes gain in power as they approach "real life", whereas Barnes's lose strength. *Laughter!* was not offensive because it told jokes about the gas chamber. There is a long tradition of gallows' humour in British theatre. Nor was it acceptable because the Author went out of his way to deplore gas chamber jokes. It was unpleasant because it lacked thought and sensitivity towards its subject: it trivialised where it could have enlightened.

Paradoxically Barnes's *Laughter!* achieved a recognition of what its stage Author insisted was the danger of laughter. Until 1978, black humour, anarchy and irreverence were all acceptable as part of a crusade against middle-class values; but there came a point where those despised standards were seen and felt to be more humane than the avant-garde's rejection of them. It may be that Barnes was aware of the appropriateness to the times of his deliberate bad taste, in which case he achieved more with this lost and forgotten play, *Laughter!*, than with his better known works. Or it may simply be that this was the point where his talent for the over-theatrical led him astray. At all events, from that moment on, it is possible in Britain to trace the change in direction from the Swinging Sixties to the Anti-Clockwise Eighties, in which the pendulum of the previous thirty years was thrown, harshly, judderingly, into reverse.

Contemporary Theatre Review, 1996, Vol. 5,1 pp. 33–50
Reprints available directly from the publisher
Photocopying permitted by license only

The Cunts, the Knobs and the Corpse: Obscenity and Horror in Howard Barker's *Victory* (1983)

I wish I could be more offensive I really do. (I.2)
Out-fucking-rageous! (Interlude)

Georges Bas

Beyond Barker's use of both obscene language and shockingly indecent situations, the play's striking originality lies in its challenging conjunction or fusion of bawdy and gruesome ingredients. Through a heightened picture of what the Restoration is commonly supposed to have been – obscene sex and venereal disease, Barker's aim is to provide a metaphorical exposure of "Reaction" as identifying with sexual violence and sexual animality, while an ambivalent portrait of Charles II as lewd but self-aware emerges out of both. And the various horrific elements, especially when they combine with obscene features, convey the similarly ambivalent comment the play makes on the self-appointed mission of the widow Bradshaw in gathering her regicide husband's remains, but, together with expressing an indictment of the Royalists, prove to be the instruments of the King's revenge against the new masters of the country. Obscenity and horror concur to bring out the structural and thematic importance of Charles, and, through the various tensions and complexities they create, show *Victory* to be one of the most achieved instances of Barker's "Theatre of Catastrophe".

KEY WORDS Bradshaw and Charles II, Character ambivalence, Reaction, Restoration period, Macabre horror, Sexual obscenity

Among the various post-censorship English playwrights, Howard Barker is undoubtedly the one – with the obvious exception of Steven Berkoff – whose plays would most seldom have passed the pre-68 required licensing unscathed, that is – as Osborne's and Bond's oft reported cases had shown – without the request of textual cuts or/and "omitting" part of a situation or the whole of a crucial scene, let alone the application of a total ban. And the one production of his most likely to have born the full brunt of the Lord Chamberlain's wrath is *Victory*, arguably his most achieved play so far, certainly a paradigmatic one. The nine "cunts" so profusely flourished in its short opening episode would have been slashed off straightaway,[1] but, most especially, the breathtaking scene which soon afterwards (I.3) displays Charles II's Court in its post-coronation bawdy talk and activities could not have been regularly staged before 1968, so daring is its visual and textual trangression of sexual taboos. Barker is known to have acknowledged "the conscious use of words conventionally described as obscene", claiming that he does it "with calculation and discrimination for their dramatic effect ... sometimes with

[1] The brief exchange "Time's a Cunt./So's God" (23) compounds obscenity with blasphemy. (References concerning the play will be to the first, separate edition [Barker, 1983] and will follow the quotations made in the text.) Barker will go much farther in *The Castle* (1985), 20–21, in the debate on "Christ's cock," "nowhere mentioned in the Bible", etc.

calculated excess, and always with the deliberate intention of creating … unease in the audience …"[2] The point about *Victory* is that such a statement should be extended beyond the "use of words" to a similar use of obscene situations and stage actions. But what is most striking is that Barker's plea about obscenity applies just as well to the other major ingredient in the play, the one concerning death – more exactly its macabre or horrific manifestations. From The *Love of a Good Man* (1978) to *The Castle* (1985), combining sex, obscene or not, and macabre horror is a standing feature in several Barker plays. But *Victory* proves really paroxystic in its exploitation of both, and in no other play are they as co-extensive with the whole action. Its indecent features outdo those of the bawdiest Restoration comedy while its grisly effects are the boldest to be met since the great Jacobeans, and in few dramatists are the two so intimately brought together. So that, beyond any identification of Eros and Thanatos, that all too familiar couple of literary criticism, the real issue in *Victory* is the raison d'être and functional roles of both obscenity and horror proper.

The two notions happen to be mentioned close to each other when the former "Secretary" of one Bradshaw, a dead Republican regicide and "Polemicist" (*Characters*) referring to "the obscene career" of his widow – the main character of the play – in those early Restoration days, wonders which event in it "gave [him] the most horror" (41).[3] In this instance, the two terms are obviously employed without any sexual or gruesome connotation, and Scrope – the Secretary – makes them nearly synonymous expressions of his moral blame. Both the semantic extension and the similarity are to be borne in mind. But in the course of the play, not only the widow but most of the characters are involved in sexually obscene situations or confronted with ghastly figures of horror. And, besides illustrating Barker's claim that a play of his is "a work of art in which the normal criteria of offence and empathy are abolished",[4] *Victory* gives ample evidence that his "calculated excess" in order to create "unease" is triumphantly justified through the way both the obscenity and the horror in it, which make up the very texture of the play, become – as Barker has argued about the former only – "a ground for moral revaluation".[5] They are dramatic vehicles meant to test the "validity and truth"[6] of the main characters and the society depicted.

The nine "cunts" of the opening scene are something like an overture to a play really resounding throughout with obscene four-letter words. Quite unsurprisingly, most of these have a sexual origin, copulation being expressed through several synonymous verbs besides "fuck" – such as "shag", "bang", "frig" or

---

[2] "On Language in Drama", in Barker (1989), 27–28.

[3] The historical John Bradshaw actually was the President of the High Court which judged and sentenced Charles I (see *Victory*, 25). Barker disclaims any historical accuracy in his "history plays" (see n. 12 below). Exerting his creative freedom as an artist in *Victory*, he renames Bradshaw "Dick" (35, 60) and turns him into the author of a fictitious utopian treatise called "*Harmonia Britannia*" [sic]. So that the lawyer with moderate, even conservative, views is reputed to have been a radical Republican ideologist. (See n. 18 below for Bradshaw's posthumous fate as a regicide.) In the play, the character of his widow is simply called "Bradshaw". The same will be done here, except when confusion is to be avoided.

[4] "On Language in Drama", in Barker (1989), 26.

[5] Ibid., 28.

[6] Ibid., 28.

"hump", and "knob" or "dick" often replacing "cock" to refer to the male organ, while "slit" or "purse" are only occasional – though picturesque – variations on "cunt" to designate the female pudenda. But scatological obscenity never lags far behind, and "poop" as well as "shit" or "fart", to which "rump" or "arse" (as well as "bum") and "piss" could be added, are common enough. The same initial "cunts" show that such "foul language" (5) can often serve merely to voice abuse and, whatever the scenes or the characters, obscene expletives or intensives are liberally flung about, as has indeed become customary in post-censorship drama. Yet, beyond "the two or three words we are so often exercised about", as Barker has put it,[7] most of the obscene slang in the play has a very definite anatomical and sexual application – as "boob", "tit" or "dug" for women's breasts, or "bollocks" for "balls", also testify. Barker's defence in answer to the objection "Do you really need those words?" has been to declare them "irreplaceable", grounding his refusal to ban them on a "responsibility" to "emotional truth", that is to the expression of "feeling", whether "fear" or "longing" and "desire", and arguing that the imputation of obscenity is only an attempt to "inhibit emotion."[8] Much more valid for whatever is erotic in a sexually obscene idiom than for a scatological one, such an argument does not quite account for the "calculated excess" also claimed by Barker. But what is most distinctive about sexual obscenity in *Victory* is that, far from being – as in Berkoff – packed within monological word spoutings, or self-contained verbal outpourings, of a lyrical and artificial nature, it is evenly distributed along the various episodes or situations and over the whole cast of dramatis personae, irrespective of class, rank, political party or gender – so that courtiers or City people, Royalists or Republicans, duchesses or Puritan matrons are all almost equally obscenely gross. The reason for this is not, Barker has made it clear, naturalistic authenticity – a "spurious realism" which would be truthful to the way all people actually speak,[9] neither is it historical verisimilitude – the language of the play being evidently anachronistic. Still, however "compellingly imaginative" it was meant to be,[10] its indecent dialogue, even when it may seem overdone, does convey the sense of real people in a real society, is true to character and situation. And their concretely felt physicality makes these words "irreplaceable" for verbal or stylistic as much as emotional reasons. Their often monosyllabic punch and their general phonetic impact combine with their semantic or/and imagistic vitality to heighten such evocative or forceful phrases as "the sun like the bald baker's bollocks" (1) by a soldier, "I'm pissed on pomp ... I'm pig hot in this ponce stuff" (9) by a courtier, "All the juice in the royal 'ores cunts will never make my fingers soft" (29) by a City builder with "clumsy paws", or "Stay there you ball of scrawn and bollocks" (42) by a threatening Cavalier, and countless others. These are an index of the inventive and vigorous stage language for which Barker is justly reputed, and to emphasize the unquestionable dramatic force of his "highly charged"[11] obscene idiom is not to purify *Victory* of any stigma of indecency.

[7] Ibid., 27.

[8] Ibid., 27.

[9] Ibid., 26.

[10] Ibid., 26.

[11] Ibid., 27.

Nevertheless, more crucial than answering "Do you really need those words?" is the other question which this suggests: "Do you really need those scenes?" This, of course, applies primarily to the daring Court scene (I.3), where the indecent nature of what is shown as well as spoken (often tactfully slurred over by critics) reaches heights of near pornographic excess unmatched even by the notorious "china scene" in Wycherley's *The Country Wife.* For the two main moments in the scene are equally outrageous. Hardly back from Westminster Abbey, still in his coronation robes and "with the anointment still damp on his forehead" (10), King Charles feels he must "grasp [the] arse" of his mistress. This will lead to the Duchess of Devonshire actually masturbating him in public, even though his courtiers' attention is drawn away from the obscene act. Whatever the staging of this is – and it can range from stylized suggestion to downright soft porn – the dialogue is quite outspoken as to what is happening: "Charlie, you are hurting my arse .../Get me then, get me in your hand ... Oh, tight in your hand!/I am –/Tighter! ... Tighter yet!" (12) And the result of the masturbation leads to a really nauseating exchange: "Charlie, I must wash my hand –/ No./I am sticky –/Lick it, then, cats do –"(13). But this has also produced a sudden fit of digust and depression in Charles, who drives his courtiers out, whereas Devonshire voices her disapproval of his altered mood in the boldest terms: "I must say I prefer you with you fist up me to this, the foul thing on your lips, altogether prefer it"... "Your knob I understand, your knob I will bow to, but not sentiment" (14). Being now sexually aroused, she vainly tries to entice him through exposing herself: "Oh, Charles, come here, catch me underneath now, quick, not in my fingers, do look, look now, see I have no knicker, look".[14] The pressing incitation to look and the *Long pause, as she poses with her skirts flung up* (14) might suggest frontal nudity and cannot but raise erotic titillations in the audience's minds. And as Charles, now *"all passion spent"* (14), frustrates her attempt with "Please tuck your cunt away"(14), Devonshire understandably bursts out into coarse invective, calling him "the most insulting man"(14), ... "And loathsome ... To the spunk, to the fart in you ... To your little weak come"(15). Loathsome certainly is the word for the various features of both the masturbation episode and the salacious duologue that follows it, both of which could invite a director to indulge in stage pornography.

Slightly different is the bare hint of visual indecency when Charles, in his self-disgust, answers Devonshire's injunction "Do up your fly" with "No, let it out!" and *"flings off his wig and trousers."*(13) This perhaps is not enough to imply any offensive exhibition. But in a later scene, a somewhat similar situation might again tempt a director to show more than is required. This is when the Royalist Ball, complaining of an "ailing foreskin" and seeking "a cure for [his] trouble," asks a doctor whom he mistakes for "a pox specialist" (22) to examine him, going into details far beyond the medical occasion: "I'll sit and unbutton. And if it rises thinking of the Bradshaw woman, tap it with some cold instrument. And blunt, mind you"... "Touch it, then, it won't bite you" ... "How is the knob, then?"(21) ... "Don't pluck it, quack, examine it!" (22) Even without any indecent exposure, the verbal boldness is enough to produce sheer obscenity.

Such shocking scenes as these undeniably run the risk of creating an "unease" that will result only in cheap sniggers or guffaws. Yet an obvious answer to the question of their necessity is that through them and others, as well as through the permanent "cock and cunt talk" (20), Barker provides – in his own words – a piece of "imagined history" which, though an artefact, is not "any the less historical."[12] In other words, set "In Good King Charles's Golden Days", *Victory* is partly meant to offer a picture of the Restoration period as public opinion most commonly supposes it to have been. True to type and, to this extent, unoriginal, the picture is as reductive as it is deliberately heightened, excessive and provocative. For, apart from the significant political features which make up another important dimension of the play, and against the idealizing official falsities trotted out in bad verse by the (fictitious) Poet Laureate (I.3, II.4), the Restoration is brought down to being little more than obscene sex and veneral disease. This is aptly summarized in a thumb-nail sketch due to Ball as he has his "knob" examined:

> Now the puritans are done for you will make a living as a cock specialist, if you're so minded. We bring from Europe every boil and sore now, it's the restoration of old lewdness and the reign of fucking.(22)

Little else needs adding. The fictitious Devonshire (any one of the King's numerous mistresses), who shows how foul-mouthed duchesses could be and how lewdly they could behave, expresses no dislike to being "Dragged out of dinners and humped in the passage before the eyes of the servants" (14). And Mc Conochie, Bradshaw's son, who wants to be a surgeon but takes Ball's advice to become a pox doctor and "live in posh" (22), ends up as "the great specialist" (56) at Court, lauded as a "prodigy" who knows how "To banish drips from sickly cocks" (56).

Emerging from most of the scenes, the picture is more especially conveyed through two of the more individualized characters, those who most markedly embody male lechery, Ball himself and Charles. More exactly, like the other characters, each is first and foremost representative or typical. Charles is "A Monarch" (*Characters*) and Ball "A Cavalier" in the same way as Devonshire is "A Mistress" and Nell Gwynn, the actress, "A Prostitute". But they are the ones in whom generic and personal features are best fused into convincing individual figures. Ball's language builds him up as the most neurotically sex-obsessed of all the characters, yet this is also expressive of a political attitude. Very aptly named, he is the iconic "randy" (32) Cavalier. Permanently abusive in the coarsest way, he pretends he is "rude because [he has] lost fifteen years" in exile, where he "swagged his hours with the bints of Calais "and licked Frenchmen's bums for nourishment and Spaniards' crotches" (3). But Ball also claims that he already "thought a lot" of Bradshaw in her "cold puritan shift" (19), and his behaviour towards the widow is an obscenely sexual expression of the Cavalier Puritan relationship. Far from thinking that the Puritans "killed old love in England" (5), he wants "a puritan woman" (21) because "They know what they do with their eyes cast down and starchy collars!" (21), because "the modesty of a real woman it does wonders to" him, he is "hard as rock" (20) as he puts it. Enraged by "this polish and this timber" in the widow's house, where "they lorded it" while he was "a pig in Calais" (20), he inveighs quite pathologically against its "disgusting cleanliness" (20). The least pathological of his sexual fantasies is that Bradshaw would "dry [his] poor wet feet in [her] lap, in [her] hot place" (19), though he adds "oh, excuse the cavalier in me, I know it offends" (19). More offensive are those in

12 "... my history plays are imagined history. I don't do research, they are an amalgam of intuitions, and the absence or misuse of facts does not make them any the less historical" – in Barker (1984), 34.

which an obviously fetishist obsession with "her starched underthings" (19) or "her starchy knicker" (20) and the compulsive mention of beds and sheets (5, 42), blending with his scatological propensity, result in "the odour of the stale old crutch and knicker" (5) or "the smell of you, a little musty, I expect, the musty hair of a sad-eyed puritan" (19–20), which betray a diseased imagination. And this also feeds on jealously conjuring up visions of love-making between the widow and her husband that lead him to ask whether she "swallowed" him (5). Obsessed with "fucking" Bradshaw from the moment he meets her (5), he pursues (22) her along her journey, eventually proclaiming "I will fuck you or I shall go mad. You have given me hell ..." (43). Ball's case does indeed border on insanity.

As to Charles, he is not the Merry Monarch but, as a City businessman calls him, "the mad shagman" (33). The self-portrait of his pre-Restoration days, when he "frigged his way through Europe, banging in the gardens, banging in the maze" (13), outdoes the usual cliché. More revealing is his identification of kingly rule with sexual activity. The words "restoration" and "monarchy" only prompt him to require the presence of "[his] duchess" and "her arse" (10), and he assures his courtiers that "mollyshagging" the same whore as an apprentice ensures "loyalty": "He grasps your flesh, he shares your monarchy." (10) To him monarchy and obscenity are obviously synonymous. His reading of recent English history is in the same vein, as is shown by the way he reacts to his father being called "Charles the martyr, noble Stuart" (9): though he declares he did not "like [his] dad" (9) but "reveres" his mother, to him the former "was in any case a sod" "who kept his cock dry for my mother", the latter "was a bint in essence", "an unfulfilled bint actually." (9) Brutally blunt, such an account of the early Stuarts leads him to draw the logical conclusion that "You cannot wonder at the revolution ... any nation governed by a bint and a sod will rise in protest" (9). His reductive cynicism is completed by fears of going "barmy" on account of his ascendancy: besides the suspicion that his father "had it" – the pox (15), there was "Sister-fucking – up nieces – down nephews – bad blood and funny bones – Stuart eggs all broken in the saucepan – " (15–16). A picturesque exaggeration, this is less significant than Charles's clear-sightedness about himself and his situation. Whereas his father "would complicate matters by being a saint as well as a sod" (9), he styles himself "a male bint pure and simple" (10), and though official rhapsodies greet him as "Our star, our moon, our radiant sun" (9), he knows he is only "a poor male bint wiping [his] knob on swan and cockatoo, draping the silk over [his] rump" (11). A grossly obscene but not inaccurate picture of what it meant to be a "monarch" after the Restoration. And if he nostalgically remarks that Bradshaw, the regicide, "when he pissed did not wince" (11), Charles voices his suspicion of Hambro, the banker and one of the Restoration "powerful men", (35) through "you ... never fuck nobody" and "I wish you fucked more" (16),[13] which are arguably meant to enlist our sympathy.

Of course, for all its "historical" dimension, *Victory* is metaphorical throughout: Barker has acknowledged using history in an Epic way, "in order to evoke, or unlock, feelings about the present."[14] Its date and its subtitle, *Choices in Reaction*, almost suffice to interpret the play as intending various parallels between the

[13] This seems enough to demolish Tony Dunn's oversubtle argument that "Capital and genital activity are intimately connected" – in Dunn (1984), 78.

[14] Barker (1984), 35.

Restoration and the anti-Left, reactionary or ultra-Right ideology of the Thatcher decade. But, besides specific capitalist/monetarist similarities, *Victory* achieves a broad, imaginative or imagistic picture of the Restoration as "Reaction", showing that it means, among other things, violence and animality expressed through obscene sex. Its Cavalier/Royalist dimension still is paramount, and again Ball and Charles are the main representatives of such "choices in reaction." Quite strikingly, both "the mad shagman" and the "randy" Cavalier happen, at some moment, to write verse letters or poems to Devonshire and Bradshaw. Having sent his duchess away from the Court, Charles keeps writing to her "beautifully" about her "rump" (40), and Ball, pursuing Bradshaw, boasts to her about composing "thirty sonnets in one night, there is cavalier art for you" (43) and being "sonnet mad for [her] " (43). The wordly-wise royal whore knows that this is "All very flattering" (39) but "a woman should never forget a poem is actually dick" (39) or, as she tells Bradshaw, that "all poems are dick" (40) – an incidental but definite debunking of "cavalier art" and poetry. But what the play actually dramatizes through Ball is that "dick" spells sexual violence. When he first meets the widow, Ball already bluntly declares: "when you stand there icy in your purity I could really dagger you with my old cavalier dick" (3). Freud would say that "dick" and "dagger" are one and the same, but the Cavalier is the permanent illustration of the political, reactionary nature of such sexual violence. Just before flourishing a sonnet allegedly "in the Italian manner" (43), he threatens Bradshaw with "I shall love you on this shore, or stab you" (43). In vain, realizing that he is about to "force" her (43), will the widow attempt to dissuade him, saying she prefers he would "read the poem" (43); she can but yield to his threats which, amounting to a rape, are quite the opposite of the love "founded on freedom of will and desire" (43) mentioned by Scrope, a witness to the scene. And Ball's most significant argument is not personal, "I am that bewildered" (43), but political, **"I am an agent of Charles Stuart, all I do is legal, naught is wrong, see?"** (43), or, as he declares a moment before, **"I am come into my rights!"** (42) Quite early in the play, he already made his own sexual obsession part of very real retaliations against the Puritans, such as "burning up and down the country, singeing rebels' widows in their empty beds" (5). Said to be "a fascist" by Barker himself,[15] Ball is the embodiment of verbal and physical violence throughout the play. But when he claims to Bradshaw that he has "come to master [her] like taking England back" (19), he makes it clear that his sexual violence is the metaphor of a reactionary sense of revengeful power and "victory."

Ball's behaviour is partly to be ascribed to an obscene animality which he shares with the monarch. His imagination is so inflamed by the expression "gone to be an animal" written by Bradshaw that, suspecting Mc Conochie of getting "in there before him "(21), "Dog-wise, yes, you did" (21) is the image that comes to his mind, and he charges the doctor with "being animal" (21), unaware that this applies much better to his own sexual ravings. The same dog image is the one employed by Charles when he acknowledges that no sooner will Devonshire have left London than his "knob will be up and barking for her" (15) or when he wishes he could follow the banker's tricks "like the dog to the bitch's arse" (16). Though this suits the lecherous monarch quite well, Charles elsewhere identifies himself quite explicitly with another and even more reputedly obscene type of animal. In

15 Barker (1986), 342, 1st col.

his post-masturbation fit of revulsion, he realizes that, much more than **"a clown!"** (13), he is a "monkey" – "a red-bummed monkey!" (13) And as Devonshire corrects this to "Blue-bummed" (13), for "Their bums are blue" (14), Charles clamours for "baboons" and "their coloured arses" (14). Accepting these as emblems of himself, he will "wear baboon skin" and paint his own bum blue, so that "the royal barge shall be babooned!" and he **"will droop** [his] **glistening arse for London out the prow!"** (14) Turning himself into a baboon, the King knows he is speaking the "truth" (13) about himself. Just before this, when he starts stripping off his clothes – "Out, bum!" (13) – and Devonshire tells him "You are always like this when you've come" (13), Charles's reply is "Yes, it is the only time I see things." (13) His own obscenity has now provided him with an occasion to "see" with undeniable self-awareness that, as a man and a king, he is not different from a baboon. And yet, beyond the monarch, animality is what defines all the Royalist party and the whole period. When, in a late scene, Hambro the banker, unable to suffer their humiliations any more, breaks out against the King and his courtiers, he says how he hates **"big arsed men who live like cattle!"** (57) and how he hopes they will "Die like – bullocks rolling in the gore" (57). Just as the dialogue of the play often coincides with the language of violence and torture,[16] it is pervaded with animal references and imagery.[17] And Bradshaw herself makes it quite clear that she has "gone to be an animal" because living in this Restoration reactionary period is to live "in time of animals" (20), or, as she also says, "Because we must crawl now, go down on all fours, be a dog or rabbit ... got to be a dog now and keep our teeth" (18). As a consequence, she accepts "being a proper four-legged bitch" (18) in order to survive.

Yielding to Ball's sexual violence, accepting the pervasive animality of what proclaims itself as a "new world" (4), Bradshaw even seems to echo its obsessive obscenity when, just after she has announced her decision, she indulges in a piece of extended and quite obvious sexual double entendre expressing how she "was shamed" (18) by her dead husband:

> Getting his ugly reason out ... showing it in public ... forever exhibiting his mind, was ever a mind hung out so much in public, dirty thing it was ... great monster of a mind so flashed and brazenly dangled? (18)

Turning a Republican's intellect into an obscene "knob", the widow shows that the very victims of the Restoration can be contaminated by it, but also that obscenity is not limited to sex and can have – as Scrope bears out – other and broader applications.

Pervasive as it is, and indubitably meaningful throughout, sexual obscenity yet becomes less insistent as the play develops, while, as this happens, macabre horror progressively looms larger. So that it could, with some simplification, be said that

---

16 "So we slit it, this draper's long nose" (2), "a tongue ... not red or roaring and at the end, ripped out" (7), "rip down the lanes and burn the manors" (21), "it's noses slit and ears off" (24), "knocking the eyeballs out of puritans" (32), "I'll split your liver" (43), "they put him on a rack ... the magistrates were out to get him chopped" (62), etc.

17 Charles to the City men: "Down, poodles, down spaniels!" (36) or Ball to a minor character: "you skinny little shivering hound" (52), are two of the numerous dog images.

Act One is the obscenity act – most so in its first four scenes, while Act Two is the horror act – with a concentration of it in the last three scenes. This structural distribution is not unrelated to the main plot-line: after Bradshaw has been informed of what is to be done to her regicide husband's disinterred body – to be dismembered and scattered, spiked and exhibited in various places ("The trunk's on Blackfriars, the legs on the Strand"(11),[18] the rest of Act One shows her starting on her errand to "collect his pieces" (18); she will do it only in the course of Act Two, which is eventually devoted to the way she manages to "pick his bits" (4). As a result, the horror of the corpse remains all but invisible in Act One, limited to verbal references until the ghastly epiphany of its head at the very end of the closing "Interlude." Then horror will intensify, reaching a peak in the compounded gruesome effects of Act Two, Scene Four, where a cruelly mutilated figure is revealed before a second appearance of the corpse's head. Indeed the play's structure consists of two movements leading up to the final disclosure – each time by none other than Charles, of all people – of the same "bonze all rotten" (10), a two-fold epiphany which thus assumes an undeniable importance.

Though the various "bits" or "pieces" of the corpse are at first decently kept out of view, the verbal vividness of the text conveys the full **"horror of being dug"** (8) and "left to freely disintegrate" (4), with what is "so disgusting" (4) about it. This is brought home by the widow, who, though her husband's head "hurt [her] so much with its arguments" (8) she "often wanted to put it on a spike [herself]" (6), yet cares for his "poor brain" (7). She does it most forcibly with her two children when she imparts the news to them, an occasion for eloquent contrasts between opposite attitudes to the horror, especially in the dialogue with her daughter:

> BRADSHAW. ... the brain I'd have thought, being soft –
> CROPPER. Shh –
> BRADSHAW. The very first thing to rot, I expect, I imagine would –
> CROPPER. Don't imagine –
> BRADSHAW. I want to imagine. Would go liquid or possibly – I have not seen a brain – dry up like a nut – a rattling nut –
> CROPPER. Shh!
> BRADSHAW, ... in the skull – a pebble – or imagine –
> CROPPER. Don't imagine –
> BRADSHAW. I will imagine! Stop telling me not to imagine!
> Alternatively, a skull full of muck, which if tipped, or tilted, would drip through the eyes, would weep its own brains out, cry muck down your skirt, splash dirty intellect on stockings and shoes – (7–8)

Barker is not out to endow Bradshaw with a morbid imagination in having her so insistently harp on nauseating details. And the graphic physicality of her idiom – "rattle", "drip", "muck", as energetic and as much meant to create unease as the

---

[18] President Bradshaw, the regicide lawyer, died in 1659 and was not "three years dead" (10) when he was exhumed at the end of January 1661; he had not been buried in "an unmarked spot" (6) or a "wet field" (10), but embalmed and granted the glory of Westminster Abbey, like Cromwell and Ireton. And he suffered the same iniquities as those inflicted on them as chief regicides: after being dragged through the streets from Holborn to Tyburn, their bodies were "hung" (4) in their shrouds, but only their heads were cut off, spiked and exposed on the top of Westminster Hall for decades to come (in the play, Bradshaw's head is visible from somewhere at Court in Whitehall – I.3). Also, his widow could not "collect and bury him" (4) after this Restoration outrage, as she died the same year as her husband; and the couple were childless, while a son and a daughter play significant though minor parts inthe play, See *DNB*; or Antonia Fraser (1973), 691–95.

numerous "cunt", "knob", and "fuck" – is aimed at the audience as much as at Cropper, relentlessly driving both fully to visualize what a rotting head actually is, making it palpably, because imaginatively, real.[19] And the widow's dauntless facing of the horrible truth as to the facts of death will again be opposed to her daughter's refusal to do the same when, having "brought Bradshaw back" after "some little inconvenience" (62) to herself – as she mildly puts it, she wants her to "Look at it, then!" (62), "In the bag, the dad" (62). Cropper, who first "turns in horror" then "concedes" (62), declares that "It is not him" because "It's bones!" (63), but the mother evinces the same inexorably factual attitude: "Yes, of course, it's bones, what did you expect? It's bones, obviously. Naturally, it's bones –" (63). So that, whatever opinion is formed of the widow's chequered journey as she carries out her macabre errand — down to the last-minute contrast between the two ways in which mother and daughter have honoured the deceased Bradshaw's memory,[20] her bold confrontation of the horror must surely be held as positive. But, most curiously, another character, Charles himself, is shown to embody a similar quality, which he twice exerts at the expense of the City men, once quite sarcastically against Hambro when the banker prefers "not to imagine" (16) that he could have the King "quietly butchered" (16) if Charles was found "barmy" (15), more ruthlessly when he forces them to look at the corpse's "bonze" – "look at his one eye" (35), "Look him in the eye, Ralph, the eye please, fix it ... **No, look at him.**" (36) It certainly is more than a coincidence that Charles should be made to share Bradshaw's unblinking courage to "imagine" and "look."

During the time it is still kept offstage, the grisly head is both safely distanced and yet unpleasantly present through verbal means in the Court scene (I.3), since, in this post-coronation moment, it is supposed to be spiked "underneath a window" (10) to which the courtiers first *"crowd"* to comment on it, then from which they will all "chuck skittles at it" (10), all "fling at the regicide's bonze" (11), *"throwing"* so much *"in earnest"* (11) that it will eventually be struck "down in the yard" (12). Here also the audience is spared no offensive detail as to what the head looks like and what is happening to it: "I touched him, he spun! ... The eyeballs are watching us, ugh!", "Jaw dropped!" (11), "Shook on its spike! ... Clipped him on the ear!/Oh, the ear drops off!" (12), "Oh, poor little ear! 'is little ear, look!" (12) Yet what is most obviously conveyed through such information is the shockingly insensitive behaviour of the courtiers themselves as they childishly exult in their game of skittles with a human skull.

When the head is at last made visible at the end of Act One, with the King surprisingly having it produced out of a bag (35), perhaps revulsion is not what is felt, as Charles, when he had asked it to be fetched him near the end of the Court scene, had required it to be washed "and the sparse hairs parted" (15), which may soften the horror when he handles it about before the amazed participants in this strange "Interlude." Against this, when Bradshaw receives the full shock of *"something black and shapeless"* – the spiked trunk – on *"A gate in Blackfriars"* (50), the widow has to conquer herself (50). And it is no doubt out of a need to distance the horror from herself – thus distancing it from the audience – that she adopts a

---

19 The same can be said of a couple of Republicans recalling the execution of Charles I: "Off came his shoe –/ An' the foot –/ The foot without the shoe was going –/ On the wooden boards –/Bang – bang /– On this frosty mornin' –/Bang – bang, the Stuart foot ..." (25–26).

20 Whereas Bradshaw has indeed managed to "collect and bury him" (4), Cropper has "learned Latin," "read his book" and is "translating it" (63).

jocular attitude towards what her husband has become. She first affects to banter about his swarthy skin: "I was deceived. Bradshaw was an African. I never stripped in daylight, nor him either. How was I to know he was an African? **No wonder we had revolution, the Moors had got into our beds**." (50) Then pretending to resent his trunk not being pecked at, she identifies it with food: "I can't think why there's flesh on it, the birds are so finicky. **What's the matter, isn't the meat good enough for you? ... That's perfectly good man you fussy buggers!**" (50) When first deciding to "get his bits" (8), Bradshaw had already turned these into unpalatable pieces of meat – "your chops and scrag, your offal and your lean cuts" (8).[21] But such picturesque – and how effective – though grim realism has now yielded to an obvious unease to be distanced. The wry joking goes on – "It's a bit well done for me" (50) – as she tries to convince a soldier on guard to "get it down, ducks" (50), with another note creeping in: Bradshaw could find a use for it as "there is a wicked shortage of cagmag, isn't there? People will use anything to make a stew. And they call it a restoration! A restoration of what, starvation?" (50) Trying to turn her disgust to tactical profit, the widow also grows dangerously provocative,[22] and her glancing private reference to the Revolution is replaced by the broad hint of a present economic crisis. A chunk of fulsome food, the trunk also becomes an indirect political weapon.

While Bradshaw only makes a brief, incidental political use of macabre horror, Charles, the embodiment of Restoration reaction, very systematically and explicitly turns two horrid Republican figures into instruments of both personal and political revenge, doing it twice, at strategic moments in the structure of the play, against those who rule in his place. Though the King had said he wanted the regicide's head to be "no mockery" (15), it serves as a visual weapon in his vain "victory" over the various "powerful men" (35) who have secretly met in "*The vaults of the Bank of England*" (28). When, at the end of this "Interlude", he has the head brought out to "**show 'em the look that stops their hearts!**" (35), that "makes their bowels go loose" (36), he does not mean it to be any *caput mortuum* general *exemplum* of human mortality; and if he calls the late Bradshaw "**The man who thinks us to death!**" (35) it is to include himself among the Restoration people now present. The reason why he so insistently wants these to look at the "scaring" (35) "bonze" and "the single eyeball" (35) is because the Republican "does look sad to be rejected" (35), because these important City men "were peas once in the pod of the Republic" (35) but have turned their backs on their former Parliament sympathies to become the real rulers in a "new world" founded on banking. So Charles flourishes the head inexorably to remind these men of business and property that their former ally – in a treatise that he can quote "word perfect" (36) – had "plotted the extinction of private property", which meant *their* extinction (35). This of course is but the transient, "shrill and squealing" (39) "victory" of a figurehead who "knows" (37) he is "only a monarch" (36), powerless before the new masters of the country. Still as vain will be the bloody "victory" achieved near the end of the play (II.4) by Ball, now become a raving Cavalier – because "called off" (35) by the new masters – who stabs Hambro the banker to death, mistakenly claiming he

---

21 Against this, in the Court scene (I.3), Cleveland – " A Female Landowner" – will turn women's breasts into enjoyable food, as she "never saw more dug, more boob out" in Westminster Abbey, which was "like a market of fresh tit," and she "never felt more like a nibble at the fruit" (9).

22 Exclaiming "Who said that!", Bradshaw " *pretends to look behind her*" (50) as if *she* had not been speaking subversively.

has thus saved the King and **"struck for England and the monarchy."** (59) But this comes just after Charles himself has wreaked another savage revenge on Hambro through having him uncover *"a large, wrapped object"* (57) – ominously guessed to be "something horrible" (57) – which, most sensationally, proves to be *"the figure of* SCROPE, *his lips cut off"* (58). For, beyond accounting for such a repellent mutilation, the King recalls that the ex-Secretary was present at the trial of his father, only to add: "Remember, Billy, you was there ...?" (58) The hideous revelation is a "Reminder of old times and gains" (57) because Scrope is "an old colleague" (58) of Hambro's, and Charles's ambiguous question subtly involves the banker in the execution of the Martyr King. The lipless Scrope may well defiantly though stammeringly anathematize the new age and exalt **"the commonwealth"** (58), he is but the helpless icon of what Charles calls "the filthy act of History" (58). Indeed Scrope's gory figure and Ball standing **"in blood and rubbish"** (59) bring the play to a climax of both lurid horror and wild violence. But soon afterwards, Charles, once more bringing forth the dead Bradshaw's "bonze", holds it close to Hambro's blood and invites it to "Drink ... at the puddle of [his] enemies" (60), thus pointing out how complexly paradoxical his macabre strategy has grown along the play: enforcing a Royalist retaliation in having the regicide exhumed and dismembered,[23] he not only has enlisted him on his own side to achieve a momentary compensation for the "humiliation" (60) of his own reduced power, but has eventually afforded him, after also enlisting an accomplice of his, a posthumous vicarious revenge against the chief representative of their now common enemies.[24] And when he declares that his gesture "ain't remorse" on his part, only that he is feeling "depressed" (60), the King probably is as clear-sighted as when his post-masturbation depression made him "see things" (13) about himself. Nearly as much as lewdness, horror leads him to self- awareness.

All the same, as this climactic scene testifies, what is so very distinctive about *Victory* is that, far from the two elements operating side by side, there is an almost permanent conjunction and combination, at times a fusion, of those two heightened versions of Eros and Thanatos. Their simultaneous presences and closeness are made obvious from the first scene, when a captain's explosive "cunts" and the erotic fantasies of digging soldiers counterpoint the exhuming of the corpse,[25] and go on right to the epilogue where Ball, still "grunting" after Bradshaw though "They had his tongue out" (62), happens to be carrying her *"bag of remains."*

The first really obscene bringing together of sex and death is of course due to the Cavalier himself, who is prompt to remind the widow that "the rat- gnawed, stinking thing you clutched in bed once" (3–4), "him who made you buck or whimper, is a nest of worms now" (4). The conventional "Way of All Flesh" motif is here simply made "offensive" – and he wishes it could be more so (4) – by Ball's diseased eroticism. But the Cavalier's ensuing reference to the corpse's "bollocks" as "very mean, shrivelled little blobs" (4) is soon to be taken up by the widow

[23] Barker (1989), 73, has said that "the state's ferocious dismembering of its enemies is of course the motor to *Victory*."

[24] Tony Dunn (1984), 83, declaring "That is the union that counts" (the one between Bradshaw and Hambro) seems to me a misreading of Charles's gesture and words in this scene.

[25] "We was in and out like the mad vicar's dick" (1) – about digging up a corpse "At low water" (1) – and "Gob open to clay and the milkmaid's hot little puddle" (2) – about another corpse in a field – are among the most telling instances. And of course the diggers *are* cunts, repeatedly identified as such by the captain!

herself, who even turns out to be more specific than Ball. Not content with forcing her daughter to imagine about the "head on a pole" and the brain (7), Bradshaw will inform her that her father's "scrotum" (she is more decorous than Ball), "though shrivelled, evidently was intact –" (8), going on in this strange way:

Did you see it? I saw it occasionally, though not in the light, his ardour was strictly nocturnal and grew rare with the strain, they will see it more clearly than I did, see it in hot sun and white light, his thing on some gate ... (8)

Besides her echo of Ball, the ex-Puritan widow's obsession with "seeing" – quite different from her final insistence on "looking" – and her erotic nostalgia in the presence of the corpse's "thing" do reveal in what peculiar conjunctions she also indulges. And some disquieting kinship with the Cavalier is again suggested as she recalls her former sexual life at the very moment when she confronts the late Bradshaw's "African" trunk (50), even venturing an openly bawdy joke to counter the scepticism of the soldier on guard as to the rotting trunk being her husband's: "What do you expect, the cock to rise?" (50)

More important perhaps than this creation of an ambivalence in her character is the more general question which the play seems to be raising as to which is the more "disgusting", the obscenity or the horror. Again Ball provides the occasion for this when, in the contrapuntal passage where Bradshaw being informed about the corpse is repeatedly interrupted by his obscene remarks, he suddenly intrudes: "There is a hole in your stocking, you slag." (4) For as the widow objects that what is going to be done to her husband is "so disgusting", Ball retorts: "No, it is the hole that is disgusting, with its six pence of white flesh –" (4). Again to be imputed to the Cavalier's own neurotic fantasies, and though leaving the issue unresolved, this short exchange is like a preparation for the extended Court scene (I.3), in which the question will be suggested through a fully sustained theatrical method. Indeed what constitutes the real character of this scene in its earlier and more complex half is the intimate fusing of the sexual and macabre happenings in it. What makes it so very provocative and **"Out-fucking-rageous!"** (37) is – most evidently – that the King is being masturbated by his whorish duchess *while* his courtiers are chucking skittles at the rotten "bonze." All along, the visual obscenity and the distanced horror are closely counterpointed and interrelated. The intricacy of the bawdy talk and excited shying is built up according to a strict dovetailing, so that "Oh, tight in your hand!" follows close upon "Oh, the ear drops off!" (12). As he is about to chuck the first skittle, Charles unmistakably joins the two together: remarking of the regicide that "no tart came near his thing –" (11), he asks "... Did it – (*He takes one.*) near – your – thing? (*He chucks one.*)" (11) And both the masturbation and the shying are clearly shown to reach simultaneous climaxes, through the overdone explicitness of "Bob done it" (12) – striking the head down – being echoed by "I done too, quicker than I wanted –" (12) – Charles's own rueful admission.[26] Perhaps it is to make up for such a piece of crude overobviousness that, when courtiers exclaim that "Horrible dust stuff flew away ..." (12), even more

[26] Are "He's down!" "It's down in the yard ..." and "Down, Charlie" (12) meant to convey a double entendre? Indeed, other features do also express the identification: Charles decides that Devonshire as well will "fling at the regicide's bonze!", soon propelling her forward to the window (11) from which the courtiers are already "Pelting" (11), where he will sexually assault her and where the masturbation, preventing her from throwing, will also take place (12). The staging clearly brings out the window as uniting the two actions.

pointedly that "grey stuff" was seen to "fly out the head" (12), Barker leaves it to the audience to imagine the other "grey stuff" which must result from the King's climax. The revolting suggestion is quite appropriate. For the aim and effect of such systematic counterpointing certainly is to raise the question: which is the more sickeningly "disgusting", the more actually obscene, action shown on stage, the sexually outrageous one or the outrage done to the corpse's head, what Charles has Devonshire do with his "knob" or what his courtiers do to the Republican's "bonze"? Surely the question is rhetorical and the answer a foregone conclusion. In this Court scene the real obscenity lies in the horror. And if the outcome is bound to be a political condemnation of the Royalists, Scrope the ex-Secretary is right: while they blend beyond any difference, both notions, transcending their separate connotations, convey the same intense moral revulsion.

Fully involved, as its initiator, in the iniquity that disgraces his courtiers, the King will nevertheless achieve his two empty "victories" over the all-powerful Hambro through two somewhat dissimilar and increasingly jarring combinations of sexual and horrific features. Already, when he decides to make use of the head in the Bank scene, his opening gambit is to ask Nell Gwynn, Nell who "can handle flesh" (35), to kiss its mouth. And as he explains that "there is no kissing like her" (35), that "she has a kiss as long as the coast" (35), his intention comes out when he asks Hambro whether the Republican was "ever done like that" when alive, then scathingly underlines that the turn-coat banker "don't remember who lipped him" (35). Transferring the horror from the "bonze" to the whorish beauty as he exclaims "she makes yer faint, she does!" (35), Charles turns this neo-Jacobean morbidly erotic kissing of a corpse's head into another reminder of the New Men's changing of sides. But his later revenge against Hambro will actually be a two-pronged one, taking place on an occasion when he presents him with two successive gifts. The gruesome disclosure of Scrope's figure is really part of a wedding ceremony (II.4) in which the King is seen "flinging cold-bummed bankers down with Lady Roaring Hips" (54) because "It takes the edge off [his] misery to inflict [Hambro] with a bitch like" Devonshire (54), even though it means enforcing an unwanted but necessary marriage on his now visibly pregnant mistress. Such a "raw old union of gain and expediency" (56) cannot go by without the courtiers indulging in salacious innuendoes about the situation (56–57) and prompts Charles to incredibly bawdy cynical remarks: "Will he shove sovereigns up your slit?" (54), **"and don't sodomize her you floppy catkin ...** Yer earldom don't give access to all her crevices –" (55). And it is after he has asked the banker made an earl to "be sweet" (55) to a "sweet virgin" (56) whom he calls his "daughter" because he is "**giving her away**" (55) that the King will have his other "present" brought in – "This gift to you from he who reigns" (57), cruelly justifying himself for inventing "**the sad present**" (58), a vast understatement for Scrope's lipless horror. Capping it all, this seems to be disclosed as a tactical counter-blast to Hambro's politically argumented outburst against "this – cock out – big balled – shagging lot – " (57), in which he proclaims he is not "mocked" by them (57).

After illustrating each in succession, this sensational scene yet ends with what is again a close conjunction of the two ingredients, but in a noticeably changed or subdued form, as Charles sits holding the "bonze" close to an also visibly pregnant Bradshaw and, though venturing an unconvinced pass at her, for he is "sick of forcing women" (60), asks if he "many touch [her] belly" (60), contrasting it with the Queen's sterile womb which is "like a walnut" (60). The latter scenes of Act

Two have shown that – to use the terms of the play – knobs in cunts may result in round bellies. The royal whore who "cannot keep from dick" (40) has noted that the widow was "not cunning enough to keep someone's cock out of her purse" (51), so "I was shagged. You were shagged" (51), as she has it, and so Scenes Three and Four have also impressed on the audience the visual images of both Devonshire's and Bradshaw's growingly rounder bellies, until Ball killing Hambro brings about one more of the duchess's numerous miscarriages (59), while the widow causes Charles to admire "the precious sight" of "a woman in late life and pregnant" (60). But the very striking and no doubt ironical upshot of this – anticipating the visual tension between Bradshaw's now born baby and the bag of remains in the epilogue – is that obscenity and horror eventually merge into the Eros and Thanatos image of a fruitful belly, "round as a football" (60), close to a death's head, before the even more deceptively tender one of "the mad shagman" in the arms of a motherly Bradshaw stroking his head (61).

The interplay of its two main ingredients is at the core of the structural and thematic complexities which make *Victory* such a richly rewarding piece of work. Focusing on it brings out that if the play of course has Bradshaw as its heroine and can be said to be "about" the ambivalent nature of her survival "odyssey" through "acquiescence" to a final ironical "victory" in her self-appointed mission,[27] Charles emerges as nearly as important and central, quite as ambivalent and an altogether very complex character. From the end of the Interlude and throughout Act Two, a singular similarity between the monarch and the widow is visually brought to our notice. Even before Bradshaw is seen with "a large bag" (50) where she collects her husband's remains, Charles has been shown with another bag (35) in which he seems to be transporting the dead regicide's head wherever he goes. This turns out to be true at the end of the wedding scene (II.4), which thus brings out that the grisly "bonze" is a prized possession and a "powerful talisman"[28] to him nearly as much as to Bradshaw. So that the bags and the head are the main stage icons of the two complementary actions which develop side by side to make up the overall inner structure of the play: the major one concerns the widow's macabre errand, but almost as significant though subsidiary is what can be called the King's own revenge. And when the two parallel lines eventually meet as Charles and Bradshaw sit close together with the head between them, the stage image is an emblem of what has united them all along. But the widow has managed to bring off her mission only at several personal costs, the most grievous of which are not sexual ones. When, near the end of the wedding scene, she claims to have ended up "perfectly all right" (59), not only with "clean drawers" and "starched underthings" but with "lips. Not rose bud. Not what they were, of course, but lips" (59), the grim juxtaposition of this with the lipless figure of the maimed yet outspoken Scrope really is an "appalling moment",[29] made even more so by the cruel taunts she lets out against him. Even the way she retrieves the last two of her husband's "bits" gives an ironical twist to her achievement: it needs a drunken and politically frustrated Ball to dislodge the trunk accidentallym so that she can "scoop up the

[27] Barker has subtitled *Claw* (1975) "An Odyssey", but several of his plays – if only *Fair Slaughter* (1977) or *No End of Blame* (1981) – could as much be called so. For the significance of "acquiescing" in the play, see Bradshaw's "Yes" speech (41) and Milton's final speech (49).

[28] Barker (1989), 73.

[29] Barker (1986), 342, 2nd col.

remains" (53), and it needs a depressed Charles who "*falls asleep on her*" (61) for her to steal the cherished "poor bald head" (8) from the King. And if sympathy is more and more balanced by judgement in the audience's developing response to Bradshaw, the bawdy and cynical yet clear-sighted monarch is anything but deprived of positive features down to his final pathetic confession – with his reminder of his actually "melancholy character" (60) and his appeal to "Pity [him] and "overlook [his] shallowness" (61) – which, adressed to the "kind woman" (61) he mistakenly sees in the widow, create in the audience the same tension, the same "intense contradiction and dilemma"[30] as Bradshaw.

These are almost enough for *Victory* to be an achieved specimen of Barker's non-Humanist and non-Epic ambitious "Theatre of Catastrophe."[31] But the play's inner structure evinces further character parallels and pairings which also result in the "internal mirrors" claimed by Barker as typical of the way his plays work.[32] One such mirror effect is that of the developing affinity between the two "cunts" in Act Two. This is symbolically initiated by the royal whore laying her cloak over the widow's shoulders (41), a "purple badge of shame" (41) in Scrope's opinion; then just as Devonshire, deciding to "go back" to Charles, declares "I will die of him ... but he makes me feel alive" (40), Bradshaw, long "untouched" by her Republican husband, acknowledges that she was "licked" yet "opened again" by Ball (44); and their growing kinship, besides their two round bellies illustrating that "It is shambles being a woman" (51), is clinched with the duchess asking "What's in the bag?" (51) and having it carried by a footman of hers, as if she were becoming a party in the widow's mission while Bradshaw is more and more involved through her in the world of the Court (II.4). From uncanny unconscious echoes of the "randy" Cavalier through an ambiguous sexual submission to him to finally taking him on as second husband, the gradual union of Bradshaw with Ball is of course an offshoot of the main action, the play ending with the two "clasped together" (63) near the bones of the first husband in the "*bag of remains*." As to the two "knobs", the monarch and the Cavalier, their affinities through differences, in their political stances and even more in their obscene prospensities, extend to Ball seeming to echo Charles's habitual post-intercourse depression (13) when he notes, after forcing the widow, that his lewdness always leads him "to come off so miserable" (44).

Together with this patterning of the major characters, with both Charles and Bradshaw at its heart, the general interweaving of indecent and gruesome features is made dramatically and theatrically effective through an outer structure in which the episodic succession of eleven scenes, each of which provides a facet of the main components, is strongly articulated along three evenly spaced more substantial tableaux that stand out as three supporting pillars of the whole fabric. Near the

---

30 Ibid., 344, 1st col.

31 "Tension," "openness," "complexity," "ambiguity," "contradiction," or "fragmentation," against "certitude" and "reconciliation," both in the play and in the audience, are Barker's main "keywords" defining what he has also called "Catastrophic Theatre", together with phrases such as "the audience doesn't quite know where it ought to be because the contradictions are insoluble." See Barker (1989), *passim* and especially "The Consolations of Catastrophe," "Beauty and Terror in the Theatre of Catastrophe" and "The Catastrophic Theatre," or Barker (1986) 344, 1st col. According to Rabey (1989), 245, "*Victory* marks his breakthrough into" this type of theatre.

32 Barker (1986), 342, 2nd col.

opening and close of the play, the Court scene (I.3), which broaches the major themes after a preamble has started the main action, and the wedding scene (II.4), which brings all the strands together just before the short epilogue, are two brilliant mirror moments reverberating every element between them. At its centre, the as masterly but more political Bank of England scene (Interlude) works like a big thematic hinge. And it is on account of its impressive overall organization as much as of the way it creates its own provocative but powerful verbal and visual world through the interplay of obscenity and horror that *Victory* ranks as one of the greatest plays of the post-68 period.

References

Barker, Howard (1983) *Victory: Choices in Reaction*. London: John Calder, Playscript 104

Barker, Howard (1984) Interviewed by Tony Dunn. *Gambit*, Vol. 11, no. 41, 33–44

Barker, Howard (1985) *The Castle*. London: John Calder

Barker, Howard (1986) Interviewed by Finlay Donesky: Oppression, Resistance, and the Writer's Testament. *New Theatre Quarterly*, Vol. 2, no. 8, 336–344

Barker, Howard (1989) *Arguments for a Theatre*. London: John Calder; New York: Riverrun Press

Dunn, Tony (1984), " Howard Barker: Socialist Playwright for Our Times." *Gambit*, vol. 11, no. 41, 59–91

Fraser, Antonia (1973, 5th rept. 1983) *Cromwell Our Chief of Men*. London: Weidenfeld and Nicolson

Rabey, D.I. (1989) *Howard Barker: Politics and Desire*. London: Macmillan

Contemporary Theatre Review, 1996, Vol. 5,1 pp. 51–61
Reprints available directly from the publisher
Photocopying permitted by license only

Gender Politics and Female Characters in Edward Bond's Plays

Ruth Freifrau von Ledebur

The paper aims at a re-evaluation of Bond's characters as essential ingredients of his plays. In the light of Bond's political theories, gender or sexual politics are considered as part of the overall political structure of a play. In his "theatre of violence" gender politics are concerned with the functions characters perform and with the distribution of the roles of aggressor and victim between the sexes. The paper concentrates on the female characters but also enquires into the nature of their relationship with the other sex. In Bond's plays, the dichotomy of the sexes prevails in the sense that domination is the ultimate aim of either sex. Women may act as violently as do men, but the deeds of extreme cruelty committed against them are even more degrading. While in some plays a fully developed female character becomes a summation of actions, in others the fragmentation of character corresponds to the discontinuity of dramatic structure. Female sexuality is exploited and dominated by male fantasies, thus adding to the ambivalence of Bond's gender politics.

KEY WORDS characters essential to dramatic structure, social theory and gender politics, women and violence, female characters as pairs, sisters, mother and daughter, lesbian lovers

Introduction

The scene is set in an "upper middle-class drawing room",[1] where a rehearsal is going on for an amateur performance in support of the coast guard fund. The play is about Orpheus and Eurydice. Mrs Rafi, who directs the play, has cast herself as Orpheus and the Vicar as Pluto, all other parts are played by young ladies. The rehearsal is interrupted several times because all the amateur actors, except Mrs Rafi, are not yet familiar with their parts or feel unhappy about them. When Pluto, the Vicar, misses his cue, because he is admiring Mrs Rafi's "bibliographical splendours", he is reprimanded by Mrs Rafi, "Never mind books now, Vicar. We're struggling with life", to which he answers: "Quite so. I await direction."[2] This scene, which could come straight from any well-made drawing room comedy in the manner of Oscar Wilde, is a parody on the 'play-within-the-play' convention and uses theatrical metaphors such as the dichotomy of 'seeming' and 'being'. One might think that its author, Edward Bond, would delight in writing plays with well-constructed plots, coherent characters and witty dialogues, plays which create illusion and yet allow us to see through the make-believe. However, this scene

[1] Edward Bond, *The Sea*, Scene 4, stage direction, p. 121.

[2] *The Sea*, Scene 4, p. 127.

and its characters, taken from *The Sea* (1973)[3], are the exception rather than the rule in Bond's dramatic works.

Ever since the notoriety of *Saved* (1965), Bond's plays have been associated with shock and violence, and critics were quick to find his roots in Antonin Artaud's 'Theatre of Cruelty'. When one of the early and most influential interviews with the playwright was published under the catchy title "Drama and the Dialectics of Violence"[4], the label stuck. And most of the plays from the first series, ending with *The Sea*, have given the critics ample space to enlarge on this theme. Bond is not out to please his audience but to educate them by a kind of shock therapy. His social criticism pivots on his theory of aggression, dealt with in numerous interviews and the prefaces of his plays, according to which aggression is the driving force behind social progress.[5] Bond's theatre is explicitly political, its target being the repressions of capitalist society. For that reason, his work has been labelled "didactic drama", and criticism draws our attention to many similarities between Bond's approach and Brechtian dramaturgy (Holland, 1978). This explains the epic nature of his plays, their "distinctive episodic quality" and the "great fluidity of scenic structure."[6] Critics claim that because Bond avoids conventional dramatic causality his characters lack coherence. "Again and again Bond appears to be moving towards the establishment of characters, only to dissolve it in the next scene. [...] The construction of the plays, then, specifically disavows the coherence of character" (Holland, 1978, p. 31). What criticism offers us is an account of how Bond conveys his perception of the world and how he judges it socially and morally. Thus, critics soon reach the point when character X turns into a mere representative of this or that social, economic or political "force", into an allegory or a symbol. This abstraction is supported if not initiated by Bond's comments on his plays, in which he prefers to develop his social and political theories.

However, characters in drama are not mere abstractions; as Mrs Rafi tells us, they have to convince the audience. On stage they are very much alive. They have "round heavy shoulders, big buttocks, bulky breasts" like the fifty-three year-old Mary in *Saved*, or like Fred in the same play, a "well-shaped, steady, powerful body and a light tenor voice."[7] As spectators or readers we perceive the *dramatis personae* as characters with their own fate and history. This Bradleyan approach to drama, condemned as naive in Shakespeare criticism but recently exculpated, has its merits in that it draws attention to the interplay between character and action, and, thereby, to the actual stage business. Pam, Len and Fred, Lear, Bodice and Fontanelle, or Victoria and Florence may still people the stage of the theatre or of the reader's imagination, while the socio-political theories of their author may have become obsolete.

---

3 In the text, dates in brackets behind the titles of the plays indicate the year of the first production. For the editions of the plays cf. List of References.

4 In *Theatre Quarterly*, No. 5 (1972), pp. 4–14.

5 Numerous articles and introductions to Bond's plays deal with this central theme, cf. J.R. Taylor (1978), M. Hay and P. Roberts (1980), T. Coult (1977). For further discussion in my article see the heading "Women and Violence".

6 "Drama and the Dialectics of Violence", p. 11.

7 See Bond's notes on the cast of the first production in the Methuen Edition of *Saved*, p. 9–10.

To re-establish Bond's characters as essential and indispensable ingredients of his plays does not mean to deny their political issues but may allow their re-evaluation. It has often been remarked that with Bond, as with many other contemporary writers, power is linked with sexuality. Political or social oppression may be exercised by sexual domination or vice versa. Sexual or gender politics are thus part of the overall political structure of a play. In drama, gender politics also concern the roles and functions the playwright assigns to the female and the male characters. These functions are not only derived from the necessities of plot development but also from stereotyped role definitions and expectations which are traditionally associated with the female and the male gender. The matrix of these stereotypes and clichés is deeply rooted in our culture and belongs to the same substratum as do our religious or social taboos.[8] In Victorian literature, for instance, we recognize the working of gender politics when domination is almost automatically expected of the male and submission of the female characters. In Bond's "theatre of violence" it is of interest to notice in what ways the roles of aggressor and victim are distributed between the sexes. Bond's portrayal of his characters and the functions they perform is also relevant to the gender politics of his plays. To discuss these issues I will mainly draw upon the female characters but I will also enquire into the nature of their relationship with the other sex.

Women and Violence

Bond's much-quoted dictum "I write about violence as naturally as Jane Austen wrote about manners" contains, apart from its provocative irony, a programmatic statement. For Bond, man is not aggressive by nature but he responds aggressively when the injustice of our social structure, or what Bond calls "social morality", deprives him of his physical and emotional needs. "Violence shapes and obsesses our society." From these basic assumptions it follows that "it would be immoral not to write about violence".[9]

With these arguments Bond not only justifies his preoccupation with violence but also endows it with a moral and political purpose. If aggression is universal, the playwright will take his principle to its logical conclusion and not draw a distinction between the sexes in this regard. However, our traditional concept of woman's nature holds that she who gives life also protects life. For women, violence and above all killing are taboos in most traditional cultures, society ostracizes the murderess far more severely than the murderer. Male ruthlessness, on the other hand, and his aggressive strategies are considered to be "natural".[10] Leaving aside Bond's political programme, women's behaviour in his plays as regards violence must also be assessed in the light of these taboos.

---

[8] I can only hint at these topics. For further controversial discussion cf. G. Greer (1971) or S. Rowbothan (1973), in terms of feminist literary criticism cf. C.G. Heilbrun (1979) or J. Todd (1988).

[9] Author's Preface to *Lear*, p. V.

[10] See C. Humphrey's review essay on recent anthropological studies, "Rituals of the Full Moon", *London Review of Books*, vol. 14, no. 5 (1992), p. 20.

It has often been remarked that in Bond's plays, violence frequently takes on the form of a ritual. As with the notorious stoning of the baby in *Saved* (1965), it may begin in an almost playful manner, gradually build up tension and draw in more participants, then gather momentum until it is finally released in bouts of communal violence.[11] In *Saved*, only boys participate in the stoning of the baby. Yet Pam, the baby's mother, is not free from blame as she left the child with the gang, and after its death her behaviour is highly ambivalent. The Cockney girl Pam is in no way a motherly type, and Bond makes it abundantly clear that neither Pam nor Fred (the child's father and leader of the gang) but society is to take the blame for the child's death.

A similar communal act of violence occurs in *The Fool* (1975), when a group of farm labourers, who are out for looting, rob and threaten their parson. Again, it is a 'mob' against one helpless individual, and as in *Saved*, the labourers stimulate each other to more cruelty. Two women take an equal share in these activities, and when the parson, recalling the moral code of his society, appeals to their female decency, they laugh at him. Shouting "Off – Pull it off – Off – Off", the mob tears off the parson's clothes. And when he stands naked, one of the women is the first to pinch him, thereby initiating physical violence against the helpless old man.[12] In this scene, the women appear to be more cruel than the men, according to traditional, gender-defined moral standards, they would qualify as 'hyenas'.[13] But Bond counteracts this by supplying the women with an ulterior reason for their cruelty. As they are too poor to feed their children, they have a special grievance against the parson as a member of the ruling class. We are faced with the dramatist's paradoxical contention that a women's maternity is used to justify her cruelty, which would normally be considered to debase her womanhood.

Perhaps the most outrageous examples of violence occur in *Early Morning* (1968). The reciprocal cannibalism in heaven, performed like a ritualistic orgy, is presided over by Queen Victoria herself. Even if these scenes are relieved of some of their shock potential because of their surrealistic improbabilities, the same cannot be said of cannibalism on earth, when a man is killed and then eaten outside a cinema because "'E pushed in the queue" (Scene 4, p.19). In the trial Len and Joyce, the two accused, describe the gruesome events, gloating over every gory detail. Again the woman takes her full share in the cruelties ("she karati-chops 'im cross the front of 'is throat with the use of 'er 'andbag [...] and she starts stabbin' 'im with 'er stilletos [sic] ...", p. 22). It is the discrepancy between the awful deed and the tone of righteous indignation with which they justify it that marks the moral insensibility of the couple. Joyce's obscene jokes reveal the sexual lust as part of the cannibalistic rite and also emphasize the dramatic function attributed to the member of the female sex in this scene. Her participation makes it even more repulsive, a reaction that is not relieved by the farcical elements of the scene.

On the whole, the dramatic roles that women play in these violent rituals are ambivalent. On the one hand, they are as deprived of human decency as the men, thus ruling out any distinction between the sexes. On the other hand, it is the

---

11 See E. Durbach's (1975) analysis of this motif.

12 Cf. *The Fool*, Scene 3, pp. 20–25.

13 Desparate women or women who plunder are often likened to hyenas, cf. Schiller's famous dictum (from his poem "Die Glocke") "Da werden Weiber zu Hyaenen ...".

women, not the men, who by word or deed draw our attention to the sexual perversion of these acts of violence. As they are violating taboos, the female characters rather than the male may be held responsible for the extreme moral discomfort caused by these scenes.

Female Characters as Pairs

Like any other dramatist, Bond uses pairs to achieve certain effects. The dualities between such figures as the hero and his adversary contribute to the development of action and are thus essential to the dramatic potential of a play. With Bond, however, this is not merely a matter of dramatic technique but primarily of the ideological concerns of his plays. In the antagonistic pairs of "victim" and "aggressor" he sees the embodiment of the "life force" and the destructive forces in society.[14] When discussing the functions of these pairs, Bond quotes only male examples, although there are numerous female pairs in his plays as well. Like their male counterparts they are indicative of the underlying ideology of a play and of the development of its action. Moreover, these women are likely to bring to light certain gender-specific stereotypes which may not be so apparent in an individual. They also allow us to evaluate the extent to which women conform to social norms or violate taboos. Three pairs will serve as examples from three very different plays, namely *Lear* (1972), *The Woman* (1977) and *Early Morning* (1968).

The Sisters in *Lear*

While pairs of brothers are plentiful in myth, fairy-tales or literature, their female counterparts are rare. From Romulus and Remus onwards, male twins hold the imagination of the story-teller: their being identical becomes the focal point of comic plots, and the ties of brotherhood serve as models for ideal friendship. No such glamour is attached to the familial ties of two sisters; they do not seem to lend themselves as paradigms of socially esteemed behaviour. Sisters usually appear in threes or any other symbolic number, such as the three Graces or the three Norns in Nordic mythology.

While we find the traditional pattern of three daughters in Shakespeare's *King Lear*, Bond's king has only two daughters and the Cordelia of his play is not a member of the family. Although Bond's alterations effect the course of action of his play, its themes and images have many similarities with Shakespeare's play.[15] The parts of the two sisters, Fontanelle and Bodice, are structured along the lines of their models. They, too, incite their husbands against the king, their rebellion causing his madness. Like Goneril and Regan, Fontanelle and Bodice despise their husbands, whom they plan to murder, lust after the same man, Warrington, and secretly plot to destroy one another. The two pairs of sisters are alike also in their cruelty and the violence they inflict upon others.

---

[14] Cf. Letter to Irene, quoted in P. Roberts (1985), p. 64. Innes (1984) calls the pairing of protagonists Bond's "central thematic symbol", p. 129.

[15] Cf. the comparative studies by H. Oppel and S. Christenson (1977) and by G. Stratmann (1980).

Apart from these similarities, Bond has cast distinctively different moulds for his two sisters. The dramatist appears to have aimed at a certain degree of differentiation between the two sisters. While Bodice is bold and controlled, continuing with her knitting even during the most violent scenes, Fontanelle is more spirited and "repeatedly in danger of losing her self-control" (Oppel & Christenson, 1974, p. 7). On the other hand, Bond emphasizes their likeness by repetitive patterns in their speech and actions. When they reveal their dark intentions concerning the murder of husband and sister respectively to reach their ultimate aim, they repeat one another's thoughts almost verbally. Fontanelle: "Then I'll marry Warrington and let him run the country for me." Bodice: "... then I'll marry Warrington and run the country through him". (*Lear*, 1.3). Similarily, when they later fear Warrington's betrayal, they both give orders to cut out his tongue. The effect Bond achieves with these repetitions is twofold. On the one hand, they stress the sisters' identical conduct and ambition, on the other hand the parrot-like repetitions add a melodramatic, grotesque note to the scenes. Fontanelle and Bodice appear like puppets moved by the same "social force". When Warrington is being tortured, Fontanelle first takes the lead. She instructs a soldier how to inflict pain and then joins in the torture, while Bodice remains outwardly cool and continues knitting. Yet her cruelty appears to be more calculated than her sister's when she orders the speechless Warrington to "ask his pardon", which she refuses, and then thrusts her needles into his ears so that he is dumb and deaf. The horrified comment of the soldier – "What a pair!" (1.4) brings home the truth about the two sisters: the cruelties they inflict upon other human beings leave out no horror. Fontanelle's passionate violence is complemented by Bodice's calculated callousness; they are indeed a pair whose atrocities cannot be surpassed.

Once the principle of this pattern has been established it is taken to its logical conclusion. Their deaths sum up the similarity of their fates: Both are captured, taken into Lear's prison, confronted with their father and then killed by the rebels. According to the political logic of Bond's play, violence breeds violence and the death of the sisters is not the work of moral justice but of the "dynamics and dialectics of aggression."[16] The play's ideology accounts for the rigidity of the dramatic structure and for the inflexibility of the sisters. Reduction and distortion are the principles on which their characters are designed. Their being sisters counts only in their common bond with Lear, or rather in the violation of this bond. They appear to be inhuman because they lack all attributes of human kindness. Their female gender is relevant only in that it qualifies their sexual lust and disdain. Lear's daughters are like the two halves of one identity, and in that sense they are true representatives of Bond's symbiotic pairs.

'Mother' and 'Daughter' in *The Woman*

With *The Woman* (1978), Bond has turned to Greek mythology and dramatized the story of the Trojan War. The two women who are of interest to us in this play are Hecuba, widow of the Trojan King Priam, and Ismene, wife of the young Greek Commander Heros, the latter two being Bond's additions to the mythological characters. Although they come from opposite sides, their relationship resembles

[16] Author's Preface to *Lear*, p. XIII.

that of mother and daughter. In fact, Bond has devised his dramatic plot so that the interaction between Hecuba and Ismene is instrumental to its development. These are not only "Scenes of War and Freedom" as the subtitle suggests, but it is also a play about sexual politics.[17] Sexist behaviour, which both Trojans and Greeks demonstrate in their distrust, contempt or fear of women, is treated as one more form of social and political violence. Yet the vigour with which Hecuba and Ismene are imbued saves them from being mere victims of male cruelty and domination.

There are hardly any other two women in Bond's plays whom he presents in such a favourable light. They are both intelligent, courageous even in the face of death and full of pity for the fate of others. Hecuba, the elder, shows all the qualities of a political leader. She is sceptical but quick in outwitting her opponents. Experience has hardened her and supplied her with a bitter irony. Ismene, on the other hand, is more enthusiastic and willing to risk everything. She devises the plan for a peaceful end to the war whereby the statue of the Goddess Fortune, stolen by the Trojans, is to be returned to the Atheneans and Troy spared. Only when Ismene offers herself as hostage is Hecuba ready to comply with her plan. Bond makes it abundantly clear that both Greeks and Trojans, lusting for power, are to be held responsible for the failure of the women's plan and the ensuing looting and destruction of Troy.

The mother-daughter relationship is established by degrees and kept in a precarious balance throughout the play. Hecuba and Ismene meet because of their mutual desire for peace, they are united by their common suffering at the hands of men. While Hecuba attempts to blind herself when Heros orders her grandson to be killed, Ismene becomes insane when she is buried alive in the Trojan Wall because of her disobedience. As in *Lear*, Bond uses the ancient symbols of blindness and madness to signify both, a higher wisdom or insight and the state of the outcast. When he invests the women with these attributes, he emphasizes their symbiotic pairing. Their mutual dependence becomes complete when Ismene leads the blind 'mother' and Hecuba guides the mindless 'child'.[18] While Ismene's behaviour oscillates between obedience and childlike obstinacy, Hecuba fully realizes the ties that bind them together: "Oh my child. [...] You love me. And look, a blind old woman covered in tears because she loves her daughter." (*The Woman*, Part II, Scene IV)

Although this image of mother and daughter is tinged with pathos, it is free of sentimentality. This is partly due to the fact that the full knowledge of the symbolic nature of their relationship is only given to Hecuba. It also results from the characteristics Bond has attributed to her: she very rarely voices her feelings, her normal diction is qualified by sarcasm and ambiguities. Bond may invite us to feel pity for this destitute pair and their tragic fate, yet he never allows us to forget our anger at those who have caused this fate.

Ismene and Hecuba are perhaps the most fully realized female characters in his plays. They incorporate most of the positive values with which womanhood is traditionally accredited and are thus also in this respect an exception among Bond's characters. As a pair, they are the very opposite of Fontanelle and Bodice

[17] Cf. Review on *The Woman* by G. Savona, *Gambit*, No. 36 (1980), quoted in P. Roberts (1985), pp. 38–39.

[18] Hecuba (to Ismene): "You child. You're my eyes – and I make you eat, and wash, and rock you to sleep when you're afraid." *The Woman*, Part II, Scene 1, p. 66.

not only because of their goodness but also because of the complexity of their characters and the fluidity they lend to the play.

Lesbian Lovers in *Early Morning*

Early Morning (1968) is perhaps the most provocative of Bond's plays, and critics have always found it difficult to come to terms with it.[19] For this play, Bond took the "icons" of Victorian England whom the English know from childhood – the Queen, Prince Albert, Florence Nightingale – and put them in "totally unhistorical, bizarre, horrific situations, transposing mental into physical cruelties".[20] Not only does the excessive violence, "a return to the intolerable",[21] offend critics and audiences alike, also the genre classification poses numerous questions. It has been termed a comic fantasy, a hard comedy, whereas Bond himself claims, paradoxically, that "the events of this play are true".[22] Accordingly, the characters of this play escape any easy definition.

Early Morning abounds with 'pairs', above all the Siamese twins George and Arthur, the prototypes of what Bond has termed the "identity between the victim and the aggressor".[23] The princes are followed by the Queen and the Prince Consort, Disraeli and Gladstone, and the two Cockneys Len and Joyce. Among the female characters Queen Victoria and Florence Nightingale are the most prominent. It is particularly with this pair that Bond satirizes the landmarks of Victorian morality and exposes the common roots of power and sexuality.[24] In trying to achieve this end, the dramatist makes use of various techniques. One of them, pertaining to all characters, is the farcical device of over-life-size representation and grotesque distortion. Thus, the clichés of the historical Victoria, such as her devotion to her husband or her love for her children, are held up to ridicule. Another means of unmasking the hypocrisy of Victorian morality is to invest the Queen with the very opposite of the 'virtues' she is usually credited with. The incarnation of the pure, loyal loving wife is revealed to be a Lesbian in love with Florence Nightingale, designated wife of Victoria's son George, the Prince of Wales. The 'pairing' of Victoria and Florence is thus marked by perversity and double standards.

Masking and unmasking becomes a basic pattern of their interaction. To hide their true relationship, Florence is dressed up as a Scotsman in attendance on the Queen, her male 'mask' leading to grotesque misunderstandings and homosexual

---

19 P. Wolfensperger (1976) gives numerous examples. Cf. his analysis of the play, pp. 66–98.

20 Review of a Glasgow production by C. Oliver in *The Guardian*, 14 May 1974, quoted in P. Roberts, (1985), pp. 17–18.

21 A Statement by E. Jonesco, describing a "theatre of violence: violently comic, violently dramatic", in his essay "Discovering the Theatre", in *Theatre in the Twentieth Century*, edited by R.W. Corrigan (New York: Grove Press, 1963), p. 85.

22 Bond's motto of the Playscript Edition.

23 Cf. Letter to Irene, quoted in P. Roberts (1985), p. 64.

24 Cf. Wolfensperger (1976), p. 78: "Es geht um den identischen Ursprung von Macht und Sexus; jede sexuelle Äusserung ist auf Machtstrukturen aufgebaut, und ungekehrt hat jede Art von Machtanwendung sexuellen Charakter."

gibes from the Lord Chamberlain. Role playing is also part of their make-up. With her cruel sentences in various trials during the play, Victoria parodies the role of the supreme judge while Florence covers up her sexual obsessions with the role of the nurse as the representative of female chastity. Apart from their 'costumes', the discrepancy between words and deeds reveals their hypocrisy. Their most cruel actions are accompanied by sententious sayings. Victoria justifies strangling her husband thus: "I don't like to see them linger – I'm a patron of the RSPCA" (*Early Morning*, Scene 5, p 36). Florence, who has been turned into the "first public hangwoman in history", comments on her work as follows: "I was better today. It's a question of taking it calmly and getting all your things ready beforehand. Like cooking" (*Early Morning*, Scene 12, p. 71).

Chaste modesty in women, double standards for men, and a perverted sexual morality, these are regarded as the prominent landmarks of Victorianism and attacked accordingly in the play. As in *Lear* and *The Woman*, sexuality and politics are also mingled in *Early Morning*. In the case of Victoria, her desire for political power is also fulfilled in sexual domination, whereas her politial regime is tinged with sexuality. In the context of the play's sexual politics, Lesbian love is yet another form of perversion. It is presented like the grotesque projection of male fantasies. Victoria rapes Florence and gloats over her friend's virginity, priding herself to have been "the first". Florence, on the other hand, reacts like a coy maiden, seeking shelter with her would-be husband George, but then submitting totally to her "friend". The same obscenity prevails in the hospital scene where it is insinuated that Florence has sexual intercourse with the dying soldiers. While the play as a whole violates almost any number of social, moral or religious taboos, the same holds true for Victoria and Florence. They are degraded as lovers and as women and are ridiculed as early representatives of women's emancipation.[25] Where it not for the bizarre exaggerations of all characters and situations, Bond might be accused of having given his play an anti-feminist stance. Of the three 'pairs' of women Victoria and Florence are certainly the most unusual and outrageous. In their artificiality, they possess a high degree of theatricality, which surpasses the ideological boundaries of the play.

Relationships between Women and Men

Gender politics are also defined by the specific functions attributed to the relationship between the sexes in the dramatic structure of the plays. Considering the negative opinion Bond holds of all traditional social institutions, it is no surprise that marriages are usually presented as a disappointment to either one or both partners. Personal feelings are clearly subordinated to political aims; if necessity commands, a partner is ruthlessly abandoned or killed, as is the case with Ismene in *The Woman*, the husband of Bodice and Fontanelle in *Lear*, or Prince Albert in *Early Morning*. Elderly couples, like Mary and Harry in *Saved*, experience little more than irritation, boredom or disgust. In many instances the economic and social factors of a marriage are predominant, as with the poet Clare and his wife

[25] Cf. Scene 12, p. 72, Florence: "I'm the first hangwoman in history – public hangwoman, that is. It's part of our war effort. And if we're being emancipated we must be consistent. So we take over any man's job that is suitable."

Patty in *The Fool*. While Patty strives hard to feed the family, Clare feels trapped in their marriage and pines after the servant-girl Mary, who occupies his sexual fantasies and inspires his poetry. Romantic love, a rare feature in Bond's plays, is definitely the domain of the male imagination. It may provide the hope for an optimistic ending, as with the rather colourless couple Rose and Willy in *The Sea* (1973), who leave the narrowness of the seaside town behind them to "change the world" (*The Sea*, Scene 8, p. 169). Or it may even lead to a sincere declaration of love, but when in one of the rare instances the words "I love you" are uttered, they come from the disembodied Arthur in *Early Morning*, during one of the most improbable 'love scenes' of the modern theatre.[26]

More often, however, the plays demonstrate how women are debased by men in word and deed. Warfare being a prevailing theme with Bond, soldiers are the most noticeable malefactors in this respect. Their obscene dialogues refer explicitly to sexual abuse and perversion; women are regarded as mere objects, like loot they are 'taken' as the rightful spoils of war.[27] Rape, the ultimate violation of female integrity, is not only frequently talked about but also carried out on stage in one of the most horrifying scenes in *Lear*, the victim being the pregnant Cordelia (*Lear* 1.7).

Even though women in Bond's plays are apt to commit deeds of extreme cruelty, those that are committed against them appear to be even more degrading. On the whole, the relationship between the sexes rephrases Bond's theme of aggressor and victim in the terms of gender politics. The dichotomy of the sexes prevails in the sense that domination is the ultimate aim of either sex. The brutalisation of both sexes is carried to an extreme which is rare in contemporary theatre.

Conclusion

In focussing on Bond's female characters, an interesting light is thrown on his dramaturgy in general and on the gender politics of his plays in particular. When the "dialectics of violence" become the sole agent of a play, as is the case with *Lear*, rigidity of structure and of characters is the consequence. As has been demonstrated with the two sisters, the portrayal of their characters does not achieve much credibility. "Bond is so clearly a didactic dramatist that the validity of his message largely determines the quality of his theatre" (Innes, 1984, p. 133). This statement points out the advantages as well as the short-comings of Bond's dramatic art. When a character like Hecuba is fully developed, she is convincing because of her complexity and ambiguity. In such instances the development of action hinges upon the development of character, and character becomes a summation of actions.[28] With such dominant characters the audience is inclined to feel sympathy, to share their joys and horrors. A "theatre of empathy", which Bond would disavow, is created almost against the intentions of its author. On the other hand, when characters constantly change their roles and 'masks', as has been shown with Victoria and Florence, the discontinuity and disparity of dramatic

[26] Scene 20, pp. 106–115. See also the first version of this scene in the Appendix. pp. 121–124.

[27] Cf. Nestor's boasting after the fall of Troy in *The Woman*, Part 1, Scene 14.

[28] Cf. P. Holland's (1978) different views, p. 31.

structure corresponds to the incongruity and fragmentation of character portrayal. When summing up Bond's gender politics, it appears that Bond holds an ambivalent position. On the one hand he seems to attempt to rule out all distinctions between the sexes, under the pressure of his own social theory. On the other hand, he makes explicit use of the qualities of the female gender either to emphasize women's maternal role or to exploit female sexuality. The latter is always conceived from a male perspective, women are dominated by male fantasies. Thereby women are treated as mere objects, a certain misogynist strain is apparent in many portrayals of female characters. In consequence, the moral and also the aesthetic discomfort we experience in many of Bond's plays is not only due to their inherent violence but also to the author's particular brand of gender politics.[29]

References

1. Primary Sources

1.1. Edward Bond's Plays

Saved. Methuen's Modern Plays series, London, 1969
Lear. Methuen's Modern Plays series, London 1972
Early Morning. Playscript 18, Calder and Boyars, London 1968
The Fool and *We Come to the River*. Eyre Methuen, London 1976
The Sea. In *Plays: Two*, Eyre Methuen, London 1978
The Woman. Eyre Methuen, London 1979

1.2 Interviews

Drama and the Dialectics of Violence. *Theatre Quarterly*, No. 5 (1972), pp. 4–14, with the editors.
Behind the Scenes: Theatre and Film Interviews from the Transatlantic Review, edited by J.F. McCrindle, pp. 125–136, New York: Holt, 1971, with G. Gordon
Die Gessellschaft erzieht die Menschen zu Mördern. *Theater heute*, 10, No. 11 (1969), pp. 35–37, with W. Asmus

2. Secondary Sources

Coult, T. (1977) *The Plays of Edward Bond*. London: Eyre Methuen
Durbach, E. (1975) Herod in the Welfare State: *Kindermord* in the Plays of Edward Bond. *Educational Theatre Journal*, 27, 480–487
Greer, G. (1971) *The Female Eunuch*. London: Paladin
Hay, M. and Roberts, P. (1980) *Bond: a Study of his Plays*. London: Eyre Methuen
Heilbrun, C.G. (1979) *Reinventing Womanhood*. New York: W.W. Norton and Co.
Holland, P. (1978) Brecht, Bond, Gaskill, and the Practice of Political Theatre. *Theatre Quarterly*, vol. 10, no. 8, 24–35
Innes, Ch. (1984) The Political Spectrum of Edward Bond: from Rationalism to Rhapsody. In *Modern British Dramatists*, edited by J.R. Brown, pp. 126–148, Englewood Cliffs, NJ: Prentice Hall, Inc.
Oppel, H., Christenson, S. (1974) *Edward Bond's Lear and Shakespeare's King Lear*. Mainz: Akademie der Wissenschaften und der Literatur
Roberts, P. (1985) Editor. *Bond on File*. London and New York: Methuen
Rowbothan, S. (1973) *Woman's Consciousness, Man's World*. Harmondsworth: Penguin
Stratmann, G. (1980) Edward Bond, "Lear". In *Anglo-amerikanische Shakespeare-Bearbeitungen des 20. Jahrhunderts*, edited by H. Priessnitz, pp. 353–374. Darmstadt: Wissenschaftliche Buchgesellschaft
Taylor, J.R. (1978) *The Second Wave: British Drama of The Sixties*, pp. 77–93. London: Methuen
Todd, J. (1988) Feminist Literary History. London: Polity Press Blackwell
Wolfensperger, P. (1976) *Edward Bond: Dialektik des Weltbildes und dramatische Gestaltung*. Swiss Studies in English 90. Bern: Francke

---

[29] This article was completed in May 1992. No reference, therefore, could be made to any study on Bond published after that date.

Contemporary Theatre Review, 1996, Vol. 5,1 pp. 63–75
Reprints available directly from the publisher
Photocopying permitted by license only

Breaking the Rules: The Plays of Sarah Daniels

Christine Dymkowski

Throughout her playwriting career, Sarah Daniels has relentlessly probed the fault-lines of contemporary society, tackling issues that are sites of contention between conservative attitudes and liberal/radical reappraisals. Daniels's handling of such potentially explosive subjects as power relations between the sexes, the position of women, lesbianism, pornography, male violence, and sexual abuse is itself subversive and challenging. By considering some of Daniels's thematic concerns, her dramatic treatment of them, and the critical responses they have provoked, this essay demonstrates the ways in which the playwright's subversion of theatrical convention and expectation challenges normative social attitudes. It concludes that the most transgressive aspect of her work is the foregrounding of female experience in a culture that is still overwhelmingly male-defined.

KEY WORDS Sarah Daniels, feminist theatre/aesthetics, theatrical representation of lesbians, theatrical representation of women, subversion of theatrical convention, gendered critical judgements

It has become a critical commonplace to label Sarah Daniels a polemical dramatist, a description not always intended as a compliment. Productions of her plays have punctuated the last decade, the Thatcher "me" years that proclaimed the demise of society and celebrated the steady rise of the unashamedly greedy self. Causes became unfashionable, caring obsolete, as the cult of the individual emerged triumphant from the dismantled welfare state. But from her earliest play, *Ripen Our Darkness* (1981), to her latest, *Beside Herself* (1990),[1] Daniels has relentlessly probed the fault-lines of contemporary society.

The issues Daniels tackles throughout her work are sites of contention between conservative attitudes and liberal/radical reappraisals: power relations between the sexes, the position of women, lesbianism, religion, class, pornography, male violence, incest, and sexual abuse. Not only are such subjects themselves potentially explosive, but Daniels's handling of them is itself subversive and challenging. By considering some of Daniels's thematic concerns, her dramatic treatment of them, and the critical responses they have provoked, I hope in this essay to show the ways in which the playwright's subversion of theatrical convention and expectation challenges normative social attitudes.

[1] At the time of completing this article (June 1992), Sarah Daniels's plays include *Ripen Our Darkness*, Royal Court Theatre Upstairs, London (1981); *Ma's Flesh is Grass*, Crucible Studio Theatre, Sheffield (1981); *Masterpieces*, Royal Exchange, Manchester (1983), transferring to Royal Court Theatre Upstairs (1983) and Royal Court (1984); *The Devil's Gateway*, Royal Court Theatre Upstairs (1983); *Neaptide*, Cottesloe, National Theatre, London (1986); *Byrthrite*, Royal Court Theatre Upstairs (1986); *The Gut Girls*, Albany Empire, London (1988); and *Beside Herself*, Royal Court Theatre (1990).

Quotations from plays are from Daniels 1989, 1991a, and 1991b, but for the ease of readers using different editions I have included act and scene references as well as page numbers.

One of the most surprising features of Daniels's writing, given the serious concerns she addresses, is its characteristic humour. Adroitly fashioning puns and oneliners, she serves up a comic feast much enjoyed by audiences and admiringly quoted by reviewers: "If home is where the heart is, I'd live in John Lewis" (*Beside Herself*, scene 2, p. 26); "My God, I wanted three daughters like the Brontës and I ended up with a family fit for a Channel Four documentary" (*Neaptide*, Part 1, scene 2, p. 247). Sometimes, the humour hits a political target, as in this opportunity afforded by the seventeenth-century dialect used in *Byrthrite* (Part 1, scene 3, p. 345):

GRACE You three climb up the tree outside and observe scene through unmended hole in the roof.
MARY Oh Grace, Thatcher still not cam?
GRACE Thatcher don't care 'bout poor folk on parish welfare.

The use of such humour is strategic: on the most simple level, laughter can enlist audience sympathy. Even male reviewers alienated by the content of Daniels's plays concede the attractions of their comedy: "It is quite a lively evening even if the dice are ludicrously loaded" (Michael Billington, *Guardian*, on *Ripen our Darkness*); Daniels "has an ear for sometimes very funny dialogue and is an unflagging feminist partisan in the sex war. ... [The play is] Entertaining, prejudiced and partial]" (Martin Hoyle, *Financial Times*, on *The Devil's Gateway*).[2] Besides evoking positive audience response through sheer enjoyment, the humour also aims at subversion. For example, the male centrist assumptions that underpin much of modern psychology are effectively exploded in this exchange between Mary and Marshall, a psychiatrist, in *Ripen Our Darkness*:

MARSHALL. And look at these letters your husband gave me. *He takes some letters from his pockets and starts to read one:*
'Dear God, if I have three grown sons, how can it be that I cannot bear to see my husband undressed? Penis running dry. I'm afraid I can't go on'.
MARY (*puzzled, looks at the letter he holds out to her*). No, my 'pen is running dry', i.e. it contains no ink. Therefore ... I couldn't write anything else after that ... You seem to be penis-mad. I haven't given the things a second thought in years. (scene 11, pp. 60–61; Daniels's ellipses)

Interviewed before the opening of *Beside Herself*, Daniels commented that "Making jokes is very risky, but ridicule is always a lot more powerful than straightforward argument" (Durrant 1990). Daniels's "always" is overstatement, but in the example given above, comic dismissal succinctly achieves what serious treatment would have failed to do: logical argument about penis-envy would only serve to validate the currency of Freud's merely speculative opinion.[3]

Daniels also uses humour in more unexpected ways – for instance, in situations where it would normally be deemed inappropriate. In *Ripen Our Darkness*, for example, Mary kills herself when her husband arranges to commit her to a mental hospital; her farewell note to him reads "Dear David, your dinner and my head are in the oven" (scene 11, p. 64). When in scene 13 (p. 66) Mary seems to waken in a

[2] Quotations from reviews, except where otherwise stated, are from the relevant issue of *London Theatre Record*; see References for further information.

[3] Although there have long been psychoanalytical critiques of Freud's theories of female sexuality, notably in the work of Jones, Horney, Klein, and Payne, the idea of penis-envy remains current in the popular imagination. See Rycroft 1968 for a discussion of some of the criticism of Freud's work.

hospital room, only to discover herself in a feminist heaven with a female Holy Trinity, the writing takes an even more unexpectedly comic turn:

> MARY (*panics*). Now hold on a minute, what sort of hospital is this?
> It's a loony bin, isn't it? He's had me committed to the bin.
> *She is frightened.*
> OLD WOMAN (*takes hold of Mary's hand*). No, Mary, you're in paradise.
> MARY (*shouts*). Christ alive. I'm dead!
> YOUNG WOMAN (*smiles*). No need to call up false images.
> MARY. But I mean, I never got the feeling that God approved of me.
> OLD WOMAN (*shrugs*). That's just as well. He doesn't exist.

In the ensuing dialogue, Mary is given the option to return "To that awful existence you call life" but, after initial temptation, decides she is "home".

Self-destruction is, of course, the archetypal ending to unhappy female lives. It is the traditional punishment for the sexually transgressing woman, like Anna Karenina or Emma Bovary. It marks the final defeat of women who have overreached their prescribed roles or can no longer bear a painful reality, like Hedda Gabler or Paula (the second Mrs.) Tanqueray. Depictions of the suicide-as-martyr celebrate woman-as-victim; the contemporary mythologizing of Marilyn Monroe and Sylvia Plath provide two of the best-known, albeit very different, examples of the syndrome. Some reviewers of *Ripen Our Darkness* responded to Mary's suicide in these usual terms of defeat and victimization: Victoria Radin of the *Observer* felt "sad that Mary does herself in instead of battling forward to selfhood", while Michael Coveney of the *Financial Times* regretted that she "goes under just at that point when she perhaps could have pulled herself together and come out fighting". However, Daniels's unconventionally comic treatment of Mary's suicide overturns the traditionally negative meaning of the act; presented as having reversible consequences, it becomes a positive choice rather than an act of despair. Without denying the harsh realities of Mary's life, Daniels contrives at once to release Mary from her domestic bondage *and* to celebrate her growth into fearless self-fulfillment:

> MARY. If I decide to go back, can you give me the power to put the fear of God –
> I beg your pardon – into those men.
> OLD WOMAN (*shakes her head and smiles*). I'm sorry, Mary, but we simply know no fear.
> MARY. In that case ... I'm home. (scene 13, p. 68; Daniels's ellipsis)

Daniels also uses humour as a way of implicating the audience in the argument of a play. *Masterpieces*, for example, opens with a scene in which three heterosexual couples are having a meal at a restaurant; the three men tell misogynist jokes, mainly about rape, at which everyone, except Yvonne, laughs. When the play was staged at the Royal Court, a theatre whose commitment to challenging political drama has been a byword since early this century, the normally aware audience joined heartily in the on-stage laughter, no doubt feeling that their response was sanctioned by the playwright's sex. However, when the hitherto-silent Yvonne finally responded with an anti-male joke ("How many men does it take to tile a bathroom? (*Pause.*) Three, but you have to slice them thinly", p. 169), the audience fell deathly silent, their discomfort palpable. Here, Daniels's humour engaged the audience in a dialectical way, raising questions about such widely divergent responses to jokes that differ only in the objects of their malice.

Heterosexism and heterosexuality are often targets in Daniels's plays, with lesbianism presented as an implicit norm against which other relationships should be, and are, judged. The structure of *Ripen Our Darkness*, for example, carefully lays the ground for such comparison: in scene 1, we see the home-life of Mary, her overbearing husband, and demanding sons; in scene 2, that of Rene and her daughter Susan, verbally abused and physically threatened by the drunken Alf; in scene 3, that of Anna and Julie. References have already been made to these two women: in scene 1, David has referred to his daughter Anna as a "disgrace" (p. 11), and in scene 2, Rene has commented that "women like [her step-daughter Julie] are never 'appy, how can they be?" Susan's ironic reply, "Not like we are then, eh, Mum? (p. 16), explicitly invites comparison of the lesbian couple with the heterosexual ones.

Anna and Julie, whose relationship is depicted in scenes 3, 7, 10, and 13, are neither idealized nor romanticized. The couple have various disagreements in the course of the play, ranging from serious arguments about practical matters (Anna objects to Julie's desire to offer her half-sister Susan a home) to more light-hearted exchanges about sexual politics:

ANNA. Hang on, is this the same person who had to be physically removed from the pub last night, screaming 'Off with their rocks!'?
JULIE. So? So?
ANNA. So? Half of my colleagues were there.
JULIE. Do you want to live a lie?
ANNA. That's not fair. They all know I'm gay.
JULIE. Gay? You're the most humourless, miserable fucker this side of the Blackwall Tunnel.
(scene 3, p. 19)

However, unlike the heterosexual relationships in which the men dominate their wives, this one is balanced, with neither woman consistently having the upper hand. The first disagreement about Julie's sister ends good-naturedly (ANNA. "Why do you always have the last word?" JULIE. "Because I ain't read the right books, thank God." (p. 22)), the second with an "*exasperated*" Anna who "*slams an exercise book on the table and goes out*" (p. 48), and the third with Julie telling Anna to "fuck off!" before leaving the room (p. 54). On the latter two occasions, however, each woman gestures towards her angry partner, Julie shrugging "Just a joke" and Anna calling "Ju?" as the other leaves; there is no sense of a final breakdown of communication.

Communication is, in fact, the hallmark of their relationship: whether they are joking, talking, or arguing about political differences and personal preferences, Anna and Julie are engaged with each other in a way totally absent from the interaction of the heterosexual couples depicted. Their sensitivity to each other is perhaps best exemplified early in scene 7 (p. 41), with Julie's response to Anna's extreme bad temper:

JULIE. You got any ideas on what I can do my thesis on? It's got to be something I'm interested in.
ANNA (*sarcastic*). Oh, that shouldn't be too hard, considering you hate everything.
JULIE. I do not. At most there are only five things I actually hate.
ANNA. Yes. Art, travel, society, anything manmade, or anything alive. Oh, sod it. What in hell's name are we doing? You with your cranky sabotage of the Open University. They're only ordinary people trying to get on as best they can – they weren't born into it.
JULIE. What do you suggest I do, become a house-mother at Eton?

ANNA. And me. What in fuck's name am I doing? Priding myself on pioneering non-sexist literature for use in my classroom.
JULIE. You didn't get a letter from your mum this week, did you?

Julie's question indicates her understanding of the unspoken worry that has surfaced in Anna's irritation and frustration; it allows Anna to subsequently voice her concern. In contrast, David does not hear what Mary in fact speaks aloud; complaining that her mind is not on the game of Monopoly he has insisted she join in, he urges her to concentrate:

MARY. Sorry, dear. It's just that I haven't caught up with the washing-up from lunch, and now the tea things ...
DAVID. ... what were you doing while I was showing Daphne the rhodendrons?
MARY. Making the tea.
DAVID. I don't think we need contradict each other all the time. (scene 4, p. 23; first ellipsis Daniels's)

The audience's final vision of Anna and Julie shows them in Mary's kitchen after the funeral, their interaction empathetic and loving:

ANNA (*looks round kitchen picking up things and putting them down*). What didn't I do?
JULIE. I don't know.
ANNA. Was I too arrogant? Did I give her enough room to say what she wanted?
JULIE. I don't know.
ANNA (*smiles*). And I thought you knew everything. C'mon, let's go home.
Both hug each other ... (scene 13, pp. 69–70; my ellipsis)

Despite Anna and Julie's positive portrayal, however, some reviewers of the play's first production insisted on the couple's negative presentation, an indication of the strength of their own assumptions and prejudices about lesbianism. John Barber, writing in the *Daily Telegraph*, commented that "the couple do nothing but quarrel, either over feminist theory or a third girl," an unnecessarily ambiguous description of Julie's half-sister designed to make her sound like a sexual threat to the relationship. Milton Shulman, who is generally vituperative about Daniels's work, went further in describing the women as "held together more by their mutual loathing of men rather than anything they seem to have in common" and in declaring their relationship "even more fragile and doomed than most marriages"; he even "suspects" that they are as responsible as the men are for Mary's suicide (*Evening Standard*). Such a self-protective misreading of the play, which ignores Mary's *rapprochement* with Anna and Julie in scenes 7 and 11, suggests the very real threat that Daniels's depiction of the lesbian relationship posed to male critics reviewing the production. Michael Coveney, writing in the *Financial Times*, seems to have sensed its use as a yardstick against which to measure other relationships without explicitly reading it as such: Anna and Julie's "relationship has an almost mock conventional flavour as Mary arrives to give [them] her blessing ... ". His language hedges the question of the relationship's meaning, at once suggesting both lesbian imitation and authorial ridicule of dominant sexuality; moreover, it implies that lesbianism is so beyond the pale that nothing could ever be "conventional" about such a relationship without being "mock".

In *The Devil's Gateway*, as in *Ripen Our Darkness*, the relationship between Fiona and Linda provides the counterpoint to the heterosexual ones depicted, juxtaposing "an obstinately patriarchal household and a free-wheeling lesbian twosome"

(Billington, *Guardian*). Like Anna and Julie, Fiona and Linda do not agree on all political issues: they spray stencilled graffiti on sex-shops together (scenes 8 & 11), but Linda does not share her partner's enthusiasm for nuclear disarmament and the women's peace camp at Greenham Common (scenes 2 & 4). Although Fiona tries to interest her in the cause, there is no sense of coercion or disapproval in their discussions:

FIONA. I want you to come down with me, for the anniversary, before the eviction.
LINDA (*lightly*). What about all the people who get evicted round here? Who's fighting for them? I ain't going all the way down there for a bundle.
FIONA. You'll like it, I know.
LINDA. Why?
FIONA. Well ... umm ... because ... because it's there ... the space ...
LINDA. I know it's an open space, so is Victoria Park.
FIONA. Naw, the space for . . . creativity . . .
LINDA. Creativity?! Ha, bourgeois crap.
FIONA. It's not, not altogether, well I liked it.
LINDA (*teasing*). Creativity? You? Your whole career [social work] is about control. What a load of rubbish.
FIONA. You can't be cynical all your life you know.
LINDA. (*playing around*). Oh, goddess of creativity come down and cleanse my cynicism.
FIONA (*laughs*). Okay, okay point taken. (scene 4, p. 104; Daniels's ellipses)

Their generous interaction provides a direct contrast to that of Jim and Betty. When Betty asks her husband for some money so that she can go to Greenham for the day, he forbids her:

JIM. You'll be right here when I git back. D'you hear me, and we'll sort it out then. I can't waste no more time gabbing about it now.
BETTY. Please ...
JIM. No way, Betty. No way. (scene 12, p. 153; Daniels's ellipsis)

Lesbians figure in most of Daniels's plays, and the fact that they do so as a matter of course rather than of scandal, grotesquerie, or melodramatic plot complication (as they have done in commercial plays like Lillian Hellman's *The Children's Hour* or Frank Marcus's *The Killing of Sister George*) itself constitutes a challenge to conventional theatrical representation and conservative values. The five lesbian characters who appear in *Byrthrite* allow Daniels to make some points about the privileges accorded to men, the persecution of women who do not conform, and the inequality of class: Jane and Rose cross-dress to gain independence (Part 1, scene 2, p. 340 and throughout the play), Ann and Mary feel vulnerable to the present witch-hunt because they are unmarried (Part 1, scene 7, pp. 362–64), and Rose remains untempted by Bridget's promise of wealth (Part 2, scene 3, pp. 384–86). However, lesbianism is not intrinsic to these issues, which could just as easily have been raised through heterosexual characters. Daniels's lesbian characters do not have a functional *raison d'être*, but simply reflect a reality long denied by mainstream theatre.

Lesbianism does emerge as an issue in itself in *Neaptide*, where Claire, the closeted deputy head-teacher of a girls' comprehensive school, must decide whether to maintain her personal integrity by defending lesbian students threatened with expulsion; such action, however, will risk the loss of an impending dispute with her ex-husband over her continued custody of their seven-year-old daughter, Poppy. The school setting of much of the action inevitably raises echoes of Hellman's *The Children's Hour*, echoes which only serve to define more clearly *Neaptide*'s crucial differences.

Hellman's play, in depicting the destruction wrought by a child's malicious lie that her schoolteachers are lesbian, ostensibly sympathizes with the victims of the lie. However, the teachers' resultant ostracization by society leads one of them to realize her latent lesbianism, and she kills herself. The truly destructive force, then, is not the original lie, but lesbianism itself, which has no place in the world of the play except as ultimate slander or unendurable reality.[4] In *Neaptide*, by contrast, lesbianism *per se* is never the issue: its realization, rather than threatening personal disintegration, engenders self-fulfillment. Any problems associated with lesbianism are firmly fixed in society's ignorant, prejudiced, and punitive reactions to it. Claire's pain, for instance, is caused not by her identity, but by the threatened loss of her daughter and her own hypocrisy; when her heterosexual flat-mate suggests she continue to compromise her principles to safeguard both her job and her custody of Poppy, Claire replies: "It's not a principle we're talking about. It's me. And what do you think I've done. I've compromised myself so much I've lied my way out of existence" (Part 2, scene 3, p. 314). Her self-negation by silence represents lesbian reality more accurately than Hellman's suicidal victim.

Crucially, Claire is not alone in her difficulties, as *Neaptide*'s dramatis personae, unlike that of *The Children's Hour*, boasts many other lesbians: the head-teacher Beatrice Grimble, the physical education teacher Linda Fellowes, students Diane and Terri, and other unseen schoolgirls who take part in an off-stage meeting. Daniels's refusal to represent lesbianism in its usual theatrical guise as an isolated and individual problem challenges the audience to accept it as the part of everyday life it so manifestly is for a significant proportion of the population. This stance was appreciated by Michael Coveney, who admired how the play "neatly dodges sexist hysteria by showing Claire and [her flat-mate] Jean as ordinary people coming to terms with real domestic problems" (*Financial Times*). Michael Billington, on the other hand, regretted the absence of "a downright confrontation between sexual freedom and social prejudice" (*Guardian*) — in other words, a clichéd denouement in which a member of an oppressed minority expected to justify its existence pleads for tolerance. Daniels's rejection of such a negative approach is reflected even in the plot mechanism, which completely inverts Hellman's: events begin not with a lie about others but with a student proudly telling the truth about her own sexuality.

Like many other contemporary women playwrights, Daniels rejects linear plot structure and substitutes a split or multiple focus that, in Mary Remnant's words, addresses

> the reality of women's lives. To a woman who fits full- or part-time work into the day between taking a child to the dentist, washing the kitchen floor, doing the shopping and boiling the potatoes, the seeming anarchy of structure of, say, *Ripen Our Darkness* . . . may make far more sense than to a man whose schedule is uncluttered by domestic considerations. (Remnant 1987, p. 10)

---

[4] Indeed, whereas heroines were once routinely killed off for any transgression of social and sexual norms or expectations, in the sexually "liberated" 1960s the lesbian was usually the only female transgressor likely to pay such a price: consider not only the 1962 film version of Hellman's play but also the 1968 screen adaptation of D.H. Lawrence's *The Fox*. However, with the advent of AIDS during the last decade, any sexually-transgressive woman who threatens the heterosexual family unit is usually dead by the time the final credits roll; the most notorious example, of course, is *Fatal Attraction* (1987).

Remnant also sees this challenge to the "all-pervading male-defined aesthetic" as one reason why women's writing, Daniels's included, is often dismissed as inferior: "the inability [of male critics] to imagine the optimum dramatic structure as anything other than singly climatic may help to relegate the episodic nature of some women's writing to the realm of 'soap opera' (with its 'multiple orgasm' of continuous climaxes)" (Remnant 1987, p. 10).

In her refusal to focus on a single character or artificially-delimited issue, Daniels reflects this new feminist aesthetic. *Ripen Our Darkness* shifts between the three households already described, while *Byrthrite* follows the varied fortunes of a group of seventeenth-century friends. The latter play, which also intersperses the story with songs about modern reproductive technology, received considerable criticism from male reviewers for this tactic: Michael Billington, for example, objected "that the arguments about methods of childbirth are grafted arbitrarily on to an upbeat story about female self-discovery" (*Guardian*). Unsurprisingly, however, a female reviewer like Claire Armitstead found the connection apt: "In an era which has just seen [obstetric consultant] Wendy Savage hounded from her job for her espousal of natural childbirth, Daniels's decision to place her plot among the witch hunts of 17th century England seems apposite enough" (*Financial Times*). Not only are there links between 17th and 20th century events, as Armitstead states, but, as she also implies, a woman's right to control reproduction is an inherent aspect of the "female self-discovery" that Billington so narrowly defines.

Similarly, in *Neaptide*, Daniels complicates the main plot with an occasional focus on Claire's married sister Val, who in fact opens the play speaking from her hospital bed; depressed, she had smashed her fists and arms through a window two days previously. Although the Val sub-plot was inadequately developed, as many reviewers complained, their main criticism stemmed from a view that it had nothing to do with the rest of the play. Such a view depends on an acceptance of conventional linear narrative, with its neat compartmentalization of issues. Val's predicament in fact functions to contextualize Claire's, raising questions about the relationship between conventional, "normal" behavior and self-realization, as well as about male judgement of female experience (medical/psychological in Val's case, legal in Claire's). *Beside Herself* likewise opens with a prologue set in a supermarket-Hell where biblical women-scapegoats like Eve, Delilah, Jezebel, and Mrs Lot tell their side of the story. Most reviewers dismissed this opening scene, failing to see its connection with the main play's concern with child abuse: the mythical, historical, and contemporary fastening of blame on women for their own victimization and the necessary rejection of such blame.

Daniels's insistence on collective experience rejects the traditional dramatic celebration of a solitary and unique protagonist, whose abilities, circumstances, feelings and/or ambitions place him (as is usually the case) outside common experience. Small wonder then that critics have been infuriated that Claire is not the sole lesbian in *Neaptide* nor Evelyn the lone survivor of sexual abuse in *Beside Herself*: apart from regarding these multiple depictions as a personal affront to manhood, they suffer an assault to their rigid sense of dramatic propriety. Notions of dramatic "realism" are invoked to reject Daniels's manipulation of reality, which is consequently dismissed as unbelievable coincidence (as, for example, the revelation that Beatrice Grimble, the headteacher in *Neaptide*, is herself a lesbian). In fact, all dramatic action, even the naturalistic, involves such manipulation: that Daniels's is directed at subverting conventional ideas opens her to attack.

Similarly, Daniels's refusal to give her action an expected shape or content demands a dialectical engagement to which most reviewers seem resistant. Paul Taylor, reviewing *Beside Herself* for the *Independent*, for example, judged the play harshly for neglecting to dramatize what he saw as Evelyn's "crucial relationships" with her unseen husband and daughter:

> this omission seems odd, especially as it throws up the chance of dramatizing, in an encounter between the damaged phantom-girl and the real-life one, the (I assume) especially charged and anxious bond between an abused mother and female child. Instead, [the play] plunges you into the life of St Dymphna, the halfway house for people discharged from mental hospital, where Evelyn does some of her voluntary work.

Taylor's comment interestingly illustrates the extent of Daniels's perceived transgression, the foremost being her failure to limit the scope of her play to a domestic world, the "natural" (and derided) sphere of the woman playwright. However, by showing how Evelyn functions (and sometimes fails to function) in a wider social context, Daniels effectively prevents the audience from seeing her simply as a victim enmeshed in the psychological and emotional difficulties caused by her father's sexual abuse of her as a child. The continued presence on-stage of Evelyn's child alter ego Eve similarly dramatizes the complexity of Evelyn's emotional and mental state. Most importantly, however, the St Dymphna's setting allows the issue of child abuse itself to be seen in a social rather than a merely personal context, as a reflection of general attitudes towards sexuality and masculinity rather than of individual pathology. This point is made perhaps most clearly in the doubling of the parts of Evelyn's abusive father, who is a respected doctor, and homosexual Dave, whose mature, consensual relationship with his partner Jon was punished by their imprisonment, the consequences of which were Jon's suicide and Dave's own subsequent mental breakdown (Act 2, scene 4, pp. 51–53).

Daniels's unconventional plotting is also evident in the interjected monologues that have become almost a personal trademark; they occur in *Ripen Our Darkness* (scene 5 and 12), *The Devil's Gateway* (scene 9), *Masterpieces* (scene 7 and, in voiceover form, scenes 1 and 8), *Neaptide* (Part 1, scene 8 and Part 2, scene 5), and *Beside Herself* (scene 5). While these monologues often give Daniels an opportunity to create wonderfully comic set-pieces, they also work on a serious level. For example, Hilary's account in *Masterpieces* (scene 7, p. 196) of how, as a teenager, she "could've got an A level, a Ph.D. even, in contraceptives" was treated by reviewers simply as marvellous stand-up comedy, but Daniels herself points out that its sub-text questions the naturalness of heterosexuality, the expression of which involves so much fuss, anxiety, denial of spontaneity, risk to health, and dependence on unreliable devices (Daniels 1992).

Another hallmark of Daniels's monologues, evident in the example given above, is that they are never spoken by any of the main characters, but by the minor ones. Such brief but intense focus goes some way towards balancing the relationship of leading and secondary characters, a strategy that complements Daniels's insistence on collective experience and rejection of the lone protagonist. In this way, she gives a voice to those who would otherwise be denied an effective one: Hilary, for example, who is generally the focus of other points-of-view (e.g., a sexual object in Ron's eyes and a victim of unwanted harassment in Rowena's) becomes a powerful present through her monologue, relating directly to the audience rather than having her experience filtered through other perspectives.

In *Ripen Our Darkness* and *Beside Herself*, Daniels goes even further, giving monologues to characters who would otherwise not appear in the play at all. Tara, in the former (scene 5), is married to the psychiatrist who later in the play is anxious to commit Mary to a mental institution; her comments on her husband's sexual anxieties provide a framework by which the audience can subsequently judge *his* judgements of Mary. Richard and Gaynor Brittain, the rate-payers who object to the presence of St Dymphna's in their neighborhood in *Beside Herself* (scene 5), extend the play's parameters in many ways, particularly in regard to the arbitrariness of definitions of mental illness and to the helplessness of children within relationships with adults.

Allied to such use of the monologue is Daniels's selective depiction of fully-rounded characters, often regarded as a fault by reviewers but in fact the result of conscious practice (Daniels 1992). Those who receive a three-dimensional flesh-ing-out are those more usually given stereotypical or cursory treatment: namely, women, working-class, and other disempowered characters. Those traditionally privileged in drama – men and those in authority or positions of power – are left as ciphers. Thus, as Nicholas de Jongh pointed out in his *Guardian* review without understanding its rationale, the eponymous Gut Girls are given realistic depictions while the Duchess of Albany is caricatured. In responding to *Masterpieces*, Michael Coveney fell into the same trap by suggesting that "Now all [Daniels] has to do [to prove her powers as a playwright] is write a good man's role" (*Financial Times*). Only Giles Gordon saw that "The women's roles, understandably, are more fully realised in the writing than the men's ... simply ... to redress the balance of centuries: why should art be *fair*? (*Spectator*).

The critical response to Daniels's unequal dramatic treatment of women and men characters deserves attention; even more than her positive portrayal of lesbians, it has made her a prey to personal and unwarranted attack. Remnant has already listed the vituperative comments aimed at Daniels herself: words like "man-hating", "fanatical", vitriolic", "embittered", "bilious", "obsessive", "strident", and "shrill" pepper the reviews of male critics (Remnant 1987, p. 9).[5] However, critical hostility goes beyond mere name-calling. Some reviewers paradoxically attempt to discredit Daniels's approach by reacting with provocative sexism: Robert Cushman, reviewing *Masterpieces* for the *Observer*, for example, commented that he "spent one whole scene happily admiring Miss Pogson's legs" and disingenuously concluded that "theatre is [a very tricky arena] for the discussion of sexism". Similarly, Giles Gordon, in an otherwise admiring review of the same play for the *Spectator*, droolingly described the actor playing Hilary as "scrumptious (sexist, yes)". This reassertion of the male "right" to objectify women marks one containing strategy against the force of Daniels's plays.

Another tactic is to distort the action of a play. Many reviews of *Masterpieces*, for instance, misled the reader about the threat to Rowena in the deserted Underground station at night. Daniels's stage directions leave no doubt about the man's aggressive and threatening behavior: he

[5] I am grateful to my colleague Liz Schafer for calling my attention to Remnant's work while I was in the course of writing this article. I have long been struck by the unbalanced critical response to Daniels's plays and have followed it with interest; however, I have quoted Remnant where her analysis anticipates my own.

casually saunters up the platform towards ROWENA who doesn't look at him. Long pause. He then says something to her which we don't hear. She turns away and … moves away from him …. He approaches her again very fast. Very close to her face. She shoves him violently. He falls on the track. (scene 14, p. 224; my ellipses)

Ann McFerran, reviewing the play for *Time Out*, found "entirely plausible [the] death of the harassing male". However, male reviewers tended to describe the man's action in innocuous terms like "approach" and "address", making a hysterical Rowena responsible for her response to it: "incensed by a porn film [she is] in terror of a Tube-station approach by a man" (John Barber, *Daily Telegraph*); "shocked by what she learns about sex magazines, films, practices and … addressed by a stranger on a railway platform, she at once retaliates by pushing him under an oncoming train" (Francis King, *Sunday Telegraph*); "reeling in shock from a snuff-movie, Rowena pushes under a train a guy who propositions her on a station platform" (Michael Billington, *Guardian*); "a leering man makes a pass at her" (Giles Gordon, *Spectator*). Whether this revisioning of the play's action is intentional or merely reflects a failure of male imagination of female experience might be debatable; however, the similar transformation of a snuff movie, in which women are genuinely killed on screen, into a simple "porn" or "sex" film suggests a deliberate strategy to undermine the play's power.

Similarly, reviews tended to twist the whole import of *Masterpieces*, which regards pornography not necessarily as the cause of violence against women, but as one symptom of a prevailing social attitude that validates and legitimizes it. It is a point along a continuum that includes misogynist jokes at one end and sexual murder and mutilation at the other. Critics nevertheless dismissed what they saw as an attempted and unproven causal connection between pornography and violence. As Remnant astutely points out, however, the press was not reluctant to proclaim a link between a sex attack on a young boy and material produced by the Paedophile Information Exchange, nor is there an unwillingness to acknowledge that racist jokes help perpetuate racism. Remnant has given another example of this strategy of distortion in Michael Billington's response to *Neaptide*; he claimed that the play shows men as "congenitally unfit for child custody" when it actually deals with the threat to make a lesbian mother appear so (Remnant 1987, pp. 8–9).

Criticism of the limited opportunities afforded to male actors and of the range of men depicted in her plays is another tactic aimed at discrediting Daniels. Michael Billington's comment, vis-à-vis *Byrthrite*, that the single male actor in the play "earns my sympathy as a series of token men" in fact incorporates both complaints. Implicit in his remark is a belief that male actors deserve challenging, fully-rounded roles and also that such roles should represent a wide variety of character types. This view, shared by many other critics, judges Daniels harshly for her depiction of certain types of men, which they regard as an intentional demeaning of all men. For example, reviewing *Ripen Our Darkness*, Billington saw her as making a "blanket dismissal of [all] men as bestial exploiters" (*Guardian*), while Francis King concluded that she aimed to show that "all men are brutes" (*Sunday Telegraph*). Mary Harron, reviewing *Byrthrite*, remarked that "men get hammered and I felt deeply sorry for [the actor] who played all the ghastly male roles" (*Observer*).[6]

[6] A survey of reviews shows that, on the whole, men tend to be hostile to Daniels's work and women sympathetic, a judgement with which Remnant concurs (Remnant 1987, p. 10). Female reviewers who object to a play usually do so from a male perspective, as Harron does in the example quoted here.

The same critics who condemn Daniels for her lack of "balance", however, conspicuously fail to comment on the shallow depiction (or, indeed, rare appearance) of women characters frequent in the works of many contemporary male playwrights.[7] Neither the absence of women nor their presentation as limited, unrounded characters or mere stereotypes – bimbo, bitch, sex goddess – is seen as problematic. An archetypal or stereotypical woman is contradictorily regarded by critics simply as herself, her presence implying nothing about women in general. Yet when Daniels draws a male character in such a cursory, albeit credible, way, she provokes outrage at what male reviewers regard as a wholesale condemnation of the sex rather than a critical representation of a particular kind of behavior. Such bias has occasionally been noted even by a reviewer: Giles Gordon, for instance, commented that "If ever the reception of a play by a woman has suggested that the imbalance between the sexes among the critics is unfair, even scandalous, it has been that accorded Sarah Daniels's *Masterpieces*" (*Spectator*).

Such gendered critical reaction in fact highlights the greatest challenge that Daniels presents to her audiences: her focus on women at once reveals and confounds the expectation that "true" drama revolves around male experience. This expectation, dependent on the corollary view that the male experience is universal and the female merely particular, helps to explain different standards of judgement not only of female and male characters, but of female and male dramatists. The presence of these unwritten laws is manifest in the critical judgements of many reviewers. Milton Shulman, for instance, reviewing *Masterpieces*, remarked that Daniels "would get more sympathy ... if [her] protests were directed at the conditioning by the visual media of generations of children to accept violence as normal. In a violent society, women can expect no special exemption" (*Evening Standard*). Implicit in his comment is the view that a condemnation of violence against women constitutes a special case, while condemning violence in general makes a more persuasive point.

That male experience is the expected dramatic norm, however, is evidenced most powerfully in critical responses to *Beside Herself*, in which Daniels explores the issue of child sexual abuse through the experience of middle-aged Evelyn. Professional wisdom on the subject generally accepts that such abuse is overwhelmingly perpetrated by men on girls, but no fewer than three male reviewers criticised Daniels for her focus on Evelyn: Paul Taylor rounded on the play for "fail[ing] to acknowledge ... that little boys get abused too" (*Independent*), while Irving Wardle plaintively asked, "Do not boys get abused too?" (*Independent on Sunday*). Michael Billington, in the *Guardian*, judged that the play's "One gaping

[7] My statement is based on many years of regularly reading reviews, but an arbitrary example may strengthen the point. For the week following the premiere of *Beside Herself*, I examined Billington's reviews of contemporary plays by male playwrights in the *Guardian*; a review of *Sugar Hill Blues*, by Kevin Hood, was the only one to appear. He commended the play, about a Geordie bricklayer who travels to Harlem to study saxophone with his black idol, for 'pack[ing] in a lot about cultural colonisation, the dynamics of jazz and English small-mindedness: typically Bernie is labelled as daft by his bricklaying mates and by the snooty Shropshire chanteuse who picks him up' (Billington 1990b). The review, like the play, concentrated on the two male protagonists; Billington's comment about the "chanteuse" was his only remark on what appears to have been a minor and stereotypical character. He offered no criticism of the play for focussing on male experience, even though the themes are as pertinent to women as to men. Billington's judgement of Hood's play illustrates the one-sidedness of his criticisms of Daniels.

flaw is that [Daniels] deals with sexual abuse entirely in terms of father-daughter relationships, ignoring the proven fact that there are male victims as well" (Billington 1990a). The exclusion of male experience from the play is seen as an active denial of that experience and consequently as a distortion of reality, invalidating the real female experience on which Daniels has chosen to focus.

In a recent feature article for the *Guardian*, Michael Billington addressed the question of "What is theatre actually for?", arguing passionately that theatre "thrive[s] on its capacity for dissent: on its ability to challenge and question the prevailing moral and political codes ... to attack the deepest values of [its society]. Drama, at its best, always fulfills the role of a disloyal opposition". He concluded with a lament for the contemporary dearth of hard-hitting political drama in Britain: "Are we really saying there is nothing left to attack?" (Billington 1992). He could, of course, have consoled himself with the plays of Sarah Daniels. At a time when even many feminist playwrights have retreated to non-contentious depictions of family life and of world politics, as for example Charlotte Keatley in her portrait of four generations of women in *My Mother Said I Never Should* (1989) and Caryl Churchill in her semi-journalistic account of the Romanian revolution in *Mad Forest* (1990), Daniels has continued to explore the very core of our personal and social relations, the arena of sexual politics. That her assault on conventional prejudice and conservative values has consistently provoked such outrage along gender lines ultimately points to the most transgressive aspect of her writing: the fore-grounding of female experience in a world still overwhelmingly male-defined.

References

Billington, Michael (1990a) "Wounded child, haunted woman", *Guardian*, 6 April 1990, p. 37

——— (1990b) "Sugar Hill Blues", *Guardian*, 11 April 1990, p. 37

——— (1992) "Thriving on the oxygen of protest", *Guardian*, 7 May 1992, p. 22

Churchill, Caryl (1990) *Mad Forest*. London: Nick Hern Books

Daniels, Sarah (1989) *The Gut Girls*. London: Methuen

——— (1991a) *Plays: One [Ripen our Darkness, The Devil's Gateway, Masterpieces, Neaptide, Byrthritel]*. London: Methuen

——— (1991b) *Beside Herself*. London: Methuen

——— (1992) Personal interview, 27 April 1992

Durrant, Sabine (1990) "Beside themselves", *Independent*, 4 April 1990, p. 12

Hellman, Lillian (1934) *The Children's Hour*, in *Six Plays* by *Lillian Hellman*. New York: Vintage, 1979

Keatley, Charlotte (1989) *My Mother Said I Never Should*. London: Methuen

London Theatre Record (reviews) 27 August–9 September 1981, pp. 445–47, for *Ripen Our Darkness*; 13–26 August 1983, pp. 673–74, for *The Devil's Gateway*; 8–21 October 1983, pp. 878–81, for *Masterpieces*; 19 November–2 December 1986, pp. 1311–13, for *Byrthrite*; 2–15 July 1986, pp. 713–17, for *Neaptide*; 4–17 November 1988, pp. 1573–74, for *The Gut Girls*; 26 March–8 April 1990, pp. 468–71, for *Beside Herself*

Marcus, Frank (1965) *The Killing of Sister George*. London: Samuel French

Remnant, Mary (1987) Editor. Introduction to *Plays by Women: Volume Six*, pp. 7–12. London: Methuen

Rycroft, Charles (1968) *A Critical Dictionary of Psychoanalysis*. Harmondsworth: Penguin, 1972

All newspapers from which quotations are taken are London publications.

Contemporary Theatre Review, 1996, Vol. 5,1 pp. 77–89
Reprints available directly from the publisher
Photocopying permitted by license only

Steven Berkoff's Orgy: The Four-Letter Ecstasy

Nicole Boireau

Steven Berkoff, a provocative theatre man, is a director, an actor and a writer. His plays are based on literary models. In some of his satirical plays, *East, West, Decadence, Greek, Kvetch,* he creates a grotesque world. His outrageous use of language is a festive celebration of the forces of life. Breaking the ultimate taboo of incest is a way of historicizing ancient myths, in order to expose the artificiality of taboos and of the repressive rules imposed by society. In his adaptations of Kafka's stories, *Metamorphosis and The Penal Colony*, of Edgar Poe's *"Fall of the House of Usher"*, as well as in his production of Oscar Wilde's *Salome*, Berkoff's use of the body is a way of laying bare the lethal mechanisms of modern mythologies and of the narcissistic society of the spectacle. Language and body make up Berkoff's theatricality. His dramatic art is a mythical journey back to origins.

KEY WORDS Grotesque world, Incest, Sex, Verbal excess, Physical stylization, Narcissism, Conformity, Modern mythologies

Creating compelling theatrical events has obviously been Steven Berkoff's mission since the beginning of his acting career in repertory in the Sixties. Whether in his style of acting (he attended Jacques Lecoq's school of mime in Paris), his ensemble directing (he founded his own company, the *London Theatre Group*, in 1968), or in his writings (he started adapting stories by Kafka in the late Sixties), Steven Berkoff, the actor-manager, director and playwright has consistently appeared as one of the most provocative theatre men of his generation. The vitality and energy which he puts into his acting and directing, the physical quality of his writing style point up his attachment to what can loosely be labelled as "total theatre", so forcefully does he cut across well-defined genres and barriers. Indeed, Berkoff achieves a symbiosis between the abstractly literary and the mythical, between the ritualistic and the subversive, between metrical control and coarse language, visual stylization and verbal excess.

Breaking with realistic conventions ("naturalism is bad for your health," says Berkoff in *The Times* in 1991), his plays are based on the archetypes conveyed by Western literary tradition. Aeschylus' *Agamemnon*, Sophocles' *Oedipus, Beowulf,* Kafka's *Metamorphosis* and *The Penal Colony*, Oscar Wilde's *Salome*, Edgar Poe's "The Fall of the House of Usher", Shakespeare's *Hamlet* are, among others, the literary mediators of his journey back to origins. Berkoff uses pre-existing models, which he places within a different historical setting thus giving a grotesquely distorted but heightened picture of Western culture. Subverting the tragedy of Oedipus, transgressing the ultimate taboo of incest, unveiling the unmentionable, putting a permanent (verbal) orgy centre-stage, Berkoff breaks the frames of reference and lays bare the mechanisms of modern mythologies. Far beyond breaking the taboos of incest and verbal decorum, the physical quality of Berkoff's drama opens the way back to myth. Myth, orgy, body, life and text are, among others, the key words of Steven Berkoff's four-letter ecstasy.

The Grotesque World: The Orgy

The world Steven Berkoff lashes at in *East, West, Decadence, Greek,* which could all be defined as "state-of-England plays" satirizing ordinary reality to the point of exploding it to mammoth dimensions, is the one he describes on his train journey to Liverpool in 1991:

> The morbid taint of British lifestyle. Non-creative, sterile, lazy, mechanical. (*Weekend Guardian* p.5)

It is a menacing world, as he says in a programme note to *Kvetch* (1991), "an American play about anxiety," as its subtitle goes, and which won the 1991 "comedy of the year" Award:

> We all live under the shadow of the bomb – cancer – carcinogens – illness – unemployment – impotence – fear of fear – blacks – whites – police – rates/.../.

Working-class passivity (*Greek*), middle-class complacency and petit-bourgeois conformity (*West, Greek, Decadence, Kvetch*) are Steven Berkoff's favourite targets. Again, the "Author's Note" in the Faber edition of *Greek* is quite explicit about the world under scrutiny:

> ... the unimaginable wastelands of Tufnell Park /.../. In my eyes, Britain seemed to have become a gradually decaying island, preyed upon ...(141)

The author's notes about the "decaying island", or the "septic isle", and about the quintessence of Englishness, are strangely reminiscent of John Osborne's angry manifestoes, in which he described royalty as "the gold filling in a mouthful of decay" in the late fifties (Osborne, 1957 p. 25); scathing attacks on the ruling classes seem to be a constant feature of contemporary English drama:

> *Decadence* is a study of the ruling classes or upper classes, so called by virtue of strangulated vowel tones rather than any real achievement./.../ So they make bad lovers but are known to be very decent to servants and extremely loyal to royalty, which to them represents the pinnacle of achievement and the sum total of Englishness (Note to *Decadence* 3–4)

Decadence is a vitriolic comedy of upper-class, adulterous manners. England is represented as the country of repressive upper classes (and repressive fathers, like Steve's), who learn buggery in public schools (11–12), and who play aggressive games that channel their sexual drives; hunting is an example:

> HELEN : Oh fuck! some kid's pet cat is torn to shreds in the wake of the enthusiastic chase / never mind there's plenty more/ ah, we've got him now / I see it caught / it's trapped / its breath is pounding out in horrible short stabs / its fear setting each hair on end / the hounds all teeth and smiles as they go in and sink their fangs into its throat / the blood with one long jet / just fabulous: I'm sure the fox was pleased to make his end this way / the fury / the chase / the ecstasy/ (24)

Helen's frenzied description brings out the extreme callousness of that sort of pastime. Hunting is also a suitable metaphor for the sexual games people play. Indeed, in *Decadence*, Steve's wife can teach us a thing or two about the sex war, namely how to hunt a rich man, play cat-and-mouse with him, titillate him and trap him into marriage:

> SYBIL: sus out the guy and check his bankability / (...) give him a taste and then withdraw a while /

he'll crave for more and more / think your pussy's made of gold and myrrh / he'll make poems to your asshole the pathetic cur / tantalize / (...) you get them by cunning skill and shrewd device / or else be sweet and honest girl and be well fucked, four kids and end in hell / liberation ?? This is it girl! (37–38)

Through Sybil's lesson, Berkoff squarely confronts the cynicism of the dominating moral patterns. Such is the prevailing mood in the country dominated by Maggot Scratcher, worshipped by Eddie's father in *Greek* (155). London, the city "in the grip of a plague," is therefore a suitable place for a transposition of Sophocles' *Oedipus*. The world of *Greek*, in Tufnell Park, is a "cess pit" and a "scum hole" where the pubs, "usually a smelly corner pub run by a rancid thick as pig shit paddy", are patronized by "boring turds" and "boozy old relatives in Marks and Sparks' cardigans" (145), who "fall asleep in front of the telly." The atmospheric area of Tufnell Park recalls the archetypal city described in *East* and also echoes Berkoff's own childhood memories: "*East* could be the east side of any city" says the "Author's Note" (43). The play is a London epic of rampant violence with "boots, chains and knives" (48), hovering everywhere and oozing from every stone. Undifferentiated violence is an infectious disease which strikes everybody, and has been inherited from previous eras:

The Black raven pub in Whitechapel the selfsame street where blessed Jack did rip and tear in cold thick nights. (47)

Children are bred on hatred in the city of decay and violence where Paddies come from "Hellfast". In the plague-ridden city, the worst consequence of the combination of hatred and apathy is the unhindered development of fascism. The older generation's xenophobia and nostalgic allegiance to fascism are frequent allusions in the state-of-England plays. Eddy's father in *Greek* never says much except, "send the darkies back to the jungle", and "Hitler got the trains running on time" (147). Working-class dad, in *East*, affectionately refers to Oswald Mosley as "Ozzie" and happily reminisces about the good old days:

Ozzie had the right ideas – put them into uniforms – into the brown shirts – gave people an identity. Those meetings were a sight. All them flags. Then, they knew what to do – take the law into your own hands when you know it makes sense. That beautiful summer in '38 was it? – When we marched six abreast to Whitechapel – beautiful it were – healthy young British men and women – a few wooden clubs – (54)

Working-class dad echoes upper-class Steve in *Decadence*: "kick out the Pakis, blackies, paddys and kikes / go back to the jungle / Belfast and Israel / don't turn our happy haven into a rancid hell." (30). Fascistic inclinations are not the privilege of a particular class. The fascist plague is evenly distributed and the burden of responsibility is equally shared by all social groups. After his father tells him about the fortune-teller's prediction, Eddy/Oedipus leaves his parents, walks into a café, kills the owner after a fist-fight. Before she marries Eddy, the widowed waitress bemoans her loss:

Whose black uniform will I press in readiness for his marches down Brixton with the other so noble men of England / whose photos will I dust in the living room of his heroes, Hitler, Goebbels, Enoch, Paisley and Maggot not forgetting our dear royals. Is it worth it any more? /I married a good Englishman /(160)

Berkoff's London is also the city whose upper classes go "to Monte Carlo for the season" (11), where old Keith "raced his Ferrari last week 'gainst Claude's Lamborghini and both bloody collided/" (15); it is the place of "crêpe Suzette, lobster Thermidor" (16), where Helen can boast of her "watch from Cartier" (18). At the other end of the social and geographical spectrum, Eddy's dad wears "tasteless shit-heap Burton ready-made trousers and his deadly drip-dry shirt that acquires BO faster than shit attracts flies ..." (147). Later on, Tufnell Park Oedipus thinks of his parents, who are "locked up in council bliss and £40 a week driving a 38 from Putney down to Waltham Cross and getting clobbered each Saturday night." (172)

The ambience of Berkoff's world is captured with geographical and sociological precision, with a taste for picturesque details the density of which reaches epic proportions. In *West*, going west involves a journey by tube early in the morning:

I would crush myself in the tube and others behind me would crush and we'd all get crushed together / which was right if you happened to have your leg wedged between the thighs of some radiant fair-skinned blushing and divine darling but not if some stinking gentleman from an exotic country of the East was breathing the shit he calls food all over your face / and as the doors slid open this composite mass of sludgy flesh would wobble like a wall of jelly / (116)

In a Lenny Bruce type of one-man show, Mike turns the early morning London world into a Grosz-like caricature. The same pictorial vividness applies to the many horrors spawned by modern society. Television is one of them, according to Eddy in *Greek*: "mum sits in front of the box watching some dozy cretin making cunts out of the cunts who go on to win a few bob /" (151). In *Harry's Christmas*, suicidal Harry kills time (before killing himself) with the "death-ray machine /.../ (which) pours evil rays into your head ..." (94). The material world also shapes Eddy's incongruous visions: "a chick who looks as if she's been fresh frozen..." (146).

What Berkoff forcefully denounces as rampant mediocrity is magnified and turned into a surreal fantasy world, out of touch with the initial reality:

no more the sawdust and preservative colouring and cat shit that you could better use to fill your walls than line your stomach /... / the listless British trance so often seen in Oxford Street or on the Piccadilly line at 8 a.m. / a nation half asleep and drugged with foul and bestial things poured out of packets /.../ muscles starved so long/limp with only holding *Daily Mirror* race results/ (*Greek* 166)

The journey east, west, from, or to central London offers the same picture of decadence. Helen and Steve, Sybil and Les in *Decadence*, Mum and Dad, Sylv, Les and Mike, in *East* and *West*, are all interchangeable (they are played by the same actors), all stylized and outrageous products of Berkoff's frenzied vision of present-day hell.

Exterior forces, social or political, which steam-roll individuals into spineless conformists, are relayed at home by the Oedipian family pattern. The archetypal family appears in the London plays and particularly in *Greek*, which reenacts and subverts the different stages of the well-known myth. Berkoff's Eddy learns the truth about the way he was found and adopted by his parents, who pulled him out of the Thames after a mine explosion, when he was two years old. He also learns, simultaneously, that his new beloved wife, who had lost a two-year-old son in the very same accident, turns out to be his mother. Confronted with the earth-shattering discovery, Eddy vents his despair with explosive lyricism, and then makes a decision. Between the taboos imposed by putrescent society and his blissful marriage with his mother-wife, Eddy chooses to commit himself to the latter:

loving cunt holy mother wife / loving source of your being / exit from paradise / entrance to heaven. (183)

Better love your mother than be a fascist, implies Berkoff in *Greek*, thus setting the myth in a contemporary context, historicizing it, therefore adjusting it to our times, trivializing it and shattering its haunting power. Whatever its manifestations, love is preferable to the evils of civilization. Berkoff turns the tragedy of Oedipus into a comedy in order to better confront and reject the strait-jacket of guilt. Beyond taboos lies guilt, the worst disease to be eradicated. One needs to be born again, metaphorically, in order to recapture primeval innocence. Berkoff's intentions are made clear in the 1988 programme:

it is healthier to love your mother than expiate your alleged sin by self-mutilation.

The simplistic and yet subversive philosophy applies to the other London plays based on the family pattern. The revolutionary potential of sexual desire, one of Marcuse's leading ideas, breaks through the repressive systems internalized by the family structure, which tends to reproduce the political and historical situation. Oedipus, "the figurehead of imperialism," according to philosophers Deleuze and Guattari in *Anti-Oedipus* (XVII), is the scapegoat who bears the burden of his guilt to its ultimate conclusion, his own punishment and his mother's. Anti-Oedipus acts differently:

Sexuality and love do not live in the bedroom of Oedipus, they dream instead of wide-open spaces, and cause strange flows to circulate that do not let themselves be stocked within an established order. (116)

Steven Berkoff's Eddy/Anti-Oedipus joyfully chooses a line of escape; so does Mum in scene fifteen of *East*, when she narrates her most enjoyable sexual adventure in a cinema, with a young man who turns out to be her son:

MUM : Some geezer started to fiddle with my skirt and then touched my suspenders./.../ I thought 'Shut up Doris behave like a bloke – dirty like – so I did. His hand was very slowly lifting my skirt up / .../ – go on boy I thought, and he was only a kid – fuck me, just a sweet kid of sixteen or seventeen – / .../. So he took my hand rather boldly I thought – and placed it on his chopper; cheeky! ... and he had a beautiful silky hot on, all ready primed and juicy – I was getting ever so flushy and each time the usherette went past we'd freeze like two statues – I kept on pumping away. (77)

At the end of the film, when Mum finds out who the young man is, after he has wiped "his spunk off the front seat", she proves very down-to-earth: "dirty bugger – takes after his dad – I copped him out when he got home."(78)

Keeping the baby with the bath-water is Eddy's and Mum's pragmatic choice in their rejection of guilt and their festive acceptance of the fertility rites. Turning everything upside down, carnivalizing ordinary reality to better confront patterns of moral oppression, is Berkoff's strategy for creating electrifying theatrical events. Exterior forces and inner forces combine to shape a baroque universe which he explores with tingling theatricality.

Language Unleashed : The Word

"My theatre is verbal", insist Berkoff in a 1988 interview. The theatrical excitement of his plays is primarily based on their literary resonance and inventive use of language. The influence of heroic literature can be felt in the narrative structure of the "evils-of-civilization" plays, namely the London plays and *Kvetch*, which are all based on the story-telling situation. In these plays the hero(ine) tells the story of his/her adventures or anxieties and, in doing so, he/she conjures up the presence of other characters who appear on the stage and tell their own stories. Each scene is therefore made of monologues which introduce dialogical sequences. In *West*, working-class Sid is engaged in a monologue that conjures up Pearl who then a ddresses him directly (126). Stories are embedded in other stories. The structure is fragmented, and the action gushes forth, fully armed, from the speaker's imagination. Such a technique, obviously inspired by classical heroic literature, gives direct access to the characters' subjective world and mental processes. Each character addresses the audience directly and captures its attention with a story-line which never varies : blissful sex in putrescent society against the background of a family situation. *East* parodies a heroic song, straight out of *Beowulf* or *Song of Roland*, in which the two "heroes" tell the story of their deeds with inserted comments in direct speech:

MIKE : ... so I said to him 'fuck off thou discharge from thy mother's womb before with honed and sweetened razor I do trouble to remove thy balls from thee.'

The humourous discrepancy between the majestic rhythm and the mixture of archaic and slangy vocabulary, functions as a distancing mechanism creating a form of estrangement like that found in *Clockwork Orange*. All possible lexical registers coexist with Babel-like variety in a permanent orgy. Berkoff fuels his verbal pyrotechnics with incongruous juxtapositions of heightened and obscene speech. In the London plays, the four-letter words that would have been forbidden by the Censor two decades before (piss, shit, turd, cunt, fuck) tend to proliferate with gusto: "those four-letter words are part of the bawdiness and colour of our language," says Berkoff, and Steve's inspired (and bored) description of the world in *Acapulco* (1992) is that of "a cake of shit" (57). Vernacular language, such as "I wanna chat to ya" (*Greek* 147), "bung us the toast"(*Greek* 150), "Wanna cuppa?" (*West* 127) rubs shoulders with the parodic use of far-fetched similes : "Our cheesecakes are all made from the nectar of the gods mixed with the dextrous fingers of a hundred virgins who have been whipped with bull rushes grown by the banks of the Ganges" (*Greek* 157–158). Berkoff's consistent lashing at naturalism, which is "bad for your health', is a way of undercutting self-complacent responses on the audience's part. In *East*, opposite tribes fight for beautiful Sylv "of legendary knockers" (48). Like Mike and Les, Sylv reports her adventures with the right dose of solemnity, and a humourous dash of triviality:

SYLV: ... they fought for me ... thy blood my royal Mick was shed for me and never shall the suds of Persil or Daz remove that royal emblem from that skirt that many times you gently lifted in the Essoldo Bethnal Green. (52)

Lexical and syntactic effects are skilfully controlled by the use of well-known rhythmic patterns such as the medieval metre, the iambic pentameter, mock-heroic style, and the staccato rhythm of rock-music, in a way, what Berkoff defines as the "stylization" he wants to introduce in his plays (Elder 40). The London plays are obvious parodies of well-known and established literary masterpieces, the Shakespearian overtone of the "septic isle" being only one among a million other examples. The importance given to nouns is directly borrowed from Old English poetry. The hypertrophy of nouns: "a tournament of hunt and crunch and blood and shriek" (*East* 51), and incongruous associations: "my hard on's getting quite bent" (*Decadence* 9) is a game Berkoff relishes. The collusion of neo-classic rhythms with derisive cockney and obscene vocabulary subverts the epic dimension of the journey into the heart of decadence. Rhythmic flamboyance is achieved by the mere accumulation of stressed monosyllables: "a big horny stiff thick hot pink one" (*Greek* 145). Lines written in verse form are underpinned by a perpetual organic movement towards sensual bliss:

LES : take your knickers off I wanna fuck/
SYBIL : Tell you the truth / I'd rather have a suck! (*Decadence* 11)

The gushing forth of language celebrates the forces of life vanquishing the forces of death and hatred; it is expressed through the predominance of the liquid element, "juicy" being a recurrent word, since it applies to both sexes. All possible bodily functions and sexual activities are an outrageous means to a satiric end; the quasi-unreality of Helen's "activity" with the French waiter holding the breakfast tray in *Decadence*, while her husband is sleeping next to her, owes much to the choice of words, the joyful rhythm and the sudden introduction of a rhyme:

so when I took him in my mouth it was a gorgeous thrill to do it there with bastard still snoring in his lair / and then he thrust and squirted fine silk jets of come and nearly dropped the tray. (19)

The cumulative impact of far-fetched and baroque images is exploited to the full by Berkoff: "I swim in her like I was plunging into the Jordan for baptism" says Eddy about his "bird who's carved out of onyx and marble and laced in the smells of the promise of sex" (146). Berkoff's festive similes, which sometimes carry archaic overtones: "pimples sprouting forth like buttercups on sunny days" (*East* 47), sacralize the body through inflated pictorial images. The clichéed animal metaphors applying to sexual matters ("cuntry matters" as Shakespeare would brazenly have it) are invested with a touch of innocence: "a dozen pussies on a bed nestled between some soft and squeezy thighs" (*Greek* 156). Nouns and adjectives are the building blocks of a metaphorical world. An area of perception can be transposed into another through mere wordplay. Syntactic games are also part of Berkoff's carnivalization of language: "/birds of a fucking feather ducky stick to fucking gether/" (*Decadence* 9)

The playful use of alliteration serves the baroque portrayal of a world vision bathed in primeval innocence: "mum's giggling in her glee" (*Greek* 151); "I lick his prick" (*Decadence* 10). The sound effects derive their cumulative impact from the systematic use of strikingly organic comparisons, whether scatological or sexual: "the City sits in a heap of shit" (152), "the shit has hit the fan" (155), "luscious English birds well trained in fuck and suck" (156). Verbal excess invades all territories at the same time. Anarchy prevails where sound takes precedence over sense. When necessary, the classical iambic rhythm merges with a more primitive chant: "SHIT GIVE UP THE GEN/SPILL YOUR GUTS/.../NOT YOUR SON. OH

BOLLOCKS AND CRACKLOCK." yells Eddy (179) when he finds out about his incestuous origins. In Berkoff's plays, language is an elemental force; its sheer physicality points to a celebration of the forces of life, and its obscene proliferation therefore becomes a transgressive strategy.

The use of obscene vocabulary is defined by Julia Kristeva as "a minimal mark of a situation of desire", and its ostentatious hypertrophy points to "the nonsemanticized instinctual drive that precedes and exceeds meaning." (1982 p. 143) Indeed, in Berkoff's plays, the Dyonisian liberation of language runs parallel to the liberation of the senses; verbal excess goes beyond itself and serves as a means to heightened consciousness. Its self-justification lies in its very existence, as the here and now of a climactic discovery of the self.

Playing (seduction) games with language implies the involvement of the self. "Words tell a story of sex and violence," says Jean-Jacques Lecercle in *The Violence of Language* (1990 p. 256), following in Gilles Deleuze's footsteps whereby "words carry with them a story of sex and love." (p. 260) "Linguistic misrule" reigns supreme with Berkoff, who hammers the materiality of language in all possible ways to the point of making it abstract. Berkoff's language exceeds itself in a ritualistic return to primeval forces immediately controlled by rhythmic patterns. Language unleashed is channelled back into recognizable literary forms. The tension between the orgiastic return to the origins of language and the distancing process of literary creation marks Steven Berkoff's special brand of outrageousness. Catharsis and distance, togetherness and division, make the most explosive of ambivalent mixtures. Once taboos have been broken, cultural models remain. Outrageousness needs tradition to operate in Berkoff's dramatic world. Berkoff destabilizes his audience by setting off his verbal fireworks against a traditional backdrop, thus foregrounding the antagonism between acceptance and rejection. Breaking taboos needs tradition, yet the burden of tradition cries to be broken. The persistent desire to challenge cultural values can also be achieved through the thematic and structural functions of the body.

The Body as Text

"The gesture comes first" says Steven Berkoff whose theatre of the voice is, as a consequence, also the theatre of the body. Berkoff expresses his disgust for conventional acting in the corporeal metaphor of vomiting, a recurring image in his plays, among all the other bodily functions:

> I'm banned from a lot of theatres now because I get sick and I vomit over the man in front of me. (Elder 38)

Berkoff attended Jacques Lecoq's school of mime in Paris and his plays involve mime as a major representational means. Mime is a demanding art, which calls upon all the emotional resources of the actor and spectator:

> Mime demands exactness as any ritual must since it is mutually shared with the audience whose imaginative participation is required to make it live. (Elder. 42)

In *Greek* the fight between the café-owner and Eddy is meant to be mimed and punctuated by words; so are the tube in *West*, the motorbike in *East*, the fox-hunting scene in *Decadence,* the connubial capers in *Kvetch*. The savage forces breaking loose in the fertility rites require an anti-psychological approach to acting. Berkoff is quite clear about it is his Author's note to *East*:

> The acting has to be loose and smacking of danger...it must smart and whip out like a fairy's wicked lash. There is no reserve and therefore no embarrassment. One critic described it as 'filthy beyond the call of duty' but in fact it is a loving appreciation of the male and female form. (43)

Sound and gesture are unleashed and yet marshalled into spell-binding ensemble acting, organized like a ballet. "Not quite dance, not quite army drill," says John Elsom (149) about the multi-faceted way of working of the London Theatre Group. Obvious aesthetic influences can be traced there, including Grotowski, the Living Theatre, Peter Brook, all linked to Artaud's seminal, yet basically theoretical, influence.

If libido is released through language, desire for fulfillment is let loose through the body, which is the centre of a nexus of social, political and sexual forces. The return to nature is achieved by the means of coded mime work. In other words, culturally recognizable signs show the way back to the order of nature. Here, again, the nature-culture tension operates to the full. It is the stuff the theatricality of Berkoff's plays is made of.

In Berkoff's universe, human beings create monstrous social and political machines. In *The Penal Colony* (1968) and *The Metamorphosis* (1969), two plays based on stories by Kafka, which Berkoff follows very closely, the body is either constricted or tortured. In *The Penal Colony,* the man-made writing machine inscribes messages in the prisoner's flesh. In the original production, the machine was not supposed to be mimed. It was meant to be present on the stage, and although it was represented in a stylized way, its effect was overwhelming. In *The Metamorphosis,* Gregory wakes up, one morning, as an insect, excluded from the family cell and trapped in a geometrical, spider-like and metallic structure. The destructive process at work in both plays is stylized and aestheticized to the point of laying bare the very machinery which, literally and figuratively, prints its mark in the body. This de-humanizing process is acted out through the actor's use of his body. The human body, capable of engineering the tools of its own destruction, becomes a metaphor of the non-human.

In his 1975 adaptation of Poe's "The Fall of the House of Usher", Berkoff captures the inherent theatricality of the original tale. Space, movements, surreal atmosphere, eerie characters are all taken into account. Mimework is central here, as the actor who does Roderick Usher is also supposed to "impersonate" the house. Pages of authorial stage directions show that Berkoff was very strict about the necessity for stylized acting. The Artaud-Usher-Berkoff continuum breaks through all possible prisons, whether social or political:

> Mime renders the actors inviolable since they are protected by a metaphor and can stretch and expand to this metaphor. (50)

The actor's body expands, reaches out and goes beyond its own limits. The protective metaphor expands in all directions and ambiguity is acted out to the full in Berkoff's *The Fall of the House of Usher*: who is who? Is the friend Usher himself or is he also the servant? Mime work enables the actor to be one person (or one thing) and its opposite, life and death, flesh and stone, all at the same time. The paradoxical and coded mode of representation turns the body into a text, the repository of signs, which need to be deciphered:

> This actor naturally must have a sternly clean mimetic technique and comic skill closer to the harlequin than the burlesque: even USHER through his torment creates a mildly comic and ironic figure at times, as if his extra-ordinary sensitivity was a parody on the delicate and aesthetic. (52)

Corpse-like Madeline, as an image of humanity degree zero, tries to get out of the coffin, represented by a square of light. As nothing is realistically shown on stage, full mimesis is achieved through the body. Usher is the house, Madeline's hands become a writing-pad, and she, herself, is like a cello; Usher "plays on her like an instrument" (70) writes Berkoff as Edgar, the friend, tries to paint the couple. A very abstract and yet highly physical system of representation turns *The Fall of the House of Usher* into a metaphor of metamorphosis, converting the human into the non-human and vice-versa. Usher and his sister are twins, and Usher himself is indistinguishable from the house. Absolute similarity and complete otherness are simultaneously achieved in mime. The prison of the body has to crumble to pieces, through theatrical excess, before it comes to life again.

Metamorphosis is a well-established literary tradition (let's take Ovid's work as an example), which finds its visual equivalent in mime. Like language, the body is a vehicle, but on the stage, its status is ambiguous:

> in theatre the ultimate and important referent is the body. In performance, the body, at the same time as being the referent, is itself made into a signifier. (Lambley 45)

The ambiguous status of the human body on stage, both "real" and "semiotized", accounts for its being a taboo-ridden territory. Whether verbal or physical, the metaphorical process illuminates a point in an oblique manner, particularly if the point is unmentionable, or if it cannot be materialized. In the particular context of Poe's tale, incestuous desires are not named but acted out in surreal dancing. Sexual anxiety comes centre stage in the work of the actor. The fear of woman is acted out bodily in Berkoff's *The Fall of the House of Usher*, in the same way as it is exorcized through verbal excess in *Greek*: "Yeh I wanna climb back inside my mum. What's wrong with that." (183). Physical stylization and verbal excess are the two possible ways of naming the unnameable.

The rule holds true again in Berkoff's 1989 production of Oscar Wilde's *Salome*, which Berkoff describes as "an orchestra of language devoted to the senses." (ix) in his introduction to the play.

The extreme slowness in dancing and movement, which is supposed to be the prevailing tempo of *The Fall of the House of Usher*, is also the distinctive feature of Berkoff's *Salome*. The legend is also a tale of the impossible, an extreme example of repressed sensuality. *Salome* is the tragedy of mimetic desire, starting with Herod's wish to triumph over his brother and carried over from Herod to Herodiad and then to Salome. Salome asks her mother what she is supposed to ask for. In adopting her mother's wish, the girl conforms, thereby destroying the man who tells the truth. Mimetic desire is imitative and false; it crystallizes on what thwarts it and it spreads hatred. The dialectic of mimetic desire, based on the tension between otherness and sameness, is central to Wilde's play, where narcissism knows no limit. In *Salome*, the symbiosis between unlimited desire and death, Eros and Thanatos, is achieved in the dance metaphor.

According to René Girard, sacrifice was meant to be the reenactment of an original murder and to hold social violence in check. As the truth is a scandal in the decadent world of *Salome*, the prophet who tells the truth has to be sacrificed. A sacrifice is a ritual murder, and in this case an unnecessary one. The reenactment of a sacrifice implies imitation or mimesis; so does the art of theatre. *Salome* foregrounds its own theatrical code of representation, and carries its self-reflexiveness to the point of showing that all mimetic process can be lethal. Wilde's play shows that what is desired, and what is made culturally desirable, can be false. *Salome* goes further than showing the truth beyond appearances; it demonstrates that the endless process of producing models that produce other models, *ad infinitum*, is in itself lethal. Berkoff plunges to the heart of the postmodern scene and Jean Baudrillard's *Fatal Strategies*. Representational theatrical codes show that the obscene has nothing to do with four-letter words and traditional taboos. It lies in conformity and all the images that produce and reproduce it.

One should note that *Salome* is often related to Strinberg's *Miss Julie*, which Berkoff also adapted in 1973, as both plays foreground sexuality as a driving force. Endless variations exist on the legend of Salome, "the goddess of decadence" (Parker 471). Berkoff's transposition of Wilde's play in the world of an upper-class dinner-party of the Nineteen Twenties was very much praised by the critics. The flamboyant artificiality of the play and its florid language were thus enhanced. Salome's dance took the form of a very effective simulated strip-tease act in which she did not drop a single stitch. Thus, the referential body remained veiled, whereas the signifier played with the audience's imagination. Mime, which not only avoids but excludes pornography, introduces a distance, shows the body as a "sign" and confronts us with our naked desires; the body is a projection of the mind, as Berkoff explains in his introduction to the play:

> Herod is "really seducing her symbolically, strewing her path with sublimated sex/.../The actor not only has the language of the writer but the body of the performer, and it may be the body is the spiritual part of the whole enterprise since it is unfettered by words and obeys deeper instincts. The body is the unconscious mind at work. (xi-xii)

Salome's dance is a tale of violence and seduction. She exercises ultimate power through her body. This haunting case of violence and seduction without love is akin to what Kroker and Cook describe as "excremental sex" in *The Postmodern Scene*. Mimetic desire takes us back to mythical sacrifice. Sacrificing life to the absolute narcissism is Salome's choice to reach her decadent ecstasy.

Extreme slowness, in the case of Roderick Usher's mimetic petrification, stops time and movement to freeze-frame an aestheticized picture of the world of appearances. The same process applies to *Salome*, where the slow pace of Berkoff's production acts out the conscious wish to return to a motionless void. Dancing is an illusion, so is acting, which mimes the power of illusion. The slower the performance, the more dreamlike and illusory its content, the closer we are to the void. If mental representations are more powerful than reality itself, it follows that the gesture that veils is the transgressive one in the sense that it uncovers the myth-making mechanism of societies. Forbidden incestuous passions are caressed in mental constructs, which mime only can represent. Simulated strip-tease points to the unlimited power of imagination and the lethal power of illusion. It squarely confronts us with the obsession of the erotic. Mental constructs, mass-produced images, alienate us from straightforward confrontations with reality. Dressing, a source of delight for Helen in *Decadence*, answers the same logic as undressing; here again, Berkoff's verbal skill serves a moral purpose; in showing that sensuality is not innocent, it reveals the power of images behind the mask of narcissistic desire:

> I'll wear a fulsome daring Chanel robe / slashed to the thigh / in black cashmere / gathered from the bellies of baby goats / it hugs every line every detail made clear / every vale of my body : every genital contour will amplify itself on my exterior /.../ so demure on the outside / such a whore within / fashion so divine it makes dressing up a sin. (31)

The outside/inside dialectic comes out forcefully in Helen's description. Fetishistic dressing veils and unveils at the same time. It serves the world of appearances, as dictated by the social order. "The truths of metaphysics are the truths of masks," says Oscar Wilde (1078), foregrounding the truth of appearances. Berkoff goes further in unveiling the lethal nature of cultural conformity; he demythologizes appearances, like Baudrillard, who sees obscenity and seduction in fashion as being the "ecstasy of the beautiful," in the same way as "simulation is the ecstasy of the real." (1990 p. 9) The signifier, all-powerful, is a source of endless fantasies; style triumphs over content; the representational mode predominates over the meaning.

Naked desire without love results in death in *Salome*. Forbidden desire, unrecognized, also ends up in death in *The Fall of the House of Usher*. In *Greek*, love and desire go hand in hand. Squarely transgressing the taboo of incest is Eddy's decision, founded on his genuine love of the female body: "pull back the sheets, witness my golden-bodied wife and climb into her sanctuary." (183) Such is the way to metaphorical ecstasy.

Conclusion

In a recent radio programme ("Desert Island Discs" on Radio 4, 1992), Steven Berkoff made it clear that the most vital preoccupation of the actor-director-writer was to "entrance" the audience, and that the means to the end was "to confess naked thoughts," "to excavate the past, write about yourself." A plea for an archaic return to the love of nature, to man degree zero, emerges from Berkoff's work. The analysis of some of the plays has shown that, in the nature-culture contest, nature can take over lethal culture with a deliberate and joyful return to origins. Primeval tensions break loose from the petrified House of Usher; sublimated sex escalates into lethal eroticism in *Salome*.

Transgressing taboos is a necessary step in the journey back to origins. Beyond heaven and hell, sin never rears its ugly head: "How decadent darling / how simply fab divine and rare to gobble the waiter with your husband lying there/" says Steve to Helen in *Decadence* (19), the iambic rhythm carrying the message with panache. In his approach to his art, Berkoff's mission is to "unleash the savage forces" of truth.

In his square confrontation of language and sexual forces, Berkoff makes a point about the cynicism and violence which dominate the society of the spectacle. Modern mythologies feed on the images engendered by materialistic values. The lurid colours of the end-of-the-century anxieties need more than bland images to be properly grasped in the theatre. Berkoff imitates and parodies destructive forces to better denounce the mimetic conformity which characterizes the contemporary world. The proliferation of taboo areas, with the outrageous but meaningful use of scatology and obscenity, lays bare the violent and pornographic image-making process at work in society. Berkoff's consistent use of literary models enables him to break away from them and introduce distance with catharsis. The invisible made suddenly visible, the unnameable loudly named, a sense of heightened recognition is the stuff catharsis is made of in Berkoff's drama. The distorting mirror is highly moral.

Bibliography

Baudrillard, Jean, (1990) *Fatal Strategies*, London: Pluto

Berkoff, Steven, (1989) *Decadence and Other Plays (East, West, Greek)*, London: Faber & Faber

Berkoff, Steven, (1985) *West and other Plays (West, Lunch, Harry's Christmas)*, London: Faber & Faber

Berkoff, Steven, (1988) *Metamorphosis*. London: Amber Lane Press.

——— (1990) *The Fall of the House of Usher* (with *Agamemnon*), London: Amber Lane Press.

Berkoff, Steven, (1986) *Kvetch, Acapulco*, London: Faber & Faber

——— (1988) *In the Penal Colony*, London: Amber Lane Press

——— (1991) "The Leavings of Liverpool." *Weekend Guardian*, May 4-5, 4-6

Berkoff, Steven, (1991) "Naturalism, Like Smoking, is bad for your Health." *The Times*, March 1, 20

Berkoff, Steven, (1992) *The Theatre of Steven Berkoff*, London: Methuen

Cohn, Ruby, (1991) *Retreats from Realism in Recent English Drama*, Cambridge and London: Cambridge University Press

Deleuze, Gilles, (1984) *Anti-Oedipus – Capitalism and Schizophrenia*, London: The Athlone Press

Deleuze, Gilles, & Guattari, Félix, (1975) *Kafka – Pour une littérature mineure*, Paris: Minuit

Elder, Bruce, (1978) "Doing the inexpressible Uncommonly Well: The Theatre of Steven Berkoff." *Theatre Quarterly*, 8, 37–42

Elsom, John, (1976) *Post-War British Theatre*, London: Routledge and Kegan Paul

Girard, René, (1982) *Le Bouc émissaire*, Paris: Grasset

———, (1982) *La violence et le sacré*, Paris: Grasset

Kristeva, Julia, (1982) *Desire in Language: A Semiotic Approach to Literature and Art*, London: Blackwell

Kroker, Arthur, & Cook, David, (1988) *The Postmodern Scene – Excremental Culture and Hyper Aesthetics*, London: Macmillan

Lambley, Dorrian. "In Search of a Radical Discourse for Theatre." *New Theatre Quarterly*, 29, 34–47

Lecercle, Jean-Jacques, (1990) *The Violence of Language*, London: Routledge and Kegan Paul

Osborne, John, (1957) "And They Call it Cricket." *Encounter*, 9, 23–30

Parker, Brian, (1989) "Strindberg's Miss Julie and the Legend of Salome." *Modern Drama*, 32, 469–484

Wilde, Oscar, (1988) "The Truth of Masks." *The Complete works of Oscar Wilde*, London: Collins

——— (1989) *Salome* (Introduction by Steven Berkoff), London: Faber & Faber

Contemporary Theatre Review, 1996, Vol. 5,1 pp. 91–102
Reprints available directly from the publisher
Photocopying permitted by license only

The Outrageous 80s: Conservative Policies and the Church of England under Fire in Steven Berkoff's *Sink the Belgrano* and David Hare's *The Secret Rapture* and *Racing Demon*

Monique Prunet

The Conservative policies pursued by Margaret Thatcher in the 1980s increasingly attracted sharp criticism from politically committed playwrights such as Steven Berkoff and David Hare. The three plays surveyed here shed a new light on their attacks of Thacherism and Thatcherite policies; the Prime Minister's foreign policy is brutally caricatured in *Sink the Belgrano*, the cynicism of politicians and their lust for power cruelly magnified in *The Secret Rapture* and in *Racing Demon* the Church of England appears as an empty shell, devoid of caring purposes.

The originality of the two playwrights is that, unlike other politically committed playwrights of the 1960s and 70s, both Steven Berkoff and David Hare do not appear to campaign for a cause but rather satirize and deride the very aspects of the Conservative Party that made it successful. The cynicism shown by Mrs Thatcher's Cabinet in *Sink the Belgrano* is paralleled by the lack of real concern for the destitute and the unemployed, and with greed for money in *The Secret Rapture*. *Racing Demon* also emphasises the paralysis of the Church of England, stultified by its hierarchy and torn by its internal rivalries.

By turning the Conservative 1980s into an empty shell the three comedies provoke a bitter laughter leaving almost no way forward to a less ruthless society.

KEY WORDS Conservative, hypocrisy, manipulation, ruthlessness, satire, Thatcher

Berkoff's and Hare's Anti-Thatcher Satire

The Conservative policies pursued by Margaret Thatcher in the 1980s increasingly attracted sharp criticism from politically committed playwrights who had emerged from "the bruised dreams of the sixties counter-culture" (Bull, 1984 p. 1). Among them, Steven Berkoff and David Hare stand out as virulent anti-Thatcherites, albeit differently. If one is to believe Eva Figes' opinion:

> The one thing that unites all critics and commentators throughout the ages is the belief that wickedness must not be shown to flourish unpunished (Figes, 1976 p. 142).

The three plays surveyed here certainly illustrate the two playwrights' belief in the wickedness of Thatcherism.

The Prime Minister's foreign policy and manipulation of the media are brutally caricatured in *Sink the Belgrano*; the cynicism of politicians and their lust for power cruelly magnified in *The Secret Rapture* and, in *Racing Demon* the Church of England is portrayed as an empty shell, devoid of caring purposes.

The originality of Berkoff and Hare is that, unlike other politically committed dramatists, they do not blatantly campaign for a cause but they use satire and derision to stigmatize the very aspects of Conservatism which made it successful in the 1980s.

Machiavellian Exercises in *Sink the Belgrano*

Berkoff's reputation as a ferocious satirist does not disappoint his audience or readers in *Sink the Belgrano*, a play in verse in the Shakespearian manner. His scorn tinged with violence is unleashed on Mrs Thatcher's foreign policy with a cruelty he had not fully displayed before the production of his play in September 1986.

> Berkoff's chosen terrain is the study of excess: his natural modes as the diatribe – sometimes the eulogy; he enjoys the ritual combat of hostile forces. (...) Language on his lips both in life and on the stage gives the impression of being edged in flame. (Warner, 1983 p. 135)

Sink the Belgrano epitomizes indeed a "ritual combat of hostile forces", a duel between evil and good: on the one hand, a satanic War Cabinet headed by Maggot Scratcher, on the other, the voices of reason and negotiation. Berkoff has concentrated his fury on a military event which aroused fierce debates: the sinking on the evening of May 2 1982 of the 44 year-old cruiser, *General Belgrano* – formerly USS Phoenix, a survivor of Pearl Harbor, sold to Argentina in 1951. Much has been said and written about the sinking of the cruiser which, at the time, was just outside the Total Exclusion Zone of 200 nautical miles south of the Falklands with a crew of 1,042 men, a majority of young conscripts among whom 368 died. The event gave rise to the most famous headline in the British press during the Falklands war: "Gotcha!", in the first edition of *The Sun* of May 4 1982, which, at the time of the news, embodied the feelings of the editorial team who "just felt excited and euphoric" (Harris, 1983 p. 13). On that very day, HMS *Sheffield* was hit by an Argentinian Exocet, with 24 dead.

In his play, Berkoff has seized the occasion to lampoon Conservative policies in general, and Mrs Thatcher's in particular, accusing her and her Cabinet of total contempt for human life, as he declares in his preface to the play:

> It was a calculated gamble to end the war at a stroke and failed miserably. (Berkoff 1987, p. 1)

According to Roger Caillois, comparing ritual celebrations and war, war is the ultimate celebration in modern societies ("La guerre réprésente bien le paroxysme de l'existence des sociétés modernes", Caillois, 1950 p.218). Indeed, the Falklands War, which took on a new turn after the *Belgrano* and the *Sheffield* episodes, began to epitomize a new mood in Britain, a new feeling of British pride and superiority, which lasted throughout the 1980s.

> Its resurrection ought to be a cause for concern for, behind the presumption that a British voice must speak out against violations of humanity elsewhere (which is welcome), lies the assertion that the Anglo-Saxon accent can and should arbitrate across all frontiers ... its core is a presumption of national superiority. (Barnett, 1989 p. 33)

In *Sink the Belgrano*, this new trend was picked up and developed by Berkoff into jingoism, uniting together the Conservative establishment and the lager louts, as is obvious from the first lines of the play:

Oh you most brave and valiant Englishmen
Who never shall, no never bear the yoke
Of shame or curdled pride beneath the boot
Of some o'erweening greasy foreign bloke (3)

Such lines echo Mrs Thatcher's proud declaration at a Conservative Party rally in early July 1982:

Britain has found herself again in the south Atlantic and will not look back from the victory she has won. (Barnett, 1989 p.153)

From the very beginning of the play, Mrs Thatcher and the War Cabinet are presented as gross caricatures, puppets straight from "Spitting Image". Their names are irreverentially distorted as shown by the most obvious examples: Margaret Thatcher into Maggot Scratcher; Pym (Foreign Secretary) into Pimp, Nott (Defence Minister) into Nit; Sir Terence Lewin, Admiral of the Fleet, Chief of Defence Staff, into Tell; Rear Admiral Sir John Woodward, Commander Task group 317.8 (in charge of the carrier group in the Falklands) into Woody. The name of the then leader of the Opposition, Michael Foot, does not escape such a fate; it becomes Feet. As for President Reagan, he is referred to as "Old Cowboy", "Old Geriatric Joe" (13), or "Cowboy Joe" (30).

The language used by Cabinet members, the Opposition, Naval Command and sailors alike is deliberately strewn with four-letter words, a language which would appear more adequate in the mouths of drunk football hooligans than on the lips of Her Majesty's government members and servants:

Pimp: Oh shit your royal sweetest Maggot,
The lousy Argy swines unleashed their bile
On us (...)
Maggot: Those bloody junta bloody swine...! (3–4)

On board the nuclear submarine *Conqueror*, which was to sink the *Belgrano*, Sailor 3 uses the same crude words in his answer to Sailor 1, who is in favour of self-determination – a reference to the 1960 United Nations declaration:

Sailor 3: Then fuck off this boat you cunt
Don't fucking swinge, you got no guts
A soldier's life's obey the Queen (10)

Inspired by Arthur Gavshon's and Desmond Rice's 1984 study, *The Sinking of the Belgrano*, Berkoff was determined to present the event as "a conspiracy by the Thatcher government to inflame the Falklands war" (Brown). Cynicism and ruthlessness therefore appear as the main characteristics of Maggot Scratcher's War Cabinet.

When at the beginning of the play, she is first informed of the Argentinian invasion, she ecstatically orders:

Call out the Fleet, get planes
And tanks, I love to have a crisis on my hands.(4)

The words of the last sentence were actually used by Mrs Thatcher on May 14 1982 when she addressed the Scottish Conservative Party Conference.

Her inflamed speeches are made ridiculous by her ignorance about the geographical location of the islands:

By the way Pimp ... where is the Falklands? (5)
Now where is this damn Falkland Isle? (7)

Up to the middle of the play, as tension rises among Cabinet members, Berkoff presents the call to war as opposed to diplomatic compromise over a background of social issues related to Conservative policies. In the second scene, the Falklands Farmers appear exploited by the Falkland Island Company; however, when in medical need, they have to resort to Argentinian services. Their complaints against the FIC monopoly are received with insults from Pimp:

How dare you pigs complain, you dogs
You curs that *want* always. (6)

or irony from Maggot:

So you think how lucky you are here
You might be back in England's drear
And pleasant land where miners strike
And other left-wing pests unite
Like filthy dogs disturb our rest. (7)

The 1984–85 miners' strike thus anticipated, rising unemployment and the dole queues are presented as matter of fact and due to traditional British apathy. Mrs Thatcher's 'free market policy' and 'enterprise culture' are thus being crudely derided.

Maggot: The Brits are such a lazy bunch of sods
No wonder there's three million unemployed
The buggers simply now refuse to work. (15)

Looming above the allusions to contemporary social issues, Maggot's growing determination to go to war – "we need a war" (7) is being vigorously developed. The familiar image of the Iron Lady is magnified to become that of a monster, reigning over a world of deadly metal. Lethal animal metaphors – "giant whales of death" (8) – conjure up visions of the war machine taking off. Death and brutal sex are linked together, whether it be in the rape-like description given by the Command of the *Conqueror* when explaining the firing of a torpedo (not a nuclear one however), or in the sailor's parody of "Rule Britannia".

War's just another way to fornicate
We'll fuck their slaggy Argy ships (17)

In a shrewd parallel, Berkoff develops his argument of a conspiracy organized by Mrs Thatcher and her Cabinet, concerned by low ratings in opinion polls at the time. Conjuring up a Shakespearian scene, Maggot, Nit and Pimp stand around their boiling cauldron like the three witches in *Macbeth*, making a Spanish omelette, "with some Argy eggs" (1.6). Maggot's cynicism and plotting intentions are emphasized by Pimp's naive questions:

Pimp: But who will eat this foul stew?
Maggot: The entire British press, you fool! (1.6)

Thus Berkoff fully deploys his attack against Mrs Thatcher's foreign and home policies by accusing her of having used a ploy so as to revive her government's flagging popularity. Negotiations on the international scene and debates in the Commons are grotesquely parodied. Maggot's Machiavellian strategy in using diplomatic delays for her war preparations is reflected in her outrageous comparison with Churchill. The new feeling of British superiority is manifest in Nit's condescending tone when referring to the "Yanks" or to "Old Cowpoke" (21), or to "those rotten greedy French" (21).

During the debate in the Commons, even the Opposition, in the person of its leader Feet, is caricatured, both in its approval of the use of force and in the language used:

Feet: The Labour Party now demands
That we avenge this bloody deed
For bloody bloomin' bleeding war
Should we declare right now (24)

From then on, an unswervingly pitiless course appears to be taken by Maggot Scratcher. Whenever Pimp comes forth with news of possible ceasefire and withdrawal of Argentine troups, Maggot flares up and brandishes the British flag. Spurred on by her will to triumph politically, she even asks Pimp to lie to the American President about an imminent peace plan.

Evil reaches a climax in the scene at Chequers, when it is officially decided to sink an Argentine ship. Banal conversation over the Sunday roast lamb provides a poignant contrast with the decision taken in cold blood by Maggot Scratcher on Tell's and Woody's recommendation. One is all the more shocked as, for a few moments, Maggot wavers; but her pride, goaded by Tell's reference to her being up to her reputation as the Iron Lady, triumphs over her hesitations. In a speech worthy of Lady Macbeth, Maggot Scratcher, after conjuring up a vision of British young men's bodies torn apart, seals the fate of the young Argentinian soldiers when she gives the order to sink the *Belgrano*. When the *Conqueror* Command recalls a cosy evening at the pub, the contrast is all the more heart-rending as a sailor deplores the lack of warning to the ship and evokes the hostile icy waters surrounding them. The final scene contrasts the British sailors' cheers with the vizualisation on a screen of the drowning men and the evocation by a sailor of the same fate awaiting the British two days later, when the *Sheffield* was hit by an Exocet.

As in Nick Perry's 1985 *Arrivederci Millwall*, the satire on Mrs Thatcher and her Cabinet in *Sink the Belgrano* embodies the development of anti-Thatcher feelings in the mid-80s among opponents to Conservative policies, in the wake of the Labour MP Tam Dalyell's public opposition, the Old Bailey trial of Clive Ponting and the publication in 1985 of the Minority Report of the Foreign Affairs Select Committee.

Berkoff's aim to sink Mrs Thatcher's policy by showing her manipulation of the media and of public opinion and her pursuit of political aims under the guise of military action might be considered as a personal exercise in his fascination for his target. In his own words:

he is filled with 'dark, sad paranoia' and his 'work is a confession...You must confess publicly, and exorcise yourself'. (Warner, 1983 p. 135)

Hence his own interpretation of facts. In the play, the *Belgrano* is said to be on her way home, whereas, according to military information, she was zigzagging with her two destroyers along the shallow Burdwood Bank and, owing to fog that night, might have attacked the British *Hermes* and *Invincible* with Exocets. As to the TEZ, it was announced to take place from April 12 at 04.00, but a British statement handed to the Argentine Government on April 23, implied that any ship or plane outside the TEZ might be attacked if it appeared to threaten British forces, which accounted for the decision taken by Mrs Thatcher's Cabinet.

However controversial the sinking of the *Belgrano* appears, Berkoff's anti-Thatcher's satire is extremely skillful and powerful on the stage. The physical caricatures of government members, the aggressive and offensive language, the brilliant manipulation of emotions in a verse play, the projected images on a large screen, and the stills so representative of Berkoff's technique contrived to make an impact on the audience, with horror and laughter mingled.

Materialism and Politics in *The Secret Rapture*

Considered as "the specific playwright of the 1970s" (Chambers & Prior, 179), David Hare's plays of the late 1980s appear to be political with a different approach. Although less vitriolic than Berkoff's, his criticism of the Thatcher years is nonetheless powerful; comedies such as *The Secret Rapture* and *Racing Demon* however conventional in their form, bite on the economic boom of the 1980s and the hypocrisy of the Establishment.

Cast by many critics in the role of prime spokesman for his generation of left-wing playwrights, Hare is nevertheless something of a loner whose plays seem distanced from the social and political forces which he acknowledges as crucial in shaping the world he is writing about. (Chambers & Prior, 180)

This opinion on Hare's plays of the 1970s remains just as valid when applied to *The Secret Rapture* and *Racing Demon.*

The Secret Rapture, first performed in October 1988 at the National Theatre, interweaves personal relationships between the members of a family with bitter criticism of Thatcherite policies.

Marion French, in her late thirties, is a Tory Junior Minister at the Department of the Environment. Her appearance in a business suit, as if it were a uniform, immediately categorizes her; she has all the trappings of a successful and promising politician: education, money and a career in the Conservative Party. The dramatist uses her in her political role as a kind of milder replica of Margaret Thatcher, whose name is never mentioned. However, when Marion is not playing her political persona, she is vulnerable and angry, something which her husband, Tom, President of Christians in Business, does not appear to understand:

She gets angry. Why? I mean, she's got everything she wants. Her party is in power. For ever. She's in office. She's an absolute cert for the Cabinet. I just don't see why she's angry all the time." (1, 2, 6)

Embodying the virtues encouraged by Mrs Thatcher, Marion is energetic, up at six, and on her way to her office. Her sense of being in power at the national level is mirrored in her personal relationships, particularly with her younger sister Isobel, a graphic designer, who owns her own small firm. Throughout the play, Isobel is used by the dramatist as a foil to her sister's ruthlessness and ambitions. Isobel is dynamic professionally, but at the same time she is very sensitive as far as family matters are concerned: she nursed their father to the end – Marion feels guilty about not being there herself, owing to her political commitments – and she hires their young stepmother, Katherine, an alcoholic, to work with her in order to rescue her from the bottle.

A permanent reminder of Marion's functions is her portable telephone which she carries in her handbag and which rings at the most unexpected moments, although she had the decency to turn it off during her father's funeral. Her being in the Conservative Party is a source of embarrassment to Katherine who exclaims:

I see there's no chance of escaping this Government. (1,2,12)

Marion's allegiance to the Conservative Party is emphasized by her sense of duty to the cause, as if it were her 'raison d'être':

Marion: ... Someone said, "Do you know what politics is? Finally? Politics is being there every day." And you know it's true. You have to be there. I'm there every day. Aren't I, darling?
Tom: You are.
Marion: And I'm there the next day. And the next day. And the next day. For ever. Isn't that right? (II,2,52)

Doggedly, she pursues and defends the aims of the Thatcherite policies of the 1980s. Hare particularly stresses the lack of concern for social issues, revealed in Marion's judgement of her young stepmother's problems. At the same time, she is determined to promote her career which is not to be marred by her association with Katherine, when she declares to Isobel that she can't offer Katherine a job:

Marion: Don't be ridiculous. I'm in the Conservative Party. We can't just take on anyone at all.
Isobel: What, and I can?
Marion: It's different.
Isobel: How?
Marion: You know perfectly well. It's quite a different world. With extremely high standards of intellect and conduct. Civil servants have an extremely competitive and highly-ordered career structure. In which you get very few marks for being an abusive alcoholic. (1,2,15)

However, the politicians' and civil servants' apparently impeccable moral façade is to be shattered and derided in the first scene of Act II, when Rhonda, Marion's young assistant researcher at the House of Commons, jokes about a senior Tory politician who has been making advances at her. One cannot help but being reminded of the various sex scandals which broke out in the 1980s, Cecil Parkinson's affair with Sarah Keyes being the most publicized. Rhonda mocks both his admirer's lust and paranoia about secrecy, thus stigmatizing the hypocrisy and holier – than – thou attitude of the Conservatives towards family values which they openly and publicly support.

Rhonda: Also, of course, he's fanatical about secrecy. So this makes him also, not only lascivious, not only a palpable scuzzbag as you might say, but also very security-conscious. He's worried sick about where and when we're going to meet. (II,1,41)

To a lesser and less gross extent than in *Sink the Belgrano*, the manipulation of the press and of public opinion is emphasized by Marion's account of her meeting with the Greens, for whom she feels only contempt:

I don't like Greens. They're so self-righteous. (1,4,29)

She asked the vicar not to mention her father's opposition to nuclear armaments at the funeral service for fear of jeopardizing her political career; she despises the Greens for their position on the issue, and defends her government's stand:

They're always going on as if their case is moral. That's what annoys me. Ours is moral too. People need power. Nuclear power is a cheap and effective way to provide it. It gives a lot of ordinary, decent people considerably improved standard of living. (I,4,30)

Marion herself has not realized that she is just as self-righteous as the Greens she despises so much. In a parody of a Thatcherian speech, she parades her manipulative skills and unashamedly boasts about her talents to influence public opinion:

That's the whole art of publicity for a politician. You roll back the boundary just that little bit. Anyway, let's face it, we've beaten them. We can all play greener-than-thou. (I,4,31)

The pursuit of ruthless personal ambitions and the greed for money encouraged by the 'enterprise culture' of the Thatcher years are magnified and caricatured when Isobel is dispossessed of her business by her sister and brother-in-law under the pretence of helping her to expand. After enticing her to give Tom – who, as a Christian businessman, makes constant references to God and Jesus and is very much involved in church and community schemes – the control of her firm through the setting up of a board in exchange for investment in the firm, Marion and Tom simply throw Isobel out when her results appear not to be up to their expectations, but not without drawing a substantial profit from their charitable operation: Tom's investment was tax-free and they will double their money owing to Isobel's improvements of the premises.

The dramatist's message is clear; Isobel has been swindled, and her tragedy illustrates one of the main criticisms addressed to Conservative policies in the 1980s: the nice and honest people get trampled in Mrs Thatcher's England by those ruthless enough to use the market forces to their own personal benefit. When expressed in Katherine's words, it is rather bluntly said:

Katherine: You know I think this government's appalling. But on the other hand, let's face it, given what's going on, it's just stupid not to go and grab some dough for yourself. (I,4,34)

Hare's thrashing of dubious practices and hypocrisy in *The Secret Rapture* is in keeping with his political views developed in previous plays. When Isobel declares that she has been "asset-stripped" (II,2,58), it echoes Hare's stance on corruption in *Brassneck* and *Knuckle* in which he took "a cynical look at the corruption of 'big business' and the moral bankruptcy of the middle-class" (Itzin, 1980 p. 335).

The Church of England at Sixes and Sevens in *Racing Demon*

Hare's involvement in contemporary issues made him say that he considered himself as a writer of history-plays, trying to awaken the audience's awareness.

What concerns him is not street politics but personal despair, 'and it is to that despair that as a historical writer I choose to address myself time and time again' ('A Lecture', in *Licking Hitler*). (Bull 1984 p. 70)

Despair is indeed the appropriate word to describe the atmosphere of *Racing Demon*, first performed in February 1990 at the National Theatre, in which the dramatist ironically presents the problems besetting the Church of England in the wider context of those which developed during the Thatcher years.

Located in South London, "just two miles from Westminster" (41), the Reverend Lionel Espy's working-class parish typifies the ills affecting underprivileged urban areas. Social services, whether it be health care, looking after the mentally ill or housing, appear totally inadequate; their failure is exemplified in the case of Stella, a young West Indian, a battered wife who has just had an abortion and who has come to Lionel for comfort. Against such a dreary background, two different views of the role of the Church are put forward: for the bishop of Southwark, Lionel's hierarchical superior, and the Reverend Tony Ferris, Lionel's young curate, the Church should concentrate on attendance and the observance of ritual. For Lionel and his other curates, 'Streaky' Bacon and Harry Henderson, the Church should try to understand and serve the people, a job which Lionel finds "more important than ritual." (I,2,3) Echoing Enoch Powell's words:

I wouldn't call myself a Christian, all I know is I am a member of the Church of England.

Southwark's reply to Lionel is harsh and cynical:

We're not talking about opinion. We're talking about authority. History. What the Church of England is. It's a disparate body held together by a common liturgy. (I,2,4)

Either to conform to the ritual and 'put on a show' in Southwark's words (3) or to try and alleviate the burden of the destitute, the choice is clear for Lionel, whose family has traditionally served the Church of England. His faith may be questioned by his bishop, but when trying to comfort Stella, one cannot doubt his compassion:

I don't know if God'll help you. But now you do have a friend. You have me. The house is always open. Whenever you're lonely. (12)

The two views appear to be irreconcilable: Lionel considers it is his duty to help people, whether they attend church services or not, whereas Southwark wants the church to be efficient and run like a business. Lionel's unwillingness to conform will cost him his job: working as a team with his curates, he gave up his freehold in favour of a five-year contract which is about to expire. In the same way as Isobel was a victim of her good deeds in *The Secret Rapture*, Lionel's future will be crushed by his bishop for the sake of appearances and power in the name of the Church. However, beyond two different views on faith and practice, Hare presents a state of the Church of England at present, torn not only by personal rivalries but also by burning issues such as homosexuality among the clergy or the ordination of women – a reference to the General Synod of November 1989. In the 1980s, the debates surrounding such issues threw the Church of England into the limelight, which was worsened by scandal cases, including suicide, because of obtrusive publicity in the press.

Southwark's reproach to Lionel in Act II: "The church has been turned into a ghastly parody of government" (77), epitomizes the conflicts within the church, between those who abide by the rules and those, such as David Jenkins, the controversial Bishop of Durham, who would like to bring God closer to every day life.

In *Racing Demon*, Harry Henderson exemplifies the issue of homosexuality in the clergy. Blackmailed by a journalist from the tabloid press, Harry is forced to leave Lionel's parish to go and retire in Malta. However, Harry is portrayed as a good priest, close to his parishioners; he would be worthy of Bishop Jenkins' appreciative judgement of such clergymen:

> I know the ministry of many homosexual priests to have been greatly blessed; I value the friendship of many such men and their caring qualities are obvious to anyone (Jenkins & Jenkins, 1991 p.76)

When Harry refers to the press writing on "the gay mafia (...) eating up the church" (II,9,83), one may bear in mind that around 5% of the London Church of England priests are gay, some promiscuous, which is not "a godly life" (Hope).

If Hare is less rough than Berkoff in his criticism of the press, particularly the tabloids, he nonetheless stigmatizes its debasing taste for scandal as being revealing of the corruption of Thatcher's Britain, in Harry's words:

> They give knighthoods to people who publish this stuff. It isn't coincidence. That's the country we're living in. (I,9,p.83)

As to another much debated issue in the Church of England, the ordination of women, it remains a bone of contention between the traditionalists and the modernists. In the play, Southwark, referring to the possibility of a woman bishop, appears adamant:

> Today I am in a position to command a schism in the Church. If I leave the Church of England because of this heretic woman, then hundreds of thousands will follow my lead. (II,8,80)

However, David Hare's main criticism places the emphasis on the wide gap between actual problems in contemporary British society and the paralysis suffered by the Church of England when facing them. When Lionel states that in his area, the Church "has no connection with most people's lives" (I,2,3), his words parallel those of David Jenkins, writing in 1991:

> It is urgent that we shift concentration from such side-issues (*ordination of women and homosexuality*) to things that really matter to people in society at large – issues such as what is happening to our world, the business of loving our neighbours in real, down-to-earth situations (Jenkins & Jenkins 1991 p. 184)

As the Church appears powerless in everyday life and devoid of caring purposes, attendance is very poor; Lionel's zealous young curate, Tony Ferris, is appalled by the distressingly low number of those who attend Sunday services:

> We feel we've had a good Sunday if between us we attract one per cent. One percent of our whole catchment area.(I,4,1.6)

Hence his zeal to change things and his rebellion against Lionel's merciful ways; through him, Hare satirizes the new evangelical trend among some members of the Church. Tony's obsession with God becomes increasingly alarming. Convinced that he is God's messenger, he triumphantly declares to Harry and Streaky: "Christ came not to bring peace but the sword." (II,1,50). Clinging to the words of the Bible, he even believes that an AIDS patient has been cured "with some oil and the power of prayer" (II,6,70). He however has quite misunderstood Stella whom he hired to clean the church for a mere pittance, £2.50 an hour, whereas her only dream is to go back to her brutal husband, which proves the failure of Tony's efforts.

On the whole the Church of England in *Racing Demon* appears stultified, cutting a poor figure, out of touch with real life, torn by internal rivalries or absorbed by administration and paperwork. But Hare's criticism bites deeper: God's silent absence is made pitiful throughout the play.

Whenever in need of advice and comfort, individuals are only met by their own doubts and anxieties. In a monologue, each of the main characters has a private session in church, addressing God or rather His absence. In the first scene, Lionel pathetically asks Him for a sign because people "need something beside silence" (I,1,1). Frances, although not a believer, challenges Him:

> If there were justice then I'd believe in you. I like the idea of justice better than God. Because God is arbitrary. (I,9,p.34)

In their prayers, Tony projects his own evangelical zeal, Streaky, his drunken happiness and Harry, his fear of being found out. Silence is the only answer, which accounts for the endless questioning, doubts and lack of faith. Perhaps, the main characters in *Racing Demon* should meditate on the Bishop of Durham's statement:

> Faith does not provide answers; it obliges us to face the facts. (Jenkins & Jenkins, 1991 p.193)

One cannot deny that both Berkoff and Hare, each with his distinctive approach, oblige their audiences to "face the facts" and assess reality through their satirical evaluation of the 1980s. However, they do not advocate social and political revolution: with the collapse of Communism, marxism has fallen into disrepute. The Thatcher years have not heralded the birth of a renewed British political theatre.

By shattering illusions and turning the very achievements of Thatcherism into derision, the three comedies emphasize the strains and constraints of contemporary British society; the bitter laughter they may provoke does not seem to point towards a brighter future, and leaves almost no way forward to a less ruthless and manipulative society, in which the individual, abused by politicians and abandoned by God, remains isolated:

> The world remains an alienating force which ultimately prevents any communication and in which each individual is left to work out his or her own existential deal. (Chambers, 187)

Bibliography

Barnett, Anthony, (1989) *Iron Britannia: why Parliament waged the Falklands War*, Allison and Bushy
Berkoff, Steven, (1987) "Why I wrote it", *Sink the Belgrano*, London: Faber & Faber
Berkoff, Steven, (1987) *Sink the Belgrano*, London: Faber & Faber

Brown, Mick, "A monstrous megalomania does battle at the box office", *The Sunday Times*, September 7 1986
Bull, John, (1984) *New British political Dramatists*, London: Macmillan
Caillois, Roger, (ed.1950) *L'homme et le sacre*, Paris: Gallimard
Chambers, Colin & Prior, Mike (1987) *Playwrights' Progress: Patterns of Postwar British Drama*, Amber Lane Press
Figes, Eva, (1976) *Tragedy and Social Evolution*, London: John Calder
Hare, David, (1988) *The Secret Rapture*, London, Samuel French
Hare, David, (1980) *Racing Demon*, London: Faber & Faber
Harris, Robert, (1983) *Gotcha! the Media, the Government and the Falklands Crisis*, London: Faber & Faber
Hope, David, Bishop of London, in *One Church, One Faith, One Sex?* BBC1, February 9 1992
Itzin, Catherine, (1980) *Stages in the Revolution: Political Theatre in Britain since 1968*, London: Eyre Methuen
Jenkins, David & Jenkins, Rebecca, (1991) *Free to believe*, BBC Books
Middlebrook, Martin, (1987) Taskforce: *The Falklands War, 1982*, Penguin Books, revised edition
Warner, Marina, "Berkoff", *Vogue*, May 1983

Contemporary Theatre Review, 1996, Vol. 5,1 pp. 103–109

Amsterdam B.V. Published in The Netherlands by
Harwood Academic Publishers GmbH

Beyond Hope: Howard Brenton's *Berlin Bertie*

"The new 'democratic' Germany is contaminated before it has even begun."
***Berlin Bertie*, Act III, p.67**

Wolfgang J. Lippke

A countless number of political speakers have celebrated the German reunification and the breaking apart of the former USSR as a heroic victory of the western democracies over the "evil" communist regimes. For the people behind the Iron Curtain the economic affluence of the West appeared to be a logical consequence of freedom and of higher moral standards. For many of them the Golden West was so tempting that they were ready to risk their lives for a chance of fleeing from their countries. Radical criticism or denial of the notion of the West's alleged superiority seems to be a political and social taboo.

The playwright Howard Brenton who has never hesitated to attack taboos in his long literary career, is one of the first dramatists to write a play on the collapse of the Berlin Wall. This article deals with one of his most provocative plays in the light of his literary development and his dramatic concepts.

KEY WORDS Howard Brenton, contemporary British playwright, German reunification, alleged Western superiority, moral and economical standards, radical criticism – a taboo, theater as provocation

The Matrix of Reference

In 1989, the world looking at Germany witnessed a most extraordinary spectacle. Thousands of East Germans fled from their communist-ruled country and arrived in the West, leaving behind them the Iron Curtain and the Berlin Wall. Television, radio and the printed media covered the flight from the "realm of evil" (Reagan) day after day on front page stories or at prime broadcast time. To everyone's amazement, neither the Russian nor the GDR army made the slightest attempt to stop the exodus. While hundreds of people had been shot at the Berlin Wall trying to escape during the three preceding decades, and while the world was holding its breath in fear of another 1953 in East Berlin, 1956 in Budapest or 1968 in Prague, East Germans were pouring into the West by the thousands until, eventually, the border and the death strip were abolished and the East German government had to step down. On October 3rd, 1990, Germany was re-united.

These German events form the matrix of reference for Howard Brenton's play *Berlin Bertie* which was premiered at the Royal Court Theatre in London, April 9, 1992. After *Moscow Gold* (Schäffner, 1992, p. 159ff), Tariq Ali's and Brenton's jointly written play on the perils of and for Russian *perestroika*, in which they forecast, with surprising clairvoyance, the coup d'état in 1991, Brenton was again bold enough to dramatise events on stage which are still in the process of development – history in the making – and are subject of a highly controversial debate in Germany and elsewhere. In fact, racist attacks on asylum seekers, a high unemployment rate in the former GDR, weak political leadership etc., tend to fill the two societies with envy and rage towards each other and provide Brenton's play about German reunification with an extraordinary momentum. Worst of all, strong forces in both societies strive to cover up the past of the GDR regime and its connections with the West, while on the other hand, the present government and the major parties see the cause of neo-nazi riots in the presence of refugees from other countries, thus stigmatizing ethnic minorities.

Attacking Taboos

The audience of Howard Brenton's plays has come to expect him to attack society's hidden, but nurtured, myths and to break taboos wherever he can. In his early plays, e.g. *The Education of Skinny Spew* (1969), the at the same time pampered and hated son, kills his parents as an act of liberation. *Christie in Love* (1969) deals with a horrible sexual murderer, but even more abominable and shocking appear to be the juicy, sexist jokes of the policeman in his play. In *Magnificence* (1973) he arouses the audience's irritation by confronting them with the question of whether the assassination of a member of the government by a youngster was a morally defensible act in order to open "Our English Public Man's" eyes to the corruption of his world. Just how controversial his plays can be, became hauntingly manifest in *The Romans in Britain* (1980) in which the British army are portrayed as invaders of Ireland and cruel torturers. (Lippke, 1987)

The Rotten West

Berlin Bertie is the rather catchy title of Brenton's play, being also the code name of the Stasi officer (secret police in the former German Democratic Republic, GDR). It is a familiar sounding name, evoking the image of a person of notoriety and reliability. And indeed, Bertie can be said to possess both qualities, but in a cynical way: he used to be a powerful Stasi officer who could destroy any person he wished to, holding a high rank in a secret police institution, known as the "firm", a network of espionage deployed, above all, for spying on the GDR's own people.

In the play he is the personal surveyor of Rosa, who is English but who has lived in the GDR for more than a decade, and is married to a pastor called Joachim. Both Rosa and her husband were opposed to the regime, trying to pursue Christian underground work in the totalitarian communist state. To her utter amazement and desperation she had to learn, however, that the Stasi has always had them firmly in their grip. Without their knowledge the secret police had planted microphones in their flat and were always fully informed of their plans, their conversations and their actions.

On the western side of the Iron Curtain, in London, lives Alice, a social worker, who is Rosa's sister. The two sisters have not met for fourteen years, but now, after the collapse of the GDR, Rosa visits Alice for the first time. Coming from a state which, for many in the West, symbolised nothing but rottenness and evil, Rosa is as shocked as the audience is to find Alice living in conditions of unbelievable filth, drugs and violence. Brenton opens the play with this very scene: the curtain comes up on a squalid London flat encrusted with dirt and muck with Alice and Joanne, a "Gothette" of twenty-five, lying fast asleep rolled up in some dirty rugs. These two women seem to be sleeping in a death-like stupor, for in spite of the noise created by Sandy, their third room mate, they are not to be woken up.

Sandy, Alice's foul-mouthed lover, opens the play with words which could be regarded as the underlying motto: "Some fucking sense o'responsibility" (I.1. p. 1). However, Brenton hurries to give an ironic twist to the notion of responsibility. Sandy does not refer to ethical standards or a sense of commitment, but to nothing more than tidying up the litter and dirt in the room so that one can walk in it without stepping on things. He is extremely disappointed that Alice cannot even comply with the most basic standards of orderliness which even his mother managed, although "fucking slag she is and all" (I.1. p. 2), and he is convinced that she will eventually end up in a crematorium as an undignified corpse like so many people at the bottom of the social ladder, "a very South London death"(I.1. p. 5).

There can be no doubt that Brenton offers this image as a mirror, possibly a concave mirror, of the Western world. Rosa, who had left England in 1975 still cherishes a quite different picture, full of romantic allusion: "England. Green, villages, Shropshire, and London... quiet pubs and mild, mild people taking the dog for a walk, children playing hopscotch on the pavements,..." (II.1. p. 31) Brenton does not hesitate to disrupt this image of the mind, this myth which also the audience might be inclined to cling to in the face of an often brutal reality which, as the play reminds them, is governed by drugs and violence.

Alice is protrayed to be in the throes of a deep personal crisis of identity. She is a burnt-out social worker who may bear responsibility for a particularly horrible murder of a baby she negligently left with a brutal and callous family. For a certain kind of daily newspaper this provides a welcome opportunity to break into her life, to chase and torment her. While she is desperately trying to get hold of all the tabloid papers with their slanderous articles about her, her heart is turned into cold stone and she is determined to no longer care for anything or anyone, including herself.

Brenton seizes upon a particularly gruesome story which really happened in England. At least for an English audience it would be quite believable that a certain kind of press was prepared to harass Alice mercilessly to a degree which could seriously upset her mental equilibrium. It is well known that the tabloid press in England, perhaps more than elsewhere, is notorious for intruding into the private sphere of anybody's life for the benefit of financial profit. Alice has experienced the trauma of being haunted by the media for two years and is still expecting a court trial to be opened against her. These years have all but destroyed her self, her ego, so that she feels she is nothing more than "excrement" (III.1.p. 52). On the other hand, and quite irrationally, her dilemma has furbished her with a sense of liberation from her social environment. She has shaken off all responsibility and commitment to so-called bourgeois values and has become submerged in the drug scene. When Rosa admonishes her and urges her to return to normal life, she is not even prepared to explain her reasons for her behaviour: "There is no WHY, we do what we do, do, do, or do what we do..." (III.1. p. 52). And even more than that, when accused by Rosa of not being "progressive", she objects: "And I am! I am light years ahead!" (ibid), Alice's progressiveness stands in absolute contrast to Rosa's concept of a young woman's life in the West. Alice is determined to no longer care for anyone or anything. It is quite evident that Brenton presents Western society as being basically mendacious and sees it as the cause for her total change of life. Sandy, although he is endowed with a sense of humour which can engage the audience's sympathy, is also shown in a negative light, i.e. quite uneducated, illiterate, incessantly swearing or losing his self-control and unable to perform the most basic tasks, such as driving a nail into a wall. His understanding of the socio-political world is practically non-existent. When Rosa brings a piece of stone from the Berlin wall, Sandy's puzzled reply speaks for itself: "What wall?" (I.4. p. 23)

However, their third room-mate, Joanne, the Gothette, seems to have reached the state of freedom which enables her to leave the world behind. She is interested in nothing but mime and standing on her head. Brenton frees her of all mundane hardships like work or earning one's living. And at the end of the play she is the one who can persuade Alice and Rosa that they have to leave everything and fly away.

The Rotten East

In sharp contrast to these characters stands 'Bertie', the Stasi officer. He is educated, skilled and well trained. His English is impeccable and he impresses everyone with literary quotations. He is an able craftsman as well and even built his own little house all by himself. At the end of the play he becomes a computer salesman with a sophisticated understanding of the capitalist market.

By attributing these character traits to a Stasiman, Brenton seems to be in danger of creating yet another myth of a communist superman. Bertie's efficiency seems hardly believable, for example, in the face of the economic catastrophe of the communist states. On the other hand, as a dramatic device, Bertie's presentation is apt to emphasise the shortcomings of the Western world. Yet, when this is said, Bertie's brilliance is nothing but varnish over a cruel and man-despising inner core, as would be expected from one of the most brutal members of Stasi's centre of power. When Brenton has Bertie corrupt Rosa's life to a degree that she becomes suspicious of her own husband and believes the Stasiman, the audience or the critics (*Theatre Record*, April 1992 8–21) might be inclined to dismiss this as pure fantasy. However, here as elsewhere, Brenton has drawn on authentic sources. Stasi's horrible policy was, indeed, to establish an atmosphere of total mistrust among its very own population. Millions of people were registered in secret files, recording all possible details about their private and political lives with the consequence that this network of espionage suffocated human relationships.

Brenton dramatizes this destruction in a potent image when Bertie meets Rosa. Rosa is shown in prayer – an allusion to the so-called Monday-prayers in Leipzig where thousands of peaceful demonstrators assembled every Monday in church to pray for peace and human rights. Bertie meets Rosa during the crucial days in October 1989 when more than 8000 members of the armed forces were waiting for the command to shoot at the civil right marchers whose number had increased to 70,000 people. Rosa, too, expects to be forcefully arrested by Bertie who enters her room with stains of blood on his shirt. But to her utter amazement, Bertie, although he uses threatening language, does not go on to do her any harm. No force is employed against Rosa and the armed forces withdraw from Leipzig because "the

KGB insisted the order was cancelled" (II.2.p. 40) as he bitterly explains. From that moment, Bertie changes his behaviour totally and becomes what is known in Germany as a *Wendehals* (literally: turn-neck), an opportunist without a moral standpoint. To a stupefied Rosa he declares that he wants to "confess his sins" and he asks her to "identify the . . . traumas. My 'interaction with the real world?' Help me. HEAL me." (II2.p. 39) A communist and a stalinist wishing to confess his sins to a Western Christian and a therapist – this is truly a breath-taking image and, in fact, constitutes the betrayal of the ideology of the former GDR.

Rosa suspects Bertie of planning another attack on her, cynical and despising. However, Bertie admits without any scruples that there was no truthful ideology, nothing he really believed in, no utopian idea. "I never had to believe 'it', I was 'it'," he says and continues: "A sense of power can sustain you, ... No, I can't say 'I have lost my faith." (II.2.p. 44)

For a socialist and left-wing author like Howard Brenton, this comes close to a condemnation of real existing communism, which he portrays as brutal and hypocritical. Although he has never hesitated to take a critical stance towards communism in his literary work he has hardly ever put a more opportunistic, even frivolous communist protagonist on stage. And while he has Bertie confess his own sins and atrocities, Brenton goes even further when he employs this very Stasi man as his mouthpiece for his radical critique of western values. "Do you know," Bertie says to Rosa, "that syphilis appeared on the planet, the same time that Christianity began? Both have merrily rotted minds for two millenia." (II.2. p. 44) At one blow Christianity and communism are equated with an illness that can drive people into insanity. Further on, this does not only apply to western Christian values, but to democracies too, as Bertie points out: Saudi-Arabia, the state which in the Gulf war was defended against Iraqi aggression in the name of democracy, showed interest in employing ex-GDR "instructors of certain techniques, you understand. The salaries are spectacular." (II.2. p. 45)

After this traumatic encounter with Bertie we find Rosa back in Alice's room in London, apparently in a demented state of mind, pouring champagne over the washing powder she had received from Bertie, "the frankincense and myrrh of the western world" (II.2. p. 38). A mentally disturbed Rosa stirring champagne and washing powder like an imbecile disoriented child – this is a powerful image of western civilisation in Brenton's play: drunkenness and cleanliness paired with a loss of orientation. The hissing sound of the bubbles have sent Rosa into a kind of trembling trance, in which she prays and sees herself as Jesus' lover and as his mother at the same time. She dreams of giving birth to a new Jesus while the old one is dead and, finally, it is Rosa herself who will be "the resurrection and the life/Not He." (II.2. p. 47)

For a short instant Brenton indulges in this romantic, almost sentimental image of a new saviour of the world who is a woman, not a man. But, abruptly, almost painfully, he destroys this image by Alice's blunt, and matter-of-fact comment on the situation in which she finds her sister: "Don't YOU go potty. If YOU go potty, I don't know what I'll do." (II.3. p. 47)

While Bertie's critique of communism is opportunistic and cynical, Alice's is straightforward and radical. For her, the communists' "attempt to remake humanity" was a fraud from the very beginning which, in the end, has nothing left but "a few pornographic fantasies." (III.1. p. 51) On the other hand, her disillusionment with western values is equally bitter when she accuses her own sister of having been the Stasiman's mistress. Nevertheless, her fundamental rejection of communism knows no compromise and she defends Rosa instinctively from Bertie who proposes to marry her since he and Rosa are "of a kind. We have both been scoured clean. I of socialism, you of Jesus." (III.1. p. 66) While Rosa is still paralysed, and unable to free herself, Alice sees that only violence can deal with "this joker": "Swat him down, Rosa. Tread on him." (III.1. p. 66, 67)

Bertie has no scruples either to admit that he is a joker and, indeed, that everything Stasi did was "a vast practical joke" (III.1. p. 67). Espionage and counter-espionage, files on collaborators and deliberate misinformation about innocent and suspicious people alike meticulously collected in files with the inevitable consequence that the terrible seed of distrust, lies and suspicion began to grow like a poisonous mushroom – this was the reality in the former GDR and this is what Brenton's cynical metaphor consistently describes. A jungle of suspicion and deliberately forged information makes it hard for all those who want to find out the truth while others have abandoned all hope of ever being able to do so and fear, as Bertie does, although cynically, that "...society would fall to pieces. How can an entire nation of collaborators gaol itself?" (III. 1. p. 65) This seems indeed to be one of the crucial questions Germany has to face after the reunification.

Flying Away

The ending of the play comes as a surprise although it has been thematically prepared for as one of the most likely possibilities: the three women leave everything behind and just fly away as "flying nuns", like in a showbizz act. It is Joanne, the Gothette, whose life is all pantomine and acting, who gives the final inducement to escape from their dreadful reality. She pursuades Alice to stop tormenting herself just because someone murdered a baby and she convinces Rosa not to "let that Berlin bastard into (her) head" (III.1. p. 73). Hesitatingly at first, but more and more relieved, they join her, realising that they achieved no good in the world while they were trying hard to do so, but hoping that in the future, "they'll achieve something by accident." (III.1. p. 76)

This seems to be a very unlikely ending for a play by a playwright like Howard Brenton, who was still convinced as late as 1986 that "the British revolution will be unstoppable." (*Plays: One*, preface). The collapse of communism and the atrocities which were discovered in its consequence have apparently rendered the playwright speechless. Language cannot grasp the new reality, cannot structure it and find a new order. On the other hand, this ending bears some similarities to his utopian play *Greenland* in which he tried to describe a free and peaceful society without any sufferings or conflicts. Remembering that *Berlin Bertie* takes place "over the three days of Easter, 1990", the resurrection theme seems to be deliberately implied, although never worked out in detail, by the dramatist, and thus the women's flight might be interpreted as a fresh start into something yet unknown rather than a flight from responsibility.

If theatre is, among other things, also an attempt to create an alternative "possible world" Brenton's new world is as yet unknown. However, it is interesting enough that the voyage to this world is undertaken by women, and only by women. They leave behind the world of men who, in this play seem to be the only persons responsible for evil both in the West and the East.

Selected Bibliography

Boon, Richard. (1991) *Brenton the Playwright*. London: Methuen

Brenton, Howard. (1986) *Plays: One*. London & New York: Methuen

——— (1980) *Plays for the Poor Theatre* (The Saliva Milkshake, Christie in Love, Heads, Skinny Spew, Gum and Goo). London: Eyre Methuen

——— (1973) *Magnificence*. London: Eyre Methuen

——— (1976) *Weapons of Happiness*. London: Eyre Methuen

——— (1980) *The Romans in Britain*. London: Eyre Methuen

——— (1988) *Greenland*. London: Methuen

——— (1992) *Berlin Bertie*. London: A Nick Hern Book

Brenton, H. & Hare, D. (1985) *Pravda A Fleet Street Comedy*. London: Methuen

Bull, John (1984) *New British Political Dramatists*. London: Macmillan

Chambers, C. & Prior, M. (1987) *Playwrights Progress. Patterns of Postwar British Drama*. Oxford: Amber Lane Press

Elsom, John (1979) *Post-war British Theatre*. London: Routledge & Kegan Paul

Lippke, Wolfgang (1987) *Contemporary British Authors: Howard Brenton* (Book and videofilm) Grünwald/ München: Institut für Film und Bild in Wissenschaft und Unterricht

Mitchell, Tony (1988) *File on Brenton* London: Methuen

Rabey, David Ian (1986) *British and Irish Political Drama*. London: Macmillan

Schäffner, Raimund (1992) Osteuropa und das englische Theater: Neue Stücke von Caryl Churchill, Tarik Ali/Howard Brenton und David Edgar. *Forum Modernes Theater*, 2/92, 154–179

Wilson, Ann (1992) Editor. *Howard Brenton*. New York: Garland Press

Contemporary Theatre Review, 1996, Vol. 5,1 pp. 111–125 © 1996 OPA (Overseas Publishers Association)
Reprints available directly from the publisher Amsterdam B.V. Published in The Netherlands by
Photocopying permitted by license only Harwood Academic Publishers GmbH

Confusion is not an Ignoble Condition

Brian Friel's Unconventional Translations as National and Universal Therapy

Christa Velten

Truths "immemorially posited" are illusive. They only bring forth division, often followed by destruction, of which the Northern Irish conflict is but one example. Truth, language and communication are inseparably linked with each other. *Translations* presents the different modes of human language. It shows that language establishes, but also prevents and even destroys communication, that truth may be revealed or veiled through language. Friel raises the question of whether or not true and lasting communication among human beings is possible. Similar to O'Casey's Juno, the wise teacher Hugh O'Donnell knows the way to communication and peace from personal experience: its essentials are self-examination and self-irony, the constant renewal of one's images, the readiness to suffer confusion rather than seeking refuge in illusions. Friel's ideas show a relationship to Nietzsche's philosophy, his call for "the revaluation of all values" and his notion of an "inventive chaos".

KEYWORDS Northern Irish Conflict, Communication, Confusion, Illusion

Continuous Myth-making, Continuous Troubles

Brian Friel was born in 1929 – the last year of a decade which was as fateful as it was ambiguous for the people of Ireland. It brought about Irish Independence – at the cost of a severed North. In 1921 the Irish Free State was established on condition that the former system was upheld in the six counties that were to reshape the Province of Ulster. This meant the continuance of political repression and social and economic deprivation of the Catholics of the North who now represented slightly more than one third of the Ulster population. Cut off from the Catholics in Donegal they were repressed by the alliance of one-time enemies, Presbyterians and Anglicans, who were then as now deadly decided to "cling for ever to Union and to Queen" (Vogt, 1973 p. 62), as goes a Unionist song of the early Home Rule movement.

While in the South, the war between 'Freestaters' and Republicans, following the 1921 Treaty, was settled in 1923, the Partition has kept age-old fires of enmity smouldering in the North. They flared up violently and ended in civil war at the beginning of the 70s when Ulster Catholics, along with a world-wide movement for social and political justice, demonstrated for their emancipation. Since then the world has witnessed the continuing guerilla warfare of the IRA.

From 1921 on the society of Northern Ireland has remained in a state of polarisation and radicalisation, which has dimmed the vision of a general humanity. As the historian F.S.L. Lyons puts it:

Because with us the sensational has become almost commonplace, it has been too easy to analyze the Irish question not just in political terms, but in terms of the politics of violence. We in Ireland are in a sense children of the revolution. (Grene, 1986, p. 47)

With their growing awareness of an agonizing political stalemate, historians, in recent years, have abandoned the conventional interpretation of Northern Irish politics in terms of violence and counter-violence. They are attempting a more complex and profound view of 'the troubles', and who should be better pioneers and guides in this endeavour than Irish – Northern Irish – poets and playwrights? If their occupation with the past has been termed an "obsession" (Pilkington, 1990, p. 28), this does not consequently imply the repetition of traditional myths. It may, on the contrary, be the strife to end myth-making and blind fixations, to initiate the necessary reversion from separation to integration, so that the country may come closer to G.B. Shaw's ideal that "a healthy nation is as unconscious of its nationality as a healthy man of his bones."

This aim, which Friel shares with some earlier Irish authors, has brought about a new, unconventional conception of Irish drama:

The sensational might seem to be the very stuff of drama, and yet twentieth century Irish playwrights, also, have tried to de-sensationalize, one might say to de-dramatize the images of political violence. Sean O'Casey, Denis Johnston, Brendan Behan and Brian Friel, each in their distinctive ways, have challenged the bold simplification of violence and dramatic action with complication and distancing ironies. (Grene, 1986 p. 47)

Of these four authors presented by Nicholas Grene in his essay on 'distancing drama', Brian Friel is the youngest and the only one to have lived long enough to experience the outbreak of the 'Ulster troubles' of the late sixties and seventies and the social and economic deterioration which they entailed.

Friels' Fifth Province

Born in Omagh/Tyrone, Friel grew up in the desolate catholic section of Derry, which nationalists, in defiance of a historical fact, still refuse to call by its official name 'Londonderry'. Like his father, Friel became a teacher, after receiving his BA at the catholic seminary at Maynooth College. In the fifties he began his literary career writing short stories, which were regularly published in the *New Yorker*. By 1960 his literary success allowed him to turn entirely to professional writing. Eight years later, after *Philadelphia, Here I Come* had increased his fame as one of the most promising modern Irish playwrights, his dramatic intentions changed, when

the society he had known all his life began to break down publicly and bloodily.

Once again the country was swept by the violence of "police and army, guerillas and assassins, bombers and torturers" (Deane, 1990, p. 16), relations and friendships were disrupted, society as a whole was militarized.

This explosion of the social and political *status quo* and the ensuing desolation had a crucial impact on Friel's writing. It caused him to revise his conception of history and incited his political commitment as an artist.

The first years of the 'troubles' saw him reject his own writing past; in those years he also began to confront what would dominate his writing in the future – the sense of a whole history of failure concentrated into a crisis over a doomed community or group. (Deane, 1990, p. 17)

It was the

search for a solution to the Northern Irish crisis through a cultural fifth province that would transcend political differences (Pilkington, 1990, p.28)

which prompted Friel and the distinguished actor Stephen Rea to establish the Derry Field Day Company, a cultural group, joined, among other Irish writers and poets, by Ireland's leading poet, Seamus Heaney. Their first play was *Translations*, which had its world première there on 23rd September, 1980.

Problems in Getting Across

A popular encyclopaedia describes the play as follows:

Translations (1979) explores the loss of identity entailed in the loss of a language centred in the 19th century Ordnance Survey's anglicization of Irish place-names. (de Breffny, 1983, p.89)

According to another assessment *Translations*

deals with the Anglo-Irish conflict and the decline of the Irish language under the impact of colonization (Pilkington, 1990, p. 282).

General summaries such as these cannot state the whole truth. Ringing the traditional bell of "colonized people and colonial master", or "oppressed and oppressor", they might rouse expectations which run contrary to the author's intentions.

However, the play contains some ambiguities which may be responsible for its controversial reception. The critic Edna Longley accuses Friel of

endorsing rather than questioning traditional nationalist conceptions of Irish history... The play does not so much examine myths of dispossession and oppression than repeat them. (Pilkington, pp. 283–284)

Seamus Heaney, on the other hand, finds that *Translations* "constitutes a powerful therapy". (Pilkington, p. 283)

Lionel Pilkington points out that Friel's diary entries of the time when he wrote *Translations*, as well as the idea of his 1982 play, *The Communication Cord*, suggest that Friel

did recognize that he may have evoked a nostalgic view of history, contrary to his actual design. (1990, p. 284)

Translations as History – History as Translations

But let us at this point focus our attention on the play itself and its historical background. It is set in Baile Beag/Ballybeg, Friel's imaginary town in Donegal – his symbol of native Ireland. Traditionally, yet no longer politically, a part of Ulster, Donegal – and hence Friel's Ballybeg – is a place where past and present, Irish cultural tradition and Anglo-Saxon culture collide. As will be shown later on in this paper, the motifs of separation and transition, and also of transgression, accompany the main theme in *Translations* throughout.

A double significance is also conveyed by the historical background of the play. Being the period between the Union of 1800 and the Great Famine of the 1840s it marks the end of Ireland's parliamentary independence and the beginning of its cultural, and – concerning the catholic population – even physical destruction. Yet out of the Famine emerged a new hope for national identity, later on manifesting itself in the modern nationalist movement that aimed at an Irish independence both cultural and political.

Between these landmarks of Irish history Friel chooses a crucial year in which the Irish cultural identity was subtly, but most effectually uprooted: it is the year 1832 when, firstly, the British Crown gave orders to map the country and to anglicize its geographical names and, secondly, when a national school system according to British principles was introduced. Both events meant an act of dispossession, a spiritual form of eviction, in the disguise of benefaction. (Bertha, 1987, p. 207) As Friel shows in *Translations*, place names, reflecting local tradition and folklore are now "standardized", which means that they are distorted, falsified or deprived of any meaning.

This mode of disregard and disqualification of a nation's values is completed by the introduction of new national schools, an act pretending to fill the educational gap of a backward people. But if there should have been a gap, it was one caused by British imperialism itself.

The 18th century Penal Laws had prohibited any education of the Irish population and even restricted the use of the Irish language. (Todd, 1989, p. 14) As a compensating reaction, illegal 'hedge-schools' were improvised under the open sky, hidden by the hedges of far-off fields. Later, when official restrictions slackened, the masters often located their schools under the protective roofs of barns or sheds. By 1832, the total number of hedge-schools operating was about 9000 – some even providing classical education. (Fitzgibbon, 1991)

Translations, however, is not a history play in the conventional sense. Friel does not exploit his source material in order to set up a "truthful" reconstruction of the past. Empirical facts are – in the terms of Archbishop Lombard in *Making History* (1989) – "deliberate achievement" and "sheer accident" combined in a "random catalogue" to which historians "offer a cohesion" (Friel, 1989, p. 67) and a structure. Yet being both subjects as well as objects in history, they must needs follow their own preconceived patterns. (Murray, 1991, p. 65) Therefore "histories are stories", (Friel, 1989, p. 68) and their respective authors, historiographers and artists, are spiritually and methodologically related.

A similar view is held by Hayden White who conceives the method of historiography as a sort of translation, of "carrying over" an idea or concept. (Schneider, 1991, p. 86) On a wider level, Friel may thus be understood as 'translating' his conception of history to readers and audience – yet a conception that – according to Christopher Murray

> employs history and the historians only to underline the irony of their methodology. (1991, p. 76)

Friel's statement

I don't want to write a play about Irish peasants being suppressed by English sappers ... The play has to do with language and language only. (Schneider, 1991, p. 86)

suggests his rejection of a traditional (mis)interpretation of history.

Human language, on the other hand, in its innumerable varieties and shades, is the fundamental expression of the complexity of the human mind. Like life itself, language is a dynamic process. Itself being subject to change, it causes, at the same time, a continuous recreation of reality. Individual languages may die, but their lasting influence may enrich other languages which then form the expression of a new age and a new interpretation of life.

The literary or dramatic re-presentation of a historical event would be a stale repetition, leading further and further away from any truth, like shaping an image after an image. Had this been Friel's concern, the critics of his play would certainly be right in accusing him of confirming traditional views and of dangerous myth-making. Taking language, however, as a subject of drama acknowledges life as a dynamic process. History changes the mind, just as the mind changes history, and the change is voiced through language. And again, language changes the mind, which in turn is capable of changing language. Thus language, being both subject and object, functions as the link between the mind and the outside world, each of which is equally subject to change, as well as capable of causing change. Through language translation, interrelation, communication – in their original sense – become possible.

Translation and Communication

These brief reflections on language and its relation to history may be helpful in trying to understand Friel's play as well as the various connotations of its title. Translation, in the play, is significant on various levels.

1. In Act I Jimmy Jack, a tramp-like character (a traditional type in Irish drama), "fluent in Latin and Greek", is translating from Virgil and Homer. According to the stage directions, "the world of the gods and the ancient myths is as real and as immediate" for him "as everyday life in the townland of Baile Beag" (Friel, 1990, pp. 383–384). He draws parallels between himself and Ulysses, turned by Athene into a homeless tramp, and between the fertility of the Irish earth, now suffering under foreign occupation, and the "rich, black soil" of Virgil's Latium.

Jimmy Jack's translations, though linguistically perfect, reflect the mind of a lonely man caught up in his fantasies and illusions. As such they evoke the mild mockery of those present, or are altogether ignored, while another sort of translation, excitingly real, is going on.

2. Sarah, a "waiflike" woman of indefinite age is practising hard to overcome her speech defect which has marked her off as another outsider of the Baile Beag community. With the patient help and encouragement from Manus, assistant and son of the hedge-schoolmaster, she has just uttered her first articutale statement: "My name is Sarah". It is the very first step on her way towards finding

her identity and social integration. She has finally crossed the border between dumbness and language, between impeded and functioning communication.

Critics have recognized in Sarah another Kathleen ni Houlihan, the symbolic figure of Ireland. Sarah's promising transition does indeed stand the comparison with Ireland's hopeful situation at the beginning of the 19th century brought forth to a large degree by Daniel O'Connell's achievement of catholic emancipation.

3. Irony, a pervasive element in *Translations*, becomes eminent in the translations which the schoolmaster Hugh O'Donnell demands of his pupils. Until Hugh's appearance, the fact that the play is written in English instead of Irish may have been taken merely as a practical device in regard to an English-speaking audience. Yet as Friel himself explains, this fact is intended as "a fundamental irony" of the play. (Pilkington, 1990, p. 282) Friel's ironic view of an Irish monolingualism becomes more specific through the translations that Hugh asks his pupils to perform. Always drunk with poteen, but never losing his dignity, Hugh has trained his pupils to explain the etymology of those words employed by him in conversation, which are derived from Greek or Latin. Thus 'baptizein', for example, is 'baptize', 'acquiescere': 'acquiesce', or 'verecundus:' 'verecund'. The audience becomes aware of the fact that it is English, not Irish which has roots in the classical languages.

Explicitly, however, Hugh is contemptuous of the English language which

> is only spoken by a few of us, on occasion, outside the parish, and then usually for purposes of commerce,

and he is convinced that

> our own culture and the classical tongues make a happier conjugation (Friel, 1990, p. 399)

than the Gaelic and Anglo-Saxon cultures. Friel's dialectical view, in part attached to the character of Hugh, makes it possible for Hugh to convincingly reverse his opinion at the end of the play.

4. Manus's fiancée Maire, about to emigrate, is concerned with the English language for a pragmatic reason, but even more so for an ideological one. She therefore surpasses the traditional type of the Irish emigrant. Facing Manus's incapability of ever sustaining a family she finds herself compelled to look for a new home in the United States. But it is not only for this reason that she cannot see any sense in learning Latin or Greek instead of English. Referring to the 'Liberator' Daniel O'Connell she holds that all Irish should learn to speak English, for – as Maire expresses in O'Connell's words:

> The old language is a barrier to modern progress. (Friel, 1990, p. 400)

Maire's attitude suggests the idea that the economic hardship which drives people into emigration may be due to a nation too much occupied with the past instead of facing the present. Glorifying a mythical past while neglecting present needs is an obstacle to a nation's well-being. Though Maire's critical mind rejects translating from "classical" languages, she is still unable to translate her own language into a new one. She draws, however, a strong motivation for learning from her belief that through language a "crossing-over" from backwardness and misery to progress and happiness will be possible.

5. This idea is directly demonstrated by Hugh's second son Owen who speaks English as well as Gaelic and who, as a consequence of his readiness to compromise, is leading a prosperous life in the capital of Dublin. He has temporarily returned to his native Baile Beag as an interpreter of the British Ordnance Survey team. The work of the sappers is largely dependent on the co-operative attitude of the native population which, however, has already, to various degrees, proved its will to resist. Owen has to act as a mediator between two worlds, he is – in the words of Lionel Pilkington – "less a translator" than "a public relations man". (Pilkington, 1990, p. 296) However, Friel's notion of the political character of language does not allow for any distinction, for a translator does set up public relations.

From a conventional point of view Owen's translation of Captain Lancey's speech cannot be regarded as a true translation. In the first place, it does not seem to be a translation at all, as the play is entirely written in English. Secondly, giving a genuinely objective translation is impossible for Owen, since the aim which he pursues is subject to his personal evaluations (in the same way in which the historiographer in Friel's later play *Making History* follows his individual desire):

> My job is to translate the quaint, archaic tongue you people persist in speaking into the King's good English (Friel, 1990, p. 404)

By paving the way for progress in Baile Beag Owen intends to change a state of reality which is, however, experienced and tackled by different characters in quite different ways.

In his mediating function Owen – whose name appears as Gaelic "(na) hAbhann", meaning 'of the river' as well as 'Roland', an entire falsification by the British sappers – has to take the edge out of Captain Lancey's justifications of his team's work. He is anxious to drop anything that might enhance the suspicions and animosities already existing among his people. Thus Lancey's announcement that the "enormous task" of mapping the country in every detail

> has been embarked on so that the military authorities will be equipped with up-to-date and accurate information on every corner of this part of the Empire (ibid., p. 404)

is turned into the harmless explanation that

> The job is being done by soldiers, because they are skilled in this work. (ibid., p. 406)

In the same way Lancey's white-washing

> so that the entire basis of land valuation can be reassessed for purposes of more equitable taxation (ibid, p. 406)

becomes almost spotless by Owen's 'translation', in which the ominous word "taxation" is wisely omitted and which conveys the impression that this large-scale map is part of a general act of liberation:

This new map will take the place of the estate agent's map so that from now on you will know exactly what is yours in law. (ibid., p. 406)

When the Captain does not desist from using the unfavourable term 'taxation', Owen simply turns the dubious announcement of "relief from unequal taxation" into the unambiguous prospect that "taxes will be reduced".

Blinded by his longing for a modern and progressive Ireland, which bases his double loyalty, Owen misses the growing cynicism in Lancey's speech. Lancey's conclusion:

Ireland is privileged. No such survey is being undertaken in England. So this survey cannot but be received as proof of the deposition of this government to advance the interest of Ireland. (ibid., p. 407)

sounds even more positive in Owen's 'translation':

This survey demonstrates the government's interest in England. (ibid. p. 407)

Thus Owen is ironically setting up another ambiguity: there may be more bitter truth in his 'translation' than he is aware of.

6. Again in ironic contrast, the following act is dominated by a young English soldier who cherishes a genuine and vital interest in Ireland, although he has the order to carry out the final act of colonial dispossession. Captain George Yolland is to translate all Irish place names of the area into English and enter them into the official Name-Book. Being anything but the type of dispossessor, Yolland proves sense of as well as respect for the deep connection between identity and name when he tells Owen that "something is being eroded." (ibid. p. 420)

Owen, indifferent, so far, to the corruption of his own name, has denied any such connection. In Act I he exclaimed:

Owen – Roland – what the hell! It's only a name. It's the same me, isn't it? (ibid. p. 408)

Now, during the process of finding English equivalents for the place names of his native home, Owen suddenly experiences a sense of tradition and identity and, consequently, he can no longer bear being called by his corrupted name. He recognizes that though names may be accidental, they nevertheless carry a private significance. They enable the individual to find his place in the world and to define his identity.

It should, however, be noted that even in this important instant, Friel dismisses any reason for an audience to become nostalgic: "Tobair Vree", a significant place for which Owen cannot find an adequate translation (the fact that it denotes a crossroads, and also the event that gave the place its name are both highly symbolic) is itself a corruption (Pilkington, 1990, p. 288). By this Friel shows that the erosion of Irish tradition is not solely due to foreign occupation; erosion of things and events of the past is a natural process.

The idea of name, language, dwelling and identity being inextricably linked together is the central theme in Act II which, in turn, forms the structural and metaphorical centre of the play. Here the representatives of two different cultures, the self-declared "go-between" Owen/Roland and Yolland, who may be termed in the same way, approach each other as closely as possible – spiritually, but also physically, as they are rolling about in laughter, their lines overlapping.

There is an almost symmetrical correspondence between them. Not only do their names rhyme, but each seems to be the mirror image of the other. Both have left their home in search of a better life. Yet while Owen/Roland is looking ahead for progress, Yolland romantically clings to the "ancient time" before the French Revolution when Man's dangerous potential, as he sees it, was still restricted. While Owen has found his spiritual home in a world shaped in the British way of life, Yolland thinks to have found his in the Ireland of the Gaels. Telling Owen about his arrival in Baile Beag he says:

> I had moved into a consciousness that wasn't striving nor agitated, but at ease with its own conviction and assurance. And when I heard Jimmy Jack and your father swapping stories about Apollo and Cuchullain and Paris and Ferdia as if they had lived down the road – I knew – perhaps – I could live here. (Friel, 1990, p. 416)

Although he has already picked up a few words in Irish and is hopeful of speaking the language fluently, he is yet aware of the fact that he will never entirely become an insider but will always remain in a state of dichotomy:

> I may learn the password, but the language of the tribe will always elude me... The private core will always be ... hermetic. (ibid., p. 416)

Now, in the centre of the play, occurs a caesura. Doubt interrupts the optimistic flow of translation. It is the doubt, whether the most essential translation in life, that of the deepest and most private core of a being is possible. The "language of the tribe" is something that semantics alone cannot grasp.

According to George Steiner, whose *After Babel* gave the impetus to Friel's concept of language, the individual draws on two fundamental linguistic sources: the "current vulgate", i.e. the language which is in common use and which can be learnt by a foreigner, and

> a private thesaurus ... inextricably part of his subconscious, of his memories so far as they may be verbalized, and of the singular, irreducibly specific ensemble of his somatic and psychological identity. (Pilkington, 1990, p. 297)

For Steiner, individual groups, cultures and epochs follow the same principle.

With this in mind, we may rightly doubt Owen's optimistic response to Yolland:

> You can learn to decode us. (Friel, 1990, p. 416)

Then, in an ironic counter-movement both Yolland and "Oland" (to signify their momentuous, almost complete identity) perceive in their translations a perfect congruence between a name and its reality, (ibid., p. 422) and eventually Yolland exchanges his uneasiness about his act of eroding for the confidence in his capability of decoding. Exhilarated he exclaims:

> I'll decode you yet! (ibid. p. 422)

Suspicion is close at hand, for at the same time Yolland is drinking poteen from Anna na mBreag – the Lying Anna …

Yolland with his love of poteen and ancient myths seemingly displays similarities with Hugh, but the latter, in ironic reversal, reveals himself as being amazingly clear-sighted in that he is keenly aware of the intertwinement of political situation and character, expressed through what Yolland calls "the language of the tribe". The richness of the Irish language that Yolland as an outsider so admires is explained by Hugh as a result of the particular fate of its people. It is

> full of the mythologies of fantasy and hope and self-deception – a syntax opulent with tomorrows. It is our response to mud cabins and a diet of potatoes; our only method of replying to … inevitabilities. (ibid., p. 418)

Not sharing a people's fate means never being able to speak its language – should this be Friel's message? If it were, Friel himself would be included in Hugh's ironic self-criticism:

> We like to think we endure around truths immemorially posited. (ibid., p. 418)

But if fate can form a people or an individual, – an individual or a people is also capable of forming fate. From this dialectical point of view Hugh cautions Yolland against the romantic search of an illusive Garden of Eden, against the self-deception of which he has accused his own people:

> Remember that words are signals, counters. They are not immortal. And it can happen – to use an image you'll understand – it can happen that a civilization can be imprisoned in a linguistic contour which no longer matches the landscape of … fact. (ibid., p. 419)

Hugh reveals a wisdom that can see beyond the confinements of outward appearances. He knows the actual values that the counters, themselves almost valueless, indicate and – what is essential in this context – he knows that all those private entities having left and still leaving their visible signatures, are of equal value and may be exchanged for or translated into one another. The same idea is borne out, as has already been shown, by Friel's treatment of the Irish and English languages: the spoken English, in the play representing the Irish vernacular, conveys the impression that the two languages are semantically equivalent. (Pilkington, 1990, p. 294) The title of Hugh's book therefore gains symbolic significance:

> The Pentaglot Preceptor or Elementary Institute of the English, Greek, Hebrew, Latin and Irish Languages; Particularly Calculated for the Instruction of Such Ladies and Gentlemen as may Wish to Learn Without the Help of a Master. (Friel, 1990, p. 419)

It may be taken to indicate that each of us have the chance to learn, by his or her own endeavour, to speak the language of the other, to overcome one's own limitations and dive into, or develop, a new consciousness. Should Semitic Hebrew – the 'odd man out' among Hugh's five languages – signify the language of the "fifth province"? It is one of Hugh's self-parodies that he himself cannot speak Hebrew, and who, in or outside *Translations*, has so far learned to speak that language of the "fifth province", a language that is intensely political in character? Will any two different groups ever be able to establish a lasting communication in that language? Friel poses this question leaving the final answer to his audience.

Communication seems to be possible, as Friel shows in the second scene of Act II, only within the most private sphere of the individual, when he or she, in ecstatic moments of love, experiences his or her identity with another soul. Then the two lovers may "speak with other tongues", as the biblical account of Pentecost puts it. They may speak English or Latin as do Maire and Yolland in this beautiful and touching scene, or be inspired by the magic sound of old Irish place-names, yet each of the two will understand the other in his own language, the common language of the human soul, where translation is no longer necessary.

Crossing the Border

While Maire wants this perfect unity to last for ever, the word "always" catches Yolland's special attention. "Always'? What is that word – 'always?'" he asks in his naive happiness, while the audience cannot miss the doubt ringing from his question.

Ecstatic moments are real, but just as Maire and Yolland experience their perfect congruence apart from the celebrating crowd, in an "outside area", so does ecstasy, on a general level, not belong to the common world of human frailty. The reality of their political situation soon gets hold of Maire and Yolland, and also of the 'tribe' each of them stands for. Still imprisoned in the past, one might view the situation as Jimmy Jack does:

> Do you know the Greek word 'endogamein'? It means to marry within the tribe. And the word 'exogamein' means to marry outside the tribe. And you don't cross those borders casually – both sides get very angry. (ibid., p. 446)

Like Romeo and Juliet, Captain Yolland and Maire have crossed forbidden borders. Viewed from the opposite side, Yolland has trespassed in more than one way. By his love relationship with Maire he has unknowingly interfered with Manus's most personal sphere. As the member of an invading power he is the common object of suspicion and hatred.

The sectarianism and hatred of the Baile Beag community are embodied in the Donnelly twins. Omnipresent throughout the play, yet always invisible, they launch their terrorist acts clandestinely. Whoever intentionally obstructs the communication between the British and the Irish, stands in some obscure relation with them – be it Manus, the intellectual nationalist, or Doalty and Bridget, the simple-minded peasants.

It is not by Manus' hands that Yolland is killed, but by the raw forces of the underground terror duo. They may also be taken as representatives of the destructive forces of the human soul – the soul that has suffered distortion by violence and oppression, and that hence can only respond through violence and destruction.

In its distinctly symmetrical structure the play now takes a dramatic turn in which the prevailing optimism of Act I, culminating in Act II in the magical moment of perfect congruence, is all undone.

Owen, again appearing as Captain Lancey's translator, is now made to translate the unveiled language of brutal violence, as Lancey announces his planned retaliation. What Yolland had called an eviction in a metaphorical sense, is now about to turn into reality, and while Owen is repeating the names of the Irish villages that will be destroyed, he becomes aware of his terrible mistake. When after the fatal announcement his father Hugh picks up the Name-Book, Owen dejectly tells him that "it's only a catalogue of names". But he now knows for certain, what there is behind a name. It is now clear to him that the process of renaming in which he has taken an active part, means the end of all communication, the end of a culture. Thus Sarah, from shock, loses again her power of speech. The baby, whose christening Hugh attended in the first act, dies. Manus, afraid of suffering retaliation for Yolland's death, must leave his home as well as the security of a new job as a teacher in the West. – Would a Manus be able to teach the people of the West something that truly avails?

Confusion Preferred to Illusion

When Hugh picks up Owen's Name-Book after having listened to those terrible announcements of the Captain representing the English military and political force, his answer to his guilt-ridden son is:

> We must learn those new names... We must learn where we live. We must learn to make them our own. We must make them our new home. (ibid., p. 444)

This proposal has called forth divergent reactions among critics and audiences. To many it does not seem to fit Hugh's image. Is it a sign of total surrender or of opportunism? Pilkington observes that "in the context of Lancey's impending attack" Hugh's words sound "theoretical and almost facetious", and he agrees with E. Longley that in this scene Hugh "appears more as a dreamer", (Pilkington, 1990, p. 292) which he obviously refers to Hugh's renewed state of drunkenness. Owen is seen as a staunch realist, while Hugh is understood as having lost all sense of reality.

Such critique, however, fails to consider Hugh's entire personality. It ignores his special gift for integration that makes him not only an ideal teacher, but which also gives him the character of a sage. With his power to 'look beyond' limitations and to recognize the general in the particular, with his ability to "decode" the meaning of the signal and the value a counter stands for, with his sense of the universal message contained in an ancient myth, it would be utterly incongruent for him to set up new borderlines or to practise any form of violence.

In the face of the impending destruction of the area, his mind, aloof with Anna's poteen, yet clear, wanders back to the year 1798 when he and Jimmy set out to take their part in the Insurrection:

> The road to Sligo. A spring morning. 1798. Going into battle. Do you remember, James? Two young gallants with pikes across their shoulders and the Aeneid in their pockets. Everything seemed to find definition in that spring – a congruence – a miraculous matching of hope and past and present and possibility. Striding across the fresh, green land. The rhythms of perception heightened. The whole enterprise of consciousness accelerated. We were gods that morning, James; and I had recently married my goddess, Caitlin Dubh Nic Reactainn, may she rest in peace. And to leave her and my infant son in his cradle – that was heroic, too. By god, sir, we were magnificent. We marched as far as – where was it? – Glenties! All of twenty-three miles in one day. And it was there, in Phelan's pub, that we got homesick for Athens, just like Ulysses. The desiderium nostrorum – the need for our own. Our pietas, James, was for older, quieter things. And that was the longest twenty-three miles back I ever made.

And toasting Jimmy he concludes:

> My friend, confusion is not an ignoble condition! (Friel, 1990, pp. 445–446)

What, in the given context, does Hugh mean by 'confusion'? That he should cynically approve of the mad acts of revenge from the opposing camps is out of the question. Does he not, in regard to retaliation, warn Owen that

> to remember everything is a form of madness? (ibid., p. 445)

The "not ignoble condition" of confusion accompanies, it seems, the adventurous act of anyone upsetting truths "immemorially posited". It is the condition those find themselves in, who have become conscious of their error and who are not desperately grasping for new securities (as must be assumed of Owen) that will prove equally delusive. In 1798, still today a celebrated landmark in Irish history, Hugh recognized that he was about to become the victim of romantic illusions and of the mock values of patriotism and national heroism. He and his companion, Jimmy Jack stopped and returned, each of them going back to his own source and centre of life. But as basic reversals never come easy, so Hugh's return was not an easy way out. His confession that it was "the longest twenty-three miles back" he ever made, indicates his inner conflict.

Hugh's attitude is not that of a dreamer. His perception that

> it is not the literal past, the 'facts' of history that shape us, but the images of the past embodied in language …

and his admonition that

> We must never cease renewing those images (ibid., p. 445)

reflect life experience and insight. His ideas call to mind the cultural philosophy of Friedrich Nietzsche. In *Beyond Good and Evil* Nietzsche describes history as the modern European's "storeroom for costumes" and he continues:

> It is in vain we parade ourselves as romantic or classical or Christian or Florentine or baroque or 'national', in moribus et artibus: the 'cap doesn't fit!' But the 'spirit', especially the 'historical spirit' perceives an advantage even in this despair: again and again another piece of the past and of foreignness is tried out, tried on, taken off, packed away, above all studied – we are the first studious age in puncto of 'costumes', I mean those of morality, articles of faith, artistic tastes and religions... (Nietzsche, 1976, p. 133)

To both Nietzsche and Friel – if we can recognize the author's view in Hugh's words – "to renew" does not mean to impose new values as "immemorial truths". Hugh's call for renewal comes close to Nietzsche's demand for the "Revaluation of All Values", which in *Ecce Homo* Nietzsche explains as his "formula for an act of ultimate self-examination". (in Kaufmann, 1974, p. 111)

Following David Ian Rabey, (Rabey, 1986, p. 191) L. Pilkington observes "a disconcerting similarity to Joxer and Boyle at the end of *Juno and the Paycock*, as in "both cases drunken pontifications" are "made in the face of disaster". (Pilkington, 1990, p. 292)

This view, however, neglects the fact that unlike Hugh, 'Captain' Boyle is truly deserted, caught in the vicious circle of failure and drunkenness. In contrast to him, Juno, the only one capable of self-examination, recognizes the lack of humanity as the source of personal as well as national tragedy. Her prayer that their hearts of stone may be replaced by hearts of flesh is answered as far as her own person is concerned, and she finds the power to reverse the tragic development of those in her family whose hope has not forsaken them.

Hugh's character is much more related to that of O'Casey's Juno than to Captain Boyle's in that he, too, proves capable of self-examination – even self-parody – and reversal. His humanity knows the value of a home – a place where both privacy and communication have their chance of existence.

The confusion Hugh is talking of is the opposite of the "terrible state o'chassis" in which Boyle finds the world – his own hopeless world. Hugh's idea of confusion is much more like the inventive chaos of which Nietzsche's *Zarathustra* tells us:

> One must have chaos in one to give birth to a dancing star. (Nietzsche, 1969. p. 46)

The Truth is Beyond

In *Translations* Friel shows to which extent we all "like to think we endure around truths immemorially posited". He reveals them as myths and illusions. The idea that we owe our identity to a particular language, nationality, culture or epoch, and the conviction that it is unbiased objectivity which guides our noble thoughts and actions, are sham premises. They obstruct, paralyze or even fossilize our minds. The truth lies beyond fixed borderlines.

Congruent with this philosophy Brian Friel does not attempt to sell any ready-made solutions, as many might wish for. He has nothing in common with his legendary old Brian of 'Tobair Vree', who tried the same way over and over again to get rid of his disfigurement – only to perish in the end as the victim of his own superstitions. Instead, Friel leads us to the crossroads nearby.

He confronts us with a choice of several roads and directions that we may already have taken before. At the same time he signposts a way into a new dimension. He encourages us to trust the life force within us and venture into the unknown.

References

Bertha, Czilla (1987) Tragedies of National Fate: A Comparison between Brian Friel's Translations and its Hungarian Counterpart Andras Sütö's A Szusai Nenyegzö. *Irish University Review*, 17 (2), pp. 207–222, Dublin

de Breffny, Brian (1983) Editor. *Ireland: A Cultural Encyclopedia*, London

Deane, Seamus (1990) Introduction to: Brian Friel *Selected Plays*, London

Friel, Brian (1989) *Making History*, London

Friel, Brian (1990) *Translations*. In *Selected Plays*, London

Fitzgibbon, Gerald (1991) Historical Obsession in Recent Irish Drama. In *The Crows behind the Plough*, edited by Geert Lernout, pp. 41–59, Amsterdam

Grene, Nicholas (1986) Distancing Drama: Sean O'Casey to Brian Friel, in *Irish Writers and the Theatre*, edited by Masaru Sekine, Irish Literary Studies No. 23, pp. 47–69, Gerrards Cross

Murray, Christopher Brian Friel's Making History and the Problem of Historical Accuracy. in *The Crows behind the Plough*, op. cit., pp. 61–77
Nietzsche, Friedrich (1969) *Thus Spoke Zarathustra*, London
Nietzsche, Friedrich Ecce Homo, quoted in Walter Kaufmann (1974) *Nietzsche – Philosopher, Psychologist, Antichrist*, Princeton, N.J.
Nietzsche, Friedrich (1976) *Beyond Good and Evil*, London
Pilkington, Lionel (1990) Language and Politics in Brian Friel's *Translations*. *Irish University Review*, 20 (2), pp. 282–298, Dublin
Rabey, David Ian (1986) *British and Irish Political Drama* in the 20th Century. London
Schneider, Ulrich Staging History in Contemporary Irish Drama: Brian Friel and Frank McGuinness. in *The Crows behind the Plough*, op. cit., pp. 79–98
Todd, Loreto (1989) *The Language of Irish Literature*, London
Vogt, Hermann (1973) Konfessionskrieg in Nord-Irland?, *Religionspädagogische Praxis*, 11, Stuttgart

Contemporary Theatre Review, 1996, Vol. 5,1 pp. 127–134
Reprints available directly from the publisher
Photocopying permitted by license only

Outrage in Dialogue: A Study of Wole Soyinka's Three Latest Comedies[1]

Nicole Vigouroux-Frey

For Wole Soyinka, the term "outrage", used as a partial titular definition of a collection of essays published in 1988, may also conveniently serve as a norm of evaluating three of his dramas: *A Play of Giants, Requiem for a Futurologist*, and *The Scourge of the Hyacinths*.

Outrage, in its dictionary as well as connotative senses, suggests a variety of attitudes and assumptions. In *A Play of Giants*, the emphasis is on political belief. In *Requiem for a Futurologist*, the outrage dimension becomes cultural creeds. And in *The Scourge of the Hyacinths*, the outrage focus shifts to contempt of the rights of man and misuse of traditions.

KEY WORDS outrage, comedy, carnival, satire, power, unmasking

The title of this paper is a deliberate echo of Wole Soyinka's celebrated collection of essays: *Art, Dialogue and Outrage*,[2] written over two decades. The title thus defines drama as a tripod, its most dynamic element being outrage or a creative challenge to any established international order, a stimulating questioning, significant of our cultural stock of beliefs and symbols.

Soyinka's audience is primarily that of drama, of a dialogued form of expression in what may be described as the international "global village":[3] radio remaining one of his favourite modes of expression. His audience is also very much concerned with the vitality of the dramatic landscape in progress proceeding from a dual cultural approach, integrating both the African and the World Stages, quietly defying the forces of history through political and social concern:

> it is because I believe the forces of history may be confronted that I believe in social and political action.[4]

In other words he believes that any individual can break the cycle and move the community toward any new road, at any stage in historical time.

---

[1] a) *A Play of Giants*, (1984) a fantasia on the Aminian theme, London, Methuen.

b) *Die Still, Dr Godspeak*, a radio play, broadcast on BBC's Africa Service on December 12th 1982 and later developed into a stage play: *Requiem for a Futurologist*, (1985) London, Rex Collins.

c) *The Scourge of the Hyacinths*, a radio play, broadcast on BBC's Africa Service in 1990. Unpublished.

[2] *Art, Dialogue and Outrage*, (1988) Ibadan, New Horn Press.

[3] Referring to Marshall McLuhan's use and creation of the term.

[4] Wole Soyinka in an interview conducted by Biodun Jeyifo, in *Transition* 42, 1973, p. 64.

If we define "outrage" as "an act of wanton violence", as "any gross violation of law or decency" or as "a violent behaviour or language",[5] then we may consider that Soyinka's present drama also epitomizes his historical vision of the syntagmatic environment in jeopardy. Theatrical dialogue enables him to commit himself to the resurgence of common plagues in a materialistic, technology consuming civilisation. Outrage is revealed. From the mid-eighties to the early nineties, Soyinka's drama appears deliberately set in an African context; but outrage soon develops a paradigmatic value through use of appropriate violence and limited language, through historical perspective as well as through a very specific interpretation of the very essence of drama.

The three plays which are to be considered are obviously centered around African forms of outrage. Yet we are invited to consider wider developments through a series of details suggesting that Africa's "tribal village" might well be an offspring of the world's "global village".

When training at the Royal Court Theatre, London, Soyinka wrote (1959):

> France had just tested her first atom bomb in the Sahara, ignoring, with that then fashionable Gaullist arrogance, the cries and protestations of Third World Countries, and of African nations in particular. My outrage found outlet in a poem which formed part of a Royal Court Theatre poetry-cum-drama night:
>
> We whom you super powers condemn
> To vague, unmeaning, future fears
> Regret we cannot sooner favour you
> By dropping dead.[6]

He justifies his present anger by declaring:

> We inhabit the same climate of terror — only the agents are different.[7]

Without being exactly an "Angry Young Man", Soyinka does belong to the tradition of dramatists such as John Arden in the sense that History should be reconsidered in the light of contemporary events.[8] In no way does he deny the importance of the past as it

> clarifies the present and explains the future, but it is not a fleshpot for escapist indulgence, and it is vitally dependent on the sensibility that recalls it.[9]

Yet he hastily asserts:

> The African writer needs an urgent release from the fascination of the past.[9]

And he leads the way out of the meshy snares of past and history in *A Play of Giants*, *Requiem for a Futurologist* and *The Scourge of the Hyacinths*, all of them vent-

[5] All definitions offered in the Webster dictionary.

[6] W. Soyinka in *Art, Dialogue and Outrage*, "Climates of Art', (1988) Ibadan, New Horn Press, p. 256.

[7] Ibid. p. 261.

[8] See *Pearl*, a radio play by John Arden.

[9] W. Soyinka, "The Writer in a Modern African State", in *Art Dialogue and Outrage*, opus quoted, p. 19.

ing a mood of satirical irony about the artist *"as the record of mores and experience of this society and as the voice of vision in his own time"*.[10]

When Soyinka walked out of prison in October 1969, his first declaration before the press was for justice for one and for all. Even then, chastising lack of justice as a form of prostitution of power was not revealing a new aspect of outrage. That form was already present in his earliest play, *A Dance of the Forests*. Among possible forms of outrage, the lust for power is the most provocative to his dramatist's imagination. He claimed the satirist's talent in his Foreword to *Opera Wonyosi*:

> an exposition of levels of power in practice by a satirist's pen,

and shaped it after Jonathan Swift in *Requiem for a Futurologist*.

Outrage, in *A Play of Giants* is immediate. President Kamini, alias Idi Amin, assembles all the reprobate heads of state of Africa in Kamini's (=Bugaran) Embassy in New York, across the street from the United Nations building. Here, outrage soon equals a psychopathic expression of power. First nothing seems to develop. Under the pretext of their life-size sculpture as a group of modern heroes to be displayed in the UN building, Kamini trapped all these African "supermen" of the time in an act of self-indulgent pride: what indeed, may appeal more strongly to such blood-thirsty dictators than to appear for ever as the life-size guarantee of the rights of man in Africa, in some privileged spot of the UN building. But where exactly? There's the rub; Kamini claims he has been guaranteed some strategic location. The UN officials deny his misinterpretation of intentions. At that stage, the initial cat-and-mouse game develops into the most grotesque, outrageous show of Kamini's persecution complexes. Revenge, in its primary stage, prompts him to have the white sculptor (from Madame Tussaud's) beaten black and blue, and to have the UN Chairman's head flushed in his personal toilet bowl, while he freezes the horrified faces of the Eastern and Western Representatives at gunpoint in a grotesque grimace. Satire spares no one as outrage proves both linguistic and cultural in some uncanny way: the audience cannot help resenting the implicit association of Mount Rushmore turning into a Neo-Tarzan Flushmore Valley.[11] In *A Play of Giants* all the masks have been removed. Power is multifaceted in essence and what Soyinka eventually satirizes is the complex nature of power. Outrage unveils the stark horror of political reality and the African demagogues' monstrous nakedness. The "heroes" on stage are exactly the opposite of what we expect; they are petty, visionless minds to whom power is the ultimate proof of existence. Those men "happen" to exist, to be African, but they might just as well belong to our Western culture. The most serious outrage is possibly the (un ? –) intentional maiming of the Sculptor, – of the Artist –, the only outsider, hence the only relevant commentator of history in progress. Beaten up, bandaged from head to toe, unable to complete his work, he is silenced for the rest of the play. For the carver, – even a carver at Madame Tussaud's – could tell the unveiled truth, could record the unveiled truth of eternal human features: it is a theme fully developed by Soyinka in *A Dance of the Forests*, when Demoke's carving is revealed as the

[10] Ibid. p. 20.

[11] The play has first been represented in the USA.

original hieroglyph. The ultimate outrage here is that even the carver/sculptor, proves powerless. Nameless, he is brutally dispossessed of his only voice: his hand. As an immediate consequence, we are to understand that, by exposing the brutal ignorance of the demagogues, Soyinka unmasks the ignorance and the brutality of would-be political figures who disrupt the original cosmogony and turn out to be no more than a bunch of international hijackers, of monsters parading, milling around in the UN circus arena:

Giants, Dwarfs, Zombies, the Incredible Anthropophagi, the Original Genus Survivanticus (alive and well in defiance of all Scientific explanations) ... ladies and gentlemen ...[12]

In this play, just as in *Requiem for a Futurologist* or in *The Scourge of the Hyacinths*, Soyinka expresses his concern and his anger by exposing a large range of sadistic temptations, hastily patched up under the cover of Machiavellianism. Cruel death, through sadistic power hunger, is the ultimate reward – or rather the ultimate outrage – one can expect from such adventure seekers, still groping their way out of the dark ages of slavery. For instance Gunema, alias Francisco Macias Nguema, is introduced in some lengthy discussion with his fellow heads of state:

GUENEMA Why you think we rule our people?
Some people are born to power.
Others are – cattle. They need ring in their nose for us to lead.
A Play, (Part I, p. 11)

The challenge to the free world equals the outrage: outrage to the people, to those anonymous labouring masses *and* to the real international elites, banned from power by such corrupted puppets; here is the coming on stage of Bara Tuboum, – alias General Mobutu – , in a typical carnival outfit:

dressed in a striped animal skin "Mao" outfit with matching fez-style hat. He sports an ornately carved ebony walking-stick. At his waist is strapped an ivory-handled side-arm stuck in a holster which is also made of Zebra skin (p. 18).

A colourful introduction which reminds us of Molière's Mamamouchi in *Le Bourgeois Gentilhomme*. The accumulation of similar details, the unmasking of real devastating forces, the flimsy device of hardly different names, all this should make us aware of the real challenge: to reveal the outrage in social as well as linguistic terms, to show the very point when mythifcation equals mystification in the guise of patchwork quilted, power hungry characters.

The last (but not the least) dimension of outrage deals with the audience implicitly forced by Soyinka into complicity. There is no possible evasion: either we acknowledge the traditional attire of the universal rogue in comedy, or we do not. If we do, we have no other alternative but to join the "castigat ridendo mores" crowd: we cannot miss the point, Harlequin's coat is that of the neo-Tarzans, of the mock-emperors, it has become the very essence of parody. We are no longer watching a comedy, let alone a fantasy; we are dealing with the parody of a tragic farce, an upside down, carnival-like situation. Hence we must prove active in the

[12] W. Soyinka, *A Play of Giants*, London, Methuen, 1984, p. 8.

"egungun"-like show, for fear of being taxed with sadistic voyeurism. In this last form of outrage geared toward the audience, Soyinka happily pleads guilty as he wants us to be aware that the responsibility is collective. African leaders, in full knowledge of events in Uganda, overrode all pleas and protestations, made Idi Amin the chairman of the Organization of African Unity. Well the African leaders did deserve him, for the choice was, for many, an instance of primus inter pares. But what about the rest of us?[13]

The very title, *A Play of Giants*, dwells on the humorous perspective; it also implies the notion of the play-within-the-play, hence of all its components. Couldn't we admit the following remark and playfully apply it to his construction of outrage-within-outrage in the celebration of Giants?

> was it Himmler or Goebbels who declared, 'when I hear the word 'culture', I reach for my gun?' Several African leaders applaud, by example, appalling variants of that sentiment.[14]

Soyinka seems to believe that human beings are incapable of learning from history. Yet, it is fundamental to listen to what they have to say as a man's language is his culture. Besides, words may be used as weapons and Soyinka certainly uses words to exemplify outrage, *"to punch holes inside people"*, to *"arrest the ears of normally complacent people"*.[15] Efficiency justifies the Giants' crude, primitive, military use of language and dealing with situations. It also sets the normal mood and pace of *Requiem for a Futurologist* (1985), with emphasis on Western religious and cultural references. Here again what is at stake is to expose an aspect of outrage; those pseudo-metaphysicians and para-psychologists are but masks for other dangerous individuals. The play is inspired by Jonathan Swift's *The Bickerstaff Papers* and a development of a former radio play *Die Still, Dr Godspeak* (1982). Obviously, as the two titles indicate, the purpose is that of a satirist. The years surrounding the work were tormented years: the Nigerian presidential elections of 1983 were predicted "to be disputed": violence, malpractice was the common lot. Soyinka expressed total distrust, in August, on BBC. He also published a series of articles which ended in his announcing his taking part in the campaign of disobedience (*The Observer*). Once again his situation was very similar to August 1967, when he was arrested. To avoid an unpleasant repetition of events, he left for London.

In his preface to *The Man Died* (his prison notes, published in 1985) which is dated October 1983, Soyinka sums up very clearly the philosophy of *Requiem*:

> Violence in politics takes many forms. All dead-end approaches to political goals – that is, political acts which create a cul-de-sac for all participants in the political process, constitute a violence which in itself breeds counter-violence. The nature of the violence can be purifying or it can be obscene. The violence which preceded, accompanied and was the predictable aftermath of Nigeria's 1983 elections, was ironically, a gross obscenity. The first thing to note is that it was unleashed by the party which was already in power. The purpose was to cow the populace into retaining the status quo, terrorizing voters away from manifesting their political allegiance.[16]

---

13 W. Soyinka in *PMLA*, "Twice Bitten: The Fate of Africa's Culture Producers", January 1990, vol. 105, 1, p. 117.

14 Ibid. p. 112.

15 Wole Soyinka to John Agetua in 1975, "Kongi Harvests", p. 14.

16 W. Soyinka, in Preface to *The Man Died* (Prison Notes), (1985) London, Arrow Books, p. xxi.

Requiem is more than a satire on astrologers, whether in Nigeria or elsewhere. It is a metaphor of Shagari's troubled time as referred to in the Preface to *The Man Died*, and yet the irony strikes us with the very first word: "Requiem". It is also the first word of the introit of the requiem mass, a mass for funeral, for the repose of the departed soul. Here the ceremony is orchestrated by the least appropriately named servant, Hosannah, which means in Catholic ritual, a shout of adoration;[17] in the play, Hosannah turns out to be the traitor, the Machiavellian Mosca in *Volpone*.

The other satirical oddity is that no one dies in the stage play; hence we are confronted with ritual for the dead with no corpse at all: another clue to suggest that astrologers do not seem to be Soyinka's real concern. The name of the "hero", the futurologist Dr Godspeak, also points in the direction of satire, and when we remember that George Orwell's *1984* includes a language specific to that totalitarian society, "Newspeak", we understand that satire presents a dual aspect, as if Soyinka meant outrage in more than one way.

Outside Godspeak's house we are aware of a large crowd, trying to get a glimpse of the dead body, or to hear gossip about him. It is some kind of exorcism in which Godspeak represents the undesirable aspect of a given life. The moment is a crucial one, a communal rite of passage in a carnival-like atmosphere. The wake is a make-believe pretext, a false one as there is no dead. As a consequence, the festive nature of the event turns out to be exactly the opposite: the new beginning proves to be a dead end. It is the world of parody, of imitation as Hosannah furthers the claims of Godspeak: the ritual is deviated. It is the first stage in outrage. Next, the press and the mob are manipulated, even the traditional masks are soon to be confronted with a pseudo-mask: the "egungun" meet what they claim to be a walking corpse outrageously disrupting their traditional ceremony. The whole play proves to be nothing but a fake situation, a corrupt social cycle, a carnival in terms of show. Hosannah (=the disciple) uses "godspeak" against Godspeak in his crave for power: the slave challenges the master, Hosannah outgodspeaks Godspeak.

Manipulation of situation through words and dialogue proves the key-word in *Requiem* just as it was in *A Play of Giants* or will be in *The Scourge of the Hyacinths*. Even the media are corrupted by the power of the printed announcement sent by Hosannah. It is printed, hence it is the truth, no need to verify the information. Two types of eye-witnessing are even balanced in a ludicrous episode: Godspeak does not know how to make it understood that he is not dead. They would not hear him, so he tries to climb out of the window and face them, standing on the window sill. No way, they are just anxious to have him back where he is supposed to be, in his coffin.

1st Man: My God, he climbing out. He's trying to balance on that narrow ledge.
2nd Man: The bloody fool! He'll kill himself.
1st Man: Na-a-ah. He can't do that. He's dead already. It's another of his tricks. (...)
1st Man: (screaming) Why don't you lie still Brother Godspeak. Lie down quiet and be buried like any decent citizen.
Crowd: (*First one voice, then another, until the entire crowd takes it up*) Lie still Brother Godspeak: lie still![18]

[17] Matthew xxi, 9, 15 etc ...

[18] *Requiem for a Futurologist*, opus quoted, p. 46.

The original title of the radio play, *Die Still, Dr Godspeak,* has become in the stage play, "lie still" or, in other words lie dead or alive if absolutely necessary, but for heaven's sake appear to be dead, lie in state, in a proper coffin, get buried.

Godspeak Alive?
Semuwe (alias HOSANNAH) Just the coffin, with trimmings of course -lying in state, book of condolences ... wake-keeping ...
Godspeak I don't see the point. Andy anyway what do I do afterwards? Emigrate?
Semuwe or resurrect.[19]

Hosannah proves a perfect Master of the Revels. Prevailing outrage here is no longer the fact of the double-dealer. It is above all the offence against the taboo of death and, consequently, its religious symbol. Godspeak proves to be a living metaphor, that of the eternal, embarrassing walking corpse. At the same time he plainly remains the symbol of the trickster ... too bad if he, at last, happens to be tricked.

Is *Requiem for a Futurologist* a comic play? Certainly, if we consider the multi-targeted satire, the carnival-like situation, the parody of most serious rituals. Yet, the message strikes us as particularly pessimistic because of the multi-levelled types of outrage. In that merry-go-round of manipulation we are eventually wondering who is being manipulated: men-in-power, crowds, media or audiences?

When the wheel has come full circle, comedy has emphasized the cyclical passage of time, of History, of Myths and symbols. The list of Cast indicates "battle disposition" with "front line", "operations" and "rear-guard", which can also be read as an insistence of the recurrence of situations. The overall message remains, in any case, ambiguous. The interest in this is not too successful play lies somewhere else; could it be in the outrageous punning of asserting that *"democracy will turn demo-crazy"* ?[20] The shouting crowd against Godspeak enables us to conclude that ignorance leads to most serious forms of outrage.

Soyinka's latest radio-play, *The Scourge of the Hyacinths,* retains in its title some of the satiric elements acknowledged before. Yet, the mood is totally different. The drama implies the Yoruba concept of time in which the dead, the living and the unborn co-exist.

Miguel Domingo has been bailed out of prison by his powerful and respected family; he is going for trial the next day. At night, he intends to flee the country because there is no hope left, there are no laws, no permanent rules; this is reckoning without his mother who considers the idea to be a treacherous blasphemy and outrage:

The Mother: The Domingos do not run, Miguel. Your ancestors only ran when they were slaves. (...) They took only their gods with them (...) May Sango's axe strike me dead, he [the ancestor] swore, if I ever allow any mortal to chase me or my offsprings off this land. (p. 13)

In spite of the help of his friends and of a very carefully worked-out plan, Miguel will prove unable to leave the country; he will be tried, found guilty, put in jail and hastily executed for fear of indignant supporters claiming his innocence.

What is new in the play, is the prevailing feeling that there is no possible escape, that

---

[19] Ibid. p. 49.

[20] *Requiem for a Futurologist*, opus quoted, "More Predictions", *Sunday Times*, 30th January, 1983.

For the Yoruba, the gods are the final measure of eternity, as humans are of earthy transience. (...) Past, present and future being so pertinently conceived and woven into the Yoruba world view, the element of eternity which is the god's prerogative does not have the same quality of remoteness or exclusiveness which it has in Christian or Buddhist culture.[21]

Yemanja, the deity of the waters, shows her disapproval of the overall political situation by an overgrowth of hyacinths all over the waters. They isolate the dutiful citizens, both protecting and trapping them inside a close mesh of roots. The waters look green around, so does the all too powerful young outrage, enslaving young men, emphasizing the cyclic character of human destiny. Yemanja's blessing to her community soon turns out to be a scourge, an absolute outrage.

If Soyinka selected radio – and not the stage –, as his medium in *The Scourge of the Hyacinths*, it is most certainly because

"verbal communication is the most penetrating means of identity within a community".[22]

The community in question is not restricted to the Yoruba, Nigerian or even African world. It is the "global village" enmeshed in the radio network, the community of free, English speaking citizens. With the "tribal village", that of the African heads of state inside the United Nations building (*A Play of Giants*), he contrasts the powerless victims of violence in the hope of gathering for their support the energy of the powerful global villagers of the air waves. To that form of outrage, he happily pleads guilty.

The Scourge of the Hyacinths can hardly be considered as a comedy. Yet it emphasizes a fundamental element of Yoruba drama as well as it reminds us of our original forms of Western drama: the Greek celebrations in honour of Dionysus. In that sense too, his exploration of outrage opens on to international concepts, on to the planet as a "global village".

In "the Fourth Stage",[23] Soyinka draws a comparison between the very nature of his favourite deity, Ogun, and our Dionysus. Ceremonies devoted to them imply a similar ritual of death: the tearing apart of a dog in Ogun's sacrifice and the dismemberment of a goat as the end of Dionysus' festive ritual. In both instances, drama can be considered as a transition between life and death, as both creative and destructive, as both festive and serious –both gods are related to wine and war through which one may discover one's own self and the true essence of communal life. Suffering is a constant factor in drama, whether on a comic or a tragic mode. Soyinka's message in exposing outrage in dialogue thus turns out to be

know then thyself, presume not God to scan,
the proper study of manking is man.[24]

His commitment is not only social; it is also individual and artistic.

---

21 W. Soyinka, "The Fourth Stage, 1973, in *Art, Dialogue and Outrage*, opus quoted, p. 23.

22 W. Soyinka, "Language as Boundary", 1978, in *Art, Dialogue and Outrage*, p. 134.

23 See note 21.

24 Pope, *Essay on Man*.

Contemporary Theatre Review, 1996, Vol. 5,1 pp. 135–138 © 1996 OPA (Overseas Publishers Association)
Reprints available directly from the publisher Amsterdam B.V. Published in The Netherlands by
Photocopying permitted by license only Harwood Academic Publishers GmbH

Personal Conflict and Political Concern in Wendy Lill's *The Occupation of Heather Rose*

Albert-Reiner Glaap

Wendy Lill's monodrama *The Occupation of Heather Rose*, premièred in 1986, is a play of rare frankness on the subject of Indian-White encounter in contemporary Canada. It is set in a Northern community, and the subject is explored through the idealism of an inexperienced Southern nurse. Wendy Lill poses provocative and thought-provoking questions about social responsibility: Heather finds it more and more difficult to understand officialdom's handling of the Natives' needs. But *The Occupation of Heather Rose* is by no means a play with a black-and-white issue. Not only the complacency of non-Native cultural assumptions and the despair of the Native population, but also the demoralization of the white workers, who try to better the situation, are put up for discussion.

KEY WORDS Native issues, culture, Whites, voice appropriation power.

The Author

Wendy Lill was born in Vancouver, grew up in Ontario and has lived and worked in Winnipeg and in the Maritimes. Moving around, never getting too comfortable, and using the perspective of the outsider seemed to be a very useful state in terms of her work. She started as a freelance journalist and broadcaster and worked for a Native newspaper, visiting reserves and doing little stories about sawmills or whatever else turned up. She started writing seriously when she lived in Northern Ontario at the age of twenty-six.

Wendy and her husband, Richard Starr, had a couple of lonely years trying to make a living and fit in. During those years they had two children. Wendy wrote *The Occupation of Heather Rose* when she was pregnant with Samuel. "There was quite a wonderful urgency 'with the play I was working on' that came with the creative burst of energy of a first pregnancy", she says. Not only did she become a mother, but she became the mother of a mentally handicapped child. And that has changed the world for her forever:

> Although I have always written and been committed to telling the stories of people who are vulnerable or at risk, I suddenly found myself committed on a personal level to another person with built-in problems (as opposed to the problems we begin to program into children from the day they are born). And as a direct result of that commitment, I am no longer an outsider. Children make that impossible. I am attached. Engaged.

The dramatist's concern about being engaged by her environment, her attempts at examining disturbing social problems, her own experiences as an outsider, her being the mother of a handicapped child, her personal observations while living in Northwestern Ontario between 1977 and 1978, her interest in Native issues – all this went into the making of her monodrama *The Occupation of Heather Rose*.

I asked Wendy Lill if she could tell me why she wrote this play. Her answer was:

> I wrote *The Occupation of Heather Rose* because I wanted to say that it is wrong to occupy another culture and by doing so, this will destroy your own culture. I wanted to show the damage that people like Heather can do to Native people, how they [the Natives] have miraculously managed to survive over four hundred years of occupation forces.

The Author's Experiences

Wendy Lill became directly interested in Native people in 1976 when she went up to Northern Ontario as a consultant for the Canadian Mental Health Association – the purpose was to try to assess the needs of people in Northwestern Ontario for a mental health branch.

It turned out to be a silly kind of boondoggle which Wendy left after about six months. Instead she began writing about the conflicts between Whites and Natives which she saw everywhere around her – cultural, spiritual, economic and political conflicts. She became quite distressed with the damage that was being done by well-meaning white helpers – nurses, alcohol workers, social workers, judges, teachers, daycare workers – both at the reserves and in the small towns where the Natives would do their shopping, send their children to school, go to hospitals. She wrote some articles for a Native newspaper called *Wawatay News*, from Sioux Lookout Ontario; for this she would fly to various reserves and talk to the residents. On one occasion, she slept overnight on the floor of one of the nurses' trailers. She began collecting images and conversations from the various white workers she found living on the reserves. "I was amazed", she says,

> at the great *need* which the Whites seem to have to talk about their lives, their work, as if they needed to justify it, understand it themselves. Writing and receiving letters was very important to them because they were alone and isolated from their friends and families in the south and did not belong on the reserve. Whether they ever really came to any kind of analysis of why they didn't belong or whether they just dumped the blame on the "Indians", the results were still often very disturbing. Resentment, bitterness, alcohol abuse, suicide attempts, abusive behaviour towards the Natives and inevitably – departure. Because they didn't belong.

The Occupation of Heather Rose – the Author's View

Wendy Lill kindly answered my questions in an interview which I conducted with her in Halifax on 12 September 1992.

> ARG: To what extent are Native issues still a taboo subject in Canada as a whole and in specific regions?
>
> WL: I am interested in the idea of taboo subjects. "Native issues" are very predominant now. Basically they involve the issues of Native self-government and the right to land and to their own social services and their legal system. These are all things that are talked about at great length everywhere. But I'm not saying they are given credence everywhere. Although I think that the majority of Canadians are more sympathetic now to Native issues than they were, say, ten years ago, I think they may be possibly less sympathetic now than they were two years ago.

ARG: In one of your letters you mentioned that you sometimes feel that when writing about Native issues as a non-Native you live off of the Natives and that things won't change until the Natives have a possibility of getting grants and can write about the Whites as well. Here we are discussing the problem of voice appropriation, aren't we? Could you comment on that in the light of the present development in Canada?
WL: I am very worried about the whole idea of voice appropriation. Personally, I wrote a story from what I considered the best and most powerful point of view that I could bring to it. When I wrote *Sisters* someone said to me, 'Why were there no Natives in the play?' I guess, I didn't want to have a token Native in *Sisters*; I didn't want to have just that one token child. If I could do it well enough, I wanted to have thousands of Native children who have gone through the homes of this place and whose ghosts and cries would make you feel their presence much more because of their absence. That would be my goal, in terms of writing it. I wanted to look at that group of people, who, in fact, so often escapes scrutiny altogether, such as the nuns. There were no bureaucrats in that play but all of those groups like the rich, you know, the sacred cows that just are never ever scrutinized, those are the groups that I like to look at if I can. I would be very angry if I was told I couldn't do that, if I couldn't represent a group of people who provoke disparate cultures, who have come together for some kind of struggle. I would certainly never not put someone from a different ethnic group into a play. It just doesn't make any sense to me.
ARG: Does voice appropriation mean that non-Natives should kindly refrain from caring about Native issues, should not write about them?
WL: Should not care about them? It's an interesting question. Should not think about them either?
ARG: You see, I think they should. Why not? You do and Linda Griffiths does.
WL: I think I said in my letter that the responsibility that you have as a writer is to say the truest thing you can about what you are seeing and about our own culture; and if the truest thing you're seeing is the oppression that it has brought on another, then you should tell that, you should show that. That's just a rule for me. I haven't personally run into this problem yet.
ARG: Has no one complained about what you are doing in that sense?
WL: Well, perhaps at the very beginning when *Heather Rose* first came out . . . but no, I've never actually had any complaints about this, although, I'm sure, there are people who do not like this play and overresent the fact that this play is out there. But I tested it out with Native friends when I wrote it and their response was quite amazing. They were astounded to hear that white voice. It's not a nice voice to hear. I mean, nobody wants to hear that woman but they had no doubt about it. They completely believed it. You sort of don't want to be the messenger but you shouldn't shoot the messenger.
ARG: And it all starts with the title. Do correct me, please, if I am mistaken. To me the title has different meanings. The word "occupation" means "being occupied with something", "doing something". "Occupation" could mean, as you put it in your letter, "occupying a different culture". (WL: Right.)
ARG: And "occupation", with reference to this play, also means "to be preoccupied", "to be obsessed". Do you agree with these definitions?
WL: Yes, I'd go along with that.
ARG: You were on the topic of *Sisters*. What is the specifically Native issue of this play? Why does this play about nuns deviating from their goals of teaching, lend itself particularly to concentrating on Native issues?
WL: The sisters of charity, the nuns in this particular school, were a teaching order. They had in their minds a specific goal of teaching as their plan and they were willing to take on any tasks that the priests asked of them. So they were basically set up in this residential school in rural Nova Scotia and they had never dealt with Native people before. So they had no understanding or experience of this kind of situation. They were basically teaching – which is what they did. And they were told they must not speak the Natives' language and they must not go home and visit. They were faced with a totally foreign culture. Yet they only had the tools that they traditionally used and these were not sufficient. Above all, they were not allowed to give love to these children. The nuns may also have felt this incredible split that the love they had was supposed to go towards God and not towards each other or towards the children. And therefore there was a real dichotomy there. But what in fact these women would have seen, if they were willing to go the distance and really look carefully, is that these children had been removed from their own homes, and they were not being given what they needed to nurture them to continue to grow as human beings. And if they thought about it, they would know that they *were* destroying these people, even though they believed that they were bringing them closer to God. So, basically, they were in this dilemma whether they were bringing these children closer to God or driving them further from their homes and their roots.

ARG: What does it mean "to go beyond the taboos" with reference to your plays?
WL: I'm writing a play right now which is about taboos. I'm looking at the whole issue of sexual abuse. But I'm trying to look at the abuse of justice in this area, at the hysteria which is now sweeping our country, I don't know about yours. But here if you are charged, if someone stands up and says, for example, that you have sexually abused me, then you have no life any more; it's over – it's ruined. I am very concerned about that. I certainly don't dismiss sexual abuse, but the fact is that there are a lot of people, I believe, who are being wrongly charged on this issue. So this is a sacred cow. The play is going to be staged in Alberta in two months. It's a hot topic, it's very hot, it's a real taboo – now!

I like to look at things. I like to look at the difference between the way things really are and the way people say they are; at the whole idea of injustice and who in fact are the real victims, and who are the scapegoats. Are you not scapegoating in some situations? There is abuse going on on every level of society. Abuse of power; sexual abuse. Abuse of power is going on in many different ways and some is far worse than others as far as I'm concerned. And I want people to not get too comfortable about it. The goal I have is to really look at abuse of power. If somebody claims it's there, I want to prove whether it is or not. If in fact it's not there, I want to *show* that it is not.
ARG: I don't know if I'm right but I would even go so far as to call your plays "cathartic plays". There is a kind of mental purification. Is that taking things too far or would you go along with that?
WL: I would like to say that sexual abuse is not the enemy. The enemy is fear and irrationality. People say we have to stamp out sexual abuse. I say that's not what you have to stamp out. You have to stamp out our willingness to be led, our inability to filter out lies and distortions. You know, I'm very interested in the media. I am married to a journalist who is a media critic. I see information as being a power.
ARG: What each of us sees going on in the media, on TV every day, has been brainwashed into us to such an extent that we do not really reflect on questions like abuse, but just let it happen, accept it at face value and believe those people who claim that each of these cases is a case of abuse.
WL: That's right. And it becomes a residue on us. Things don't add up. They pile up; a pile of violent images; a pile of toxic waste in our heads. But we don't immediately recognize it as such because our comprehension isn't moving at the same speed or the same level as the amount.
ARG: A recurrent motif or theme in all your plays is the paternalism in public institutions as a source of social demoralization.
WL: Am I trying to make the point that Whites have to change instead of trying to change the Natives? Absolutely. I think Whites have to change their ideas towards Native living and thinking.
ARG: If *The Occupation of Heather Rose* is a play "in favour of the Natives", why is it that Heather survived and not the Native person [Naomi]?
WL: I wrote two versions and they have two endings. In the one ending Heather has a breakdown and she leaves. I thought it was very important that Naomi died because that is what's actually happening – and it is wrong. I mean, what is happening has to stop – the death of Native people and their culture has to stop. And there is no way Heather can escape that. But I'm not trying to say that there is no hope for Native people. I do not want to believe that, I cannot believe that, I don't think there's really hope for anything if there isn't hope for the frame of beliefs that Native people dream. That is such a fundamentally compatible view of the world which we all have to get closer to if any of us are going to survive.
ARG: Could you define the difference between the two endings?
WL: As regards the other ending, I wanted to say: 'Okay, I've taken the responsibility out of Heather', and I basically moved it into the Native population. I'm saying that the last act is a curse with a Native girl. What in fact I then decided I had to do was get it right back to Heather. It's got to continue to be Heather's journey. She becomes more critical and doubtful about where she is coming from and she eventually, one assumes, just cracks up when she has a nervous breakdown or a mental breakdown and she leaves the reserve. So then what we have is this spiral downward.

To Wendy Lill *The Occupation of Heather Rose* was a very important story to tell. As she put it herself in an interview with Judith Rudakoff:

I don't know how people hear it, what they hear when they see the play. I don't know whether they see it as totally dark or whether they understand that Heather's actually gone on a journey that's essential to everyone. It's a journey that has to happen.

Contemporary Theatre Review, 1996, Vol. 5,1 pp. 139–141
Reprints available directly from the publisher
Photocopying permitted by license only

A Review of After Brecht: British Epic Theater by Janelle Reinelt

The University of Michigan Press, 1944, 209p, £27.00
ISBN 0-472-10321-0

Anthony Shrubsall

This is a thoughtful and erudite study which approaches the subject of Brecht's influence on certain contemporary British playwrights with an enthusiasm for political theatre that is noticeably lacking in present day Britain. The author's outsider status as an American academic enables her to view the British theatre scene dispassionately. However, whilst there is a distinct clarity and objectivity throughout the book this is constantly offset by the deliberate imposition of the author's own subjective voice. It is a voice that makes a refreshing change from that characteristic of much Brecht criticism to date, neither self congratulatory nor self important; it is simply honest and unafraid in its assertion that the author's own socialist convictions will illuminate the entire work.

The basic contention of Janelle Reinelt's book is that part of Brecht's legacy in Britain is the creation of a unique school of contemporary British theatre that has moved sufficiently away from its own definitively Brechtian beginnings as to be deserving of consideration in its own right. Her argument claims that within the form and content of certain playwrights' work identifiable common characteristics (gestus, epic structure and historicisation) exist to characterise what she terms British epic theatre as a political and stylistic force. Since the subject of Brecht's influence on modern British theatre and its playwrights has received substantial previous coverage, the central premise which Reinelt builds upon is not exactly an original one, particularly since the playwrights covered (Howard Brenton, Edward Bond, Caryl Churchill, David Hare, Trevor Griffiths and John McGrath) have all acknowledged a response to Brecht at some point in their creative lives. Her treatment of this central argument is, however, particularly interesting in the selection of plays, the attempt to place the 'school' against the rising tide of Thatcherism and its concomitant disastrous cultural effects, and her desire to bring everything up to date.

Following an introduction which discusses the Brechtian practices referred to above, the book is subsequently divided up into six chapters, one for each playwright. The playwrights, with the exception of Edward Bond, represent what Reinelt suggests are the second wave of Brecht influenced writers, coming after Arden, Wesker, Delaney etc. Whilst Reinelt invites the reader to add their own selections to her list, the omission of David Edgar is particularly surprising. This is especially so when one considers that some of the plays selected for analysis here, for example, Howard Brenton's *Moscow Gold* and Caryl Churchill's *Mad Forest*, represent something of British theatre's attempts to deal with a post-communist world. David Edgar's play *The Shape of the Table* surely deserves equal consideration given its parity in epic terms with the others. The fact that his latest work, *Pentecost*, continues in similar vein while other playwrights have for the present at least, turned away from this very contemporary engagement with our own time confirms the sense that the omission is a major one.

The quality and significance of Reinelt's analysis varies considerably from playwright to playwright throughout the book. The opening chapter on Howard Brenton begins with an overly earnest discourse concerning the significance of public spaces in Brenton's work and proceeds to discuss three plays from the writer's oeuvre, *The Genius, Bloody Poetry*, and *Moscow Gold*. The discussion of the first two plays works perfectly well as the British epic model, as constructed by Reinelt, fits, when applied to *Moscow Gold*, however, the model unfortunately ceases to work. A fact due mainly to the production's Meyerholdian conception, as acknowledged by Reinelt.

Where the author's critique of playwrights' work really takes off is in her application of gender analysis to Edward Bond's *The War Plays* and the works of Caryl Churchill, notably *Top Girls* and *Serious Money*. Concerning the former, the personal, subjective voice effectively works to problematise the notion of parenting and, in particular, the idea of motherhood, as expressed in Bond's triptych. With the latter, the author's deconstruction of gender roles in relation to Brecht's spectatorial triangle is also impressive. On David Hare, Reinelt writes with perception and authority on his early epic play *Fanshen* and continues to further explore his oeuvre arguing that his subsequent work encapsulates the slogan 'the personal is political' in respect of both his approach to characterisation and his concern with distanciation through filmic techniques. Reinelt effectively argues that Hare has, along with some of the other writers, ultimately moved beyond Brecht into an altogether more rarefied stream of political playwriting. Whether this is true is debatable, and at times the author's own enthusiasm for her project leads her away from the most important elements of this study.

The final two chapters most clearly reveal the book limitations. The coverage of Trevor Griffiths begins well enough and the critique of *Comedians* is particularly incisive. However, in attempting to get to grips with what she calls Griffiths' 'post-Brechtian/post-Lukacsian style' through Griffiths' recent play *Piano*, Reinelt becomes caught up chasing a Chekhovian world that although undoubtedly political, is far removed from Brechtian inspiration in terms of both form and content. Following on from the rather shaky analysis of *Piano* Reinelt applies the epic test to Griffiths' 1991 play *The Gulf between Us*. Whilst the results are infinitely stronger than those achieved on *Piano* there are distinct moments where the reader senses that Reinelt's personal voice, sympathy and commitment to the cause almost get in the way of authorial application and responsibility. Similarly, just as John McGrath's work is easily and successfully reined into Reinelt's epic model, one is left slightly curious as to the almost unquestioning approach employed by her in relation to the demise of the 7.84 Company as a force fashioned by McGrath himself.

The book's conclusions are unreservedly optimistic. Reinelt admits that the golden age of British epic theatre has passed. But, just as the political left has begun the necessary process of reformation and re-evaluation in order to face the challenges of the next millenium, so too, Reinelt implies, has the political theatre in Britain. Unfortunately, there is little evidence either in this book or in the current

British theatre scene to warrant such optimism. The playwrights covered here have all, so to speak, moved on. As to whether their subsequent work will improve upon what they have done previously, we will have to wait and see. Most importantly, Reinelt refrains from pointing out the next generation of British political playwrights; she suggests that our hopes will lie, at least for the moment, with the present generation.

Finally then, Janelle Reinelt's book *After Brecht: British Epic Theater* provides a welcome addition to contemporary theatre studies. In general the book provides valuable source material in relation to the subject of Brecht's lasting influence on British theatre for both undergraduates and postgraduates. I would certainly recommend it to colleagues and students alike.

Contemporary Theatre Review, 1996, Vol. 5,1 pp. 143–146 © 1996 OPA (Overseas Publishers Association)
Reprints available directly from the publisher Amsterdam B.V. Published in The Netherlands by
Photocopying permitted by license only Harwood Academic Publishers GmbH

Notes on Contributors

John Arden was born in Barnsley, Yorkshire, in 1939. While studying architecture at Cambridge and Edinburgh universities, he began to write plays, four of which have been produced at the Royal Court Theatre: *The Waters of Babylon, Live Like Pigs, Serjeant Musgrave's Dance, The Happy Haven*, while a fifth, *The Workhouse Donkey*, was produced at the Festival Theatre, Chichester. For a year, he held an annual Fellowship in Playwriting at Bristol University. The Bristol Old Vic produced *Ironhead*, his free adaptation of Goethe's *Goetz von Berlichingen. Armstrong's Last Goodnight* was first produced at the Glasgow Citizens' Theatre and later at the National Theatre. *Left-Handed Liberty* was specially commissioned by the Corporation of London to commemorate the 750th Anniversary of Magna Carta, and was produced at the Mermaid Theatre. He is married to Margaretta D'Arcy with whom he has collaborated on several plays. Arden has written three novels – the first of them, *Silence Among the Weapons* (1982), was short-listed for the Booker Prize. A collection of essays written with Margaretta D'Arcy entitled *Awkward Corners* was published in 1988.

Georges Bas is Emeritus Professor at the University of Paris IV (Paris-Sorbonne). He has specialized in drama and theatre, from Elizabethan drama onwards. His main field of interest and research has come to be contemporary British drama, especially "political" drama. He has edited a volume of essays on "English Drama in the 1970s and 1980s", published by the periodical *Etudes Anglaises* (1983). He has published papers on John Osborne (*A patriot for Me*, 1977), Edward Bond (*The Sea*, 1980; *The Fool*, 1983; the "answer plays," 1986), Tom Stoppard (*Jumpers*, 1984), John Arden (*Pearl*, 1986). He has co-written *British Drama* (Paris: Longman France, 1993) with Victor Bourgy.

Nicole Boireau is Professor of English literature at the University of Metz. Her fields of interest for teaching and research are: theatre studies, twentieth century British drama and fiction, feminism, theory or criticism. She wrote her State Doctorate on contemporary British drama and politics. She has written articles on contemporary dramatists (Arnold Wesker, Brendan Behan, Trevor Griffiths, David Edgar, Howard Brenton, Tom Stoppard, Sarah Daniels, Alan Ayckbourn, James Saunders, Sam Shepard). She is a member of the inter-university research group RADAC. She has contributed post-war British theatre entries to *Histoire universelle des littératures* (Paris: Presses Universitaires de France, 1993).

Margaretta D'Arcy is Irish and has worked with improvisational and theatre techniques since the fifties. Her work with Arden includes *The Business of Good Government* (1960), *The Happy Haven* (1960), *Ars Longa, Vita Brevis* (1963), *Friday's Hiding* (1965) *Muggins is a Martyr* (1968), *The Hero Rises Up* (1968), *The Ballygombeen Bequest* (1972), *The Island of the Mighty* (1972), *Keep the People Moving* (for radio, 1972),

The Non-Stop Connolly Show (1975), *Vandaleur's Folly* (1978), *The Little Gray Home in the West* (1978), *A Suburban Suicide* (1994). Her play *A Pinprick of History* was performed at the Almost Free Theatre, London, in 1977. *Tell Them Everything* (1981) is an account of her imprisonment in Armagh Gaol. She is a member of Aosdána, the Irish Artists' Association, and receives from it a grant to explore alternatives to Judaeo-Christian patriarchal culture, in pursuit of which she is one of the founder-members of an autonomous women's group, Women in Media and Entertainment, and of a women's pirate radio-station in Galway, "Radio Pirate-Woman 102 FM."

Christine Dymkowski is Lecturer in Drama and Theatre Studies at Royal Holloway, University of London. She is the author of *Harley Granville Barker: A Preface to Modern Shakespeare* (Folger Shakespeare Library, 1986). She is currently completing a theatre history edition of *The Tempest* for Cambridge University Press. Besides writing articles and papers on E. Craig, Cicely Hamilton, Susan Glaspell, Caryl Churchill, Sarah Daniels, and Timberlake Wertenbaker, she has also written introductions to thirteen plays by Eugene O'Neill, reissued by Nick Hern Books in ten separate volumes.

John Elsom currently leads the MA in Arts Criticism in the Department of Arts Policy and Management at City University. He was a founder of the Bush Theatre. He has worked as a free-lance writer and broadcaster. He was the theatre critic of *The Listener* (1972–1982), and a regular contributor to many papers. In the field of drama criticism he has published: *Theatre Outside London* (Macmillan, 1969); *Erotic Theatre* (Secker, 1972); *Post-War British Theatre* (Routledge, 1976 and 1980); *The History of the National Theatre* (with Nicholas Tomalin, Cape, 1978); *Post-War British Theatre Criticism* (Routledge, 1981); *Is Shakespeare Still our Contemporary?* (Routledge, 1989); *Cold War Theatre* (Routledge, 1992). He has contributed post-war British theatre entries to *The Cambridge Guide to World Theatre* (1988 and revised 1994), to *The Cambridge Guide to Literature in English* (1994) and to *The World Encyclopaedia of Contemporary Theatre* (forthcoming, 1995). He is also the author of plays: *Peacemaker* (with Sally Mays, 1956); *How I Coped* (1969); *The Man of the Future is Dead* (1986); *Malone Dies* (an adaptation of Samuel Beckett's novel, 1984).

Albert-Reiner Glaap was born in Wuppertal, North Rhine-Westphalia on September 1st., 1929. Having attended the local grammar school, he went to the University of Cologne in 1950, where he took his degree in English, Latin and Philosophy. From 1952 to 1953 he was a student at King's College, London, and in 1955 he was awarded a doctorate for his dissertation, entitled "Bishop Hall's Virgidemiarum, seen as written in imitation of Juvenal: A contribution to the beginnings of English satire."

A.-R. Glaap began his career as a teacher of English and Latin at the Luisengymnasium in Düsseldorf, where he taught from 1956 until 1971. During this period he took a year off to teach at the William Penn Charter School in Philadelphia (1961/62), and also became tutor in charge of trainee teachers of English in the Düsseldorf area from 1963 to 1971. In 1971 he became director of the Pedagogical Institute (an institute for in-service teacher training) in Düsseldorf before being offered a Professorship at the Teacher Training College of North Rhine-Westphalia in Neuss in 1973. Since 1980 he has held the post of Professor of English at the Heinrich Heine University of Düsseldorf.

His main fields of interest and study have been Canadian literature, especially Canadian drama, contemporary English literature, New Zealand literature, methodology of English language teaching and problems of literary translation. He has published numerous articles and books in all these fields, and in 1992 was made an Officer of the British Empire for his outstanding merits.

MaryBeth Inverso was born in Philadelphia, attended Villanova University, earning her M.A. in English. In 1978, after a month's stay she decided to pursue her studies of English literature and drama at the University of Pennsylvania, where she earned her Ph. D. She returned to England in 1985 under a Mellon Foundation grant to interview British playwrights. She is currently an Assistant Professor of English at Bentley College in Waltham, Mass. She has published *The Gothic Impulse in Contemporary Drama* (Theatre and Dramatic Studies, 63) UMI Research, 1990.

Wolfgang J. Lippke was born in Danzig in 1940. He studied at the Universities of Göttingen, Hamburg, and Münster, where he took his degree in English and Physical Education and began his career as a teacher at a Gymnasium.

In 1973 he was offered a position in the Department of Modern Languages at Siegen University where he currently holds the post of Akademischer Direktor.

His main fields of interest and study have been contemporary literature in English, methodology of English language teaching and problems of teacher education. He has published widely in these fields. In 1992 he became President of the German Society of Contemporary Theatre and Drama in English.

Monique Prunet is Lecturer in English at the University of Paris IV (Paris-Sorbonne). She currently lectures on contemporary British Civilization and Economy. Her field of research is contemporary British Theatre from the 1960s to the present day. She belongs to a French inter-university research group on British and American drama (RADAC). She has published a number of articles in various journals, and has given papers related to her field of research at many symposiums in France and in England. She is also co-author of *Initiation à la civilisation britannique* (Paris: Masson, 1988, 3rd ed. 1995).

Christa Velten was born in 1943 in Limburg, Germany. She graduated in English and theology at the University of Frankfurt/Main and has taught English at a German Gymnasium since 1969. Since 1985 she has been a member of the International Association for the Study of Anglo-Irish Literature (IASAIL). She is the co-translator of John Dewey's *Art as Experience* (published by Suhrkamp in 1980) and the author of studies on Sean O'Casey and Brian Friel, published in the proceedings of IASAIL.

Nicole Vigourous-Frey is Professor of Drama and Cultural Studies at the University of Rennes (Haute-Bretagne). Her fields of teaching and research are English-speaking drama and media. She is responsible for a Research Programme on the Performing Arts. She is the Editor of *Le Spectaculaire* (Presses Universitaires de Rennes): *Traduire le théâtre aujourd'hui?* (1993), Voix de femmes (1994). She is a member of RADAC, and the Editor of *Coup de Theatre*. She is a member of the Erasmus Network: Theatre Arts and Media. She holds a long-standing partnership with the CNRS (Arts du Spectacle).

Ruth Freifrau von Ledebur was born in 1929. She was Professor of English Literature at the universities of Bonn and Siegen until 1989. Her fields of interest for teaching and research are English literature and teaching methodology. She has been a Board Member of the German Shakespeare Society since 1993. She has published more than thirty articles in books and scientific journals, on Shakespeare, modern English literature and teaching methodology. She has written or edited: *Deutsche Shakespeare-Rezeption seilt 1945* (Frankfurt a.M., Ahtenaion, 1976); The *English Short Story*, ed. with Annotations and Commentary (Frankfurt a.M., Hirschgraben, 1982); *Slaughterhouse Five*, by Kurt Vonnegut Jr., ed. with Annotations and Commentary (Düsseldorf: Bagel, 1985); *Schreibfest: Modisches und Methodisches aus Englischen Gefilden*, ed. with Reimer Jehmlich (Siegen, 1987).

Contemporary Theatre Review, 1996, Vol. 5,1 pp. 147–148 © 1996 OPA (Overseas Publishers Association)
Reprints available directly from the publisher Amsterdam B.V. Published in The Netherlands by
Photocopying permitted by license only Harwood Academic Publishers GmbH

Index